THE V
CONFEDER
HENRY T. OWEN

HENRY T. OWEN - 1831-1921
CAPTAIN, COMPANY C, 18TH VIRGINIA
CONFEDERATE STATES OF AMERICA

Kimberly Ayn Owen, Graham C. Owen and Michael M. Owen

WILLOW BEND BOOKS
2004

WILLOW BEND BOOKS

AN IMPRINT OF HERITAGE BOOKS, INC.

Books, CDs, and more—Worldwide

For our listing of thousands of titles see our website
at
www.HeritageBooks.com

Published 2004 by
HERITAGE BOOKS, INC.
Publishing Division
65 East Main Street
Westminster, Maryland 21157-5026

COPYRIGHT © 2004 KIMBERLY AYN OWEN,
GRAHAM C. OWEN AND MICHAEL M. OWEN

All rights reserved. No part of this book may be reproduced or transmitted in any form or
by any means, electronic or mechanical, including photocopying, recording or by any
information storage and retrieval system without written permission from the author,
except for the inclusion of brief quotations in a review.

International Standard Book Number: 1-58549-969-2

DEDICATION

We dedicate this book to the memory of Henry Thweatt Owen, whose letters and writings made this work possible and to Emerson G. Whiteside, one his great-grandsons, who donated Henry's letters and other documents to the Library of Virginia for preservation.

TABLE OF CONTENTS

LIST OF ILLUSTRATIONS

ACKNOWLEGEMENTS AND SPECIAL NOTES

Many of the letters, documents, and other material published in this book are from the original documents. These originals are owned and archived by the Library of Virginia as "Henry T. Owen Papers 1822-1929 (Accession 28154) Personal Papers Collection, Archives Research Services. The Library of Virginia, Richmond, Virginia."

We are grateful to the Library of Virginia for their permission to publish this material. Unless otherwise specified, the letters and documents in this work are copied from the originals in the archives of the Library of Virginia.

Some of the names in the letters, places and dates were researched from Dr. James I. Robertson's book, "18th Virginia Infantry," Copyright 1984, H. E. Howard, Inc. We would like to thank Dr. Robertson for his permission for using this source.

Some of the letters, documents and other material published in this book are from the original documents and are the personal property of some of the descendants of Henry T. Owen and Michael Melancthon Owen. The papers published in this book from this collection are designated "Owen Family Papers."

We are also grateful to Julia M. Owen, who spent many hours helping with the transcripts.

The authors.

INTRODUCTION

The War Between the States - 1861-1865, was and remains the most devastating of all wars fought by the men of the United States of America. The casualties of that war were greater than in all other wars combined fought by Americans. It was a war that left the South in ruins and it was nearly seven decades later before the South would begin to recover. For the South, there was no Marshall Plan. Reconstruction was not, nor was it intended to be, a re-building of the South. The South, with the help of some of the industrialist of the North, in reality re-built itself. The railroads, hotels and resorts built by such men as John D. Rockefeller, Henry Plant, Henry Flagler and others helped the South recover. We should remember however, that a large portion of the funds, used by the wealthy industrialist of the North, were made by those industrialists during the war. Henry T. Owen was a participant in that war and was a participant in that re-building.

Henry Thweatt Owen fought the War of 1861-1865 on several fronts. As the commander of Company C, 18th Virginia Infantry Regiment, Army of Northern Virginia, Confederate States of America, he fought against the Union Army. He fought also on a second front in frequent battles with the commander of the 18th, Colonel Robert Enoch Withers. His battles with Colonel Withers resulted in Henry finding himself in a great deal of trouble, but true to his Welsh heritage, he came out the winner. Henry also fought minor skirmishes with his wife, Harriet. These skirmishes usually involved his attempts to keep Harriet's spirits up during the war and during some very trying times for all the wives of soldiers, who were left to take care of the homesteads and, in many cases, small children.

When we began this project, it was our intent to gather as much information about Henry T. Owen as we could, and to preserve this information for future generations of the Owen family. The more we delved into the life of our ancestor, the more we realized that his story was a personal history of the War Between the States and further, his letters, documents and diaries were in such detail as to make that devastating war become more of a reality to those of us who had not lived through it.

The life and times of Henry T. Owen are somewhat condensed in this book. His story is told much in his own words.

There are perhaps, hundreds or even thousands of men who lived much the same experiences. The difference between Henry's life and many of the others is that Henry recorded those experiences on paper. After his death one of Henry's great grandsons, Emerson G. Whiteside of Richmond, Virginia, gave the papers to the Library of Virginia. We are eternally grateful to this cousin and to the Library of Virginia for preserving the papers.

In this work, we edited the letters and documents only when necessary for clarification. In an effort to preserve the integrity of the originals, we left the style of writing (few punctuation marks), wording and other characteristics of the documents just as they were written.

This book is not intended to be a tribute solely to Henry T. Owen. It is a tribute to both Confederate and Union soldiers and sailors and to the wives, children and other loved ones they left behind. It is our hope that our readers will find, in this work, that there were many young men of both the North and South who held high standards of conduct and principles in their lives. Following the war, thousands of young men, like Henry T. Owen, returned to their homes to try and put together the broken pieces of their lives and to heal the nation's wounds. It was not an easy task.

The descendants of both Union and Confederates should know that both sides fought a gallant fight. It was the last war of gentlemanly conduct. It was probably the last war where brother fought against brother and it was, we hope, the last war that would divide this great nation.

Kimberly Ayn Owen - Richmond, Virginia
Michael M. Owen - Marietta, Georgia
Graham C. Owen - Interlachen, Florida

CHAPTER 1 - THE HERITAGE

"John Owen, the son of Thomas Owen, the son of William Owen, who worked his way across, then a boy, and his son Thomas was father of John, the father of Jesse, the father of William Jack, who was my father." *Henry T. Owen 1896*

Owen Family Papers

****

The people of Wales have a long-standing heritage of being warriors. In some of the first recorded history, we find Caractaceus, King of the Silures, the most numerous of the three tribes then occupying the country we now know as Wales. In about 55 B.C., following his conquest of Gaul, Julius Caesar sent his Roman army to the islands, then known as Britannic, to conquer the Celts. After fifteen years of battling the Romans, Caractaceus was captured and taken to Rome in chains. The spirit of the Welsh people was not broken, however, and eventually they drove the Romans from their homeland.

For almost fifteen hundred years, following the invasion of Wales by the Romans, various tribes and principalities fought to preserve the freedom of their country. When Wales was finally annexed into the British Empire, many of its inhabitants sought a new life in other parts of the world.

On August 30, 1650, William Owen, born in Wales in 1635, then fifteen years of age, worked his passage on a British ship and landed in the colony of Virginia. As a good sailor, he was appointed by the Royal Governor of Virginia as a pilot on the James River and for the next few years acquired several hundred acres of land in Henrico County. William's son, Thomas, added to that estate and became a prominent landowner in Henrico County.

In the third generation, of this Virginia Owen family, John Owen, son of Thomas Owen, acquired over three thousand acres or land, lying in Henrico and other counties later carved out of Henrico. His largest tract was in what became Prince Edward County and it was here he built his last home on the banks of Sandy

Plat Showing Property of John Owen in 1749, Prince Edward County, Virginia

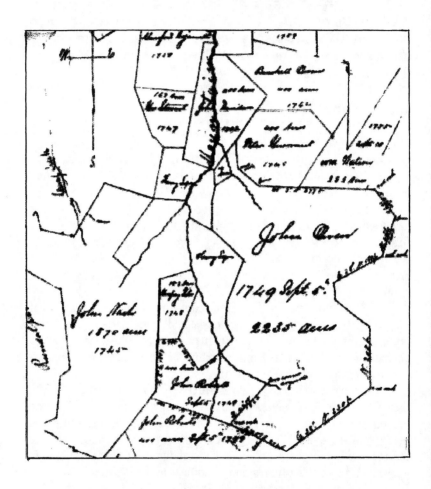

From Henry T. Owen Papers, 1822-1929 (Accession 28154), Personal Papers Collection, Archives Research Services, The Library of Virginia, Richmond, Virginia

River. His large family, six children by his first wife, Sarah Brackett, and six by his second wife, Phoebe Brackett, became prominent citizens of Prince Edward, Halifax and Shelby County Kentucky. His youngest son, Jesse Owen, a Captain in the Revolutionary War, settled in Prince Edward County, married Ann Crawford and had eleven children. The youngest, William Jack Owen, born March 10, 1786, married Sally Marshall on October 28, 1812. To this couple were born seven children. William Jack Owen died suddenly at his plantation in Prince Edward County on July 26, 1841. His youngest son, Henry Thweatt Owen was only nine years of age at the time.

Born on July 28, 1831, Henry Thweatt Owen grew up on his father's plantation near the Sandy River in Prince Edward County, Virginia. Disliking the life of a planter, he taught himself to telegraph at a young age. In early1850, he was employed as depot agent for the South Side Railroad at Nottoway Court House and on November 13, 1850, he married Harriet Adelena Robertson at her father's home "Rock Castle" in Crewe, Nottoway County, Virginia.

For the next eleven years, Henry and Harriet led a quiet and peaceful life. Henry's work at the depot was rewarding. The South Side Railroad was one of the smaller Pre-War lines linking the City of Petersburg, Virginia to Lynchburg. On its route across the South end of the State it passed through the small towns of Five Forks, Burkeville, Farmville, Nottoway Court House, Danville and Appomattox. The South Side Railroad also connected to one of the main rail lines to Richmond. During those years, Henry and Harriet had four children, Elizabeth Mildred born February 11, 1852, Henry Clay born May 15, 1853, Michael Melancthon born March 19, 1856 and Harriet Louisa born November 26, 1860. Their home, on the outskirts of Nottoway Court House, was a gathering place for Harriet's many relatives as well as some of Henry's kin from nearby Prince Edward County. Harriet's family helped to found a Presbyterian Church and a building was constructed on a lot next door to the Court House. The Court House had been constructed of brick in 1842-1843. The church was also built of brick, said to have been salvaged from an old outbuilding on Harriet's grandfather's plantation "Eleven Oaks."

In addition to his job as depot agent, Henry served one year in 1859 as Post Master of Nottoway Court House. His handwriting was precise and meticulous and his ability to add, subtract and multiply figures made him a good candidate for this position.

3

Having been tutored on his father's plantation and other nearby plantations, Henry put much stock in education and insisted that his children should also become scholars.

In the census of 1800, the population of Nottoway County was shown at 9,401. By 1830 that figure had grown to 10,130, however by 1850 the population had declined to 8,437. There were no major industries, the economy was based on agriculture and Henry's small farm on the edge of town produced sufficient food to provide for his family.

Henry T. Owen was probably typical of many young men of that era in the South. From his father, he had inherited some land and a few slaves. It is apparent from some of his letters and from conversations, he later held with one of his sons, Michael M. Owen, that he did not believe the institution of slavery was just or right. He looked upon the few slaves he inherited as a responsibility, they were considered by Henry to be part of the family and he felt it was his obligation to take care of them as best he could. He held no large tracts of land and thus did no large scale planting. The slaves he inherited, mostly women, helped Harriet in the care of the children and helped in performing the daily household tasks.

Though certainly not justified by these facts, slavery had existed since the earliest times. The ancient civilizations including Rome, Egypt and many other nations had slavery as a part of their economic structures. In the fifteenth, sixteenth and seventeenth centuries, the major countries of Europe, including England, France and Germany, had slaves in their colonies. In addition, the practice of indentured servants was a form of slavery and was practiced worldwide. Soon after this country was settled, the ship owners of the Northern colonies saw the potential of big profits in slave trading. By sailing to the coast of Africa, they could bribe many of the tribal leaders, on that continent, to enslave members of nearby tribes, and in some cases people from their own tribes, sell them to the ship owners, then bring them to the American colonies and re-sell them to the settlers. For a time, even after the beginning of the War Between the States, slaves were owned by both Northerners and Southerners. The Africans, however, were considered best suited to the fields of the South and it was here that the practice of owning slaves was most prevalent.

During the war, Henry stated in his letters, several times, his concern for his slaves. He also expressed his concern for the welfare of his children. Henry T. Owen, like many other Southern

4

men with families, cherished his wife and children. He wanted his children to have a good education and above all to enjoy good health. The medical technology of that day was crude and unreliable. The few doctors were mostly "self-made" and had received sparse training. A good portion of the population of the South relied upon "home remedies" to cure their ailments. Cures for many common diseases had not been found or perfected and many died from measles, typhoid, yellow fever and even chicken pox.

Henry and Harriet were both hospitable people. Their home was open to friends and relatives and Henry was especially adept at making friends. The ancient Owen family motto found on the coat-of-arms in Wales read "Honestas-Optima-Politia" - " Honesty is the Best Policy." Henry had no patience with deception or dishonesty. He educated his children to follow the same principles and after the war spent countless hours seeking the truth of various events of the war. He also spent countless hours researching and compiling his family's genealogy and history.

During almost two decades prior to 1861, the storm clouds of war were gathering across our nation. The Federal government in Washington D.C., controlled by the Northern States, began passing legislation that many Southerners felt were infringements on their liberties. As debates heated up in the halls of Congress and as the South resisted some of the new laws, various militias were formed "to protect the South against possible Northern aggression."

Henry T. Owen was not particularly concerned with the issue of slavery. The few slaves he owned were not an absolute necessity to the welfare of his family. He was concerned that his beloved Virginia was losing many of its rights to a centralized power in Washington, D.C.

Prior to the Revolutionary War, the colonies established local militia. These groups of armed men were under the command of the territorial governors and their main purpose was to protect the citizens from Indian raids. During the war for America's independence, they were called upon to serve in the Continental Army and following the war were kept mobilized for the purpose of protecting the citizens of the newly formed states. The militia units, for the most part, were under the command of the governors of the individual states and were the forerunner of the present day National Guard.

Sometime during the 1850's, Henry formed a militia company. "The Nottoway Rifle Guards" trained on the Nottoway

5

Court House lawn. With some assistance from the State of Virginia, the Company equipped themselves with uniforms, arms and equipment. The small company elected Henry T. Owen as their Captain. Henry's company consisted of men from all stations of life. There were merchants, a blacksmith, farmers and teachers. Many of his company were Robertson men, relatives of his wife, Harriet Robertson Owen.

A second infantry company was formed at Nottoway Court House, first known as Company G of the Nottoway Rifle Guards, the name was later changed to the Nottoway Grays. In addition other companies were formed in Nottoway County, including the Jeffress Artillery, Company E of the 3rd Virginia Cavalry and the Nottoway Reserve C.S.A.

As matters grew worse, and with the election of Abraham Lincoln as President of the United States, Southern leaders began holding meetings. Although there were still slaves in the North and although Lincoln had not indicated he would attempt to abolish slavery, the Southern leaders felt other measures were being taken by "Northern radicals" to cripple the South's economy. The Southern leaders apparently did realize that slavery would eventually "have to go." They also realized that if slavery were abolished suddenly, it would probably bring economic ruin to the South. They evidently felt the most practical solution was to phase out slavery over a period of time.

The constitution of the Confederate States of America contained a clause that prohibited the importation of any more slaves. It is believed, by many, that slavery, as an institution, would have been phased out in the South without the war. This, of course, we will never know. We do know that slavery was and remains today an evil abomination in a so-called "civilized" world. To Henry T. Owen, the right to own slaves was a small part of the issues of the War of 1861-1865. To him, his homeland had been invaded and his home, his family and his individual freedoms were in jeopardy. The warrior of Prince Edward and Nottoway County, true to his Welsh heritage, fought a good fight. He never hung his head in shame for a cause he felt was just and right.

CHAPTER 2 - 1856 - THE BEAUTY OF VIRGINIA - A TRIP TO THE MOUNTAINS

"I would give right smart if you were with me, and if I have one, two or three years, you will see this country, it is certainly the finest land on the face of the globe." *Henry T. Owen - July 5, 1856.*

Henry T. Owen, together with some other gentlemen of Nottoway, made a trip to the Virginia Mountains. Henry had traveled some in the southeastern part of Virginia, but on a visit in 1856 to the Blue Ridge Mountains of upper Virginia, Henry was awe struck by the sights. As a part of the Appalachian chain of mountains, running from Northeast Georgia to Maine, the Blue Ridge were and remain one of the most beautiful places in America. In a letter to his wife, Harriet, dated July 5, 1856, Henry describes some of the countryside.

****

Blacksburg, Montgomery Co. Virginia
Saturday, July 5, 1856

Dear Wife,
We are here safe and sound and in a fine flow of spirits. Don't know where we will be by night. We are now going down hill on the other side of the world and expect as there can't be much more worth seeing, we will see the balance and go right through.
This place is about ninety four miles from Lynchburg and there we are handedly one hundred and seventy five miles from home. Our company and J. Chappell, Griffin, Wesley, Bill and myself we got off the cars at Liberty, Bedford Co. and took stage ten miles to the peaks of Otter, this was Tuesday. Wednesday morning we were up two hours before day and after waking the owner man and getting straight, I next commenced the assent, got up to the top after real vast deal of fatigue and some stance and resting spells. But if we had been at some considerable trouble to get to the top, we felt proud unashamedly when there, not only for that, but for the whole trip from Nottoway. We could take a vision of a vast deal of the finest looking country in the world. There were peak after peak until the eye could see no farther. Lofty ranges of hills and

mountains South, East, North and West. We could see more than a thousand farms below us worked. They looked more like they were about as large, most of them, as you Pa's garden while they had seven hundred and a thousand acres in them.

You must see the peaks and if we do buy land up here I am going to take you up here. The first time we get in a notion to go to the Richmond fair, for this is worth four times as much for again, we can see some of the finest cattle in the world and certainly the best land. I have passed through fields of corn yesterday in Roanoke Co. that were as high as a man's head on horse back and a mile long by a half our side to appearances. One farm, Mr. Brussels, extended along the R.R. for three miles. Corn on one side, splendid wheat on the other as high as my head and Chappell swore they might take his hat. We have come through cuts that appeared to me at least a hundred feet deep and over. We have come over some mountains, though mostly trains by mountains, under mountains and along the edge of a mountain hundreds of feet high, where the least tilt would have capitulated us into eternity without a doubt. We have come through a moles hole under ground three times. Look for us about next Saturday, though we may come earlier. I would give something right smart if you were with me, and if I have one, two or three years you will see this country, it is certainly the finest land on the face of the globe. I have seen land that sold at auction for eighty dollars per acre and the cheapest land within any distance of this place is now offered for thirty five dollars per acre. But good bye and kiss the babies for their daddy. You can see I am in a tremendous hurry as the boys are calling me. I will write again soon.

Yours, Henry

****

Henry never realized his dream of purchasing land in the Blue Ridge Mountain region. In less than six years, the war would break out and all of his resources would be
lost in that war and its aftermath.

His experiences of seeing the mountain region would be a fleeting moment in time but he probably never forgot that sojourn into a world very different from his surroundings in Nottoway, Henrico and Prince Edward Counties.

CHAPTER 3 - THE FAMILY MAN AND A CALL TO ARMS

"Harriet, I will take care of myself, your brothers and your cousins. We will fight only if we have to."
Henry T. Owen, Nottoway Courthouse, April 23, 1861
Owen Family Papers

****

In 1861, Nottoway Courthouse was only a small village. The population, according to the 1860 U.S. Census, for the entire county was 8,836 inhabitants. The county seat, Nottoway, was a center of activity on court day, but the developing towns of Crewe, Burkeville and Blackstone had the larger population.

In that era, tobacco was one of the chief money crops in Virginia, although some corn and wheat were grown. The chief means of transporting agriculture goods and people were by rail. As, at times, inclement weather made the roads almost impassable, the stage lines to Richmond and other larger towns and cities were unreliable. The small, South Side Railroad passing through Nottoway was an important link to the outside world.

At Nottoway Courthouse in addition to the depot, there was an imposing brick structure that housed the Court and office of Clerk of the Court. There were two or three stores, a doctor's office and "Old Brick" Presbyterian Church.

"Old Brick" had been built in 1837 by the efforts of several of the families in the area and a young minister, Rev. Theodorick Pryor. At the end of the dedication service, in 1837, Rev. Pryor christened a two-year-old girl named Harriet Adelena Robertson. On November 13, 1850, Rev. Theodorick Pryor performed the marriage ceremony for Harriet Robertson and Henry T. Owen.

Harriet Adelena Robertson was the daughter of John Archer Robertson of "Rock Castle" in Crewe. Harriet's grandfather, Archer Robertson of "Eleven Oaks" was one of the early settlers of Nottoway County. His plantation and home, between Nottoway and Crewe, also served as a stagecoach stop for one of the routes between Charleston, South Carolina and Richmond, Virginia.

In the early morning of April 23, 1861, Governor John Letcher sent a message for all militia units to report at once to

Richmond. Henry T. Owen received the message by telegraph at the depot in Nottoway. He immediately dispatched one of his brothers-in-law, instructing him to "round up the men and have them meet in the Courthouse yard." Henry then made arrangements to be relieved of his duties at the depot. He awoke the Rev. Theodorick Pryor of "Old Brick" Church and asked him to conduct a prayer service for he and his men.

As the men of the Nottoway Rifle Guards gathered on the Courthouse lawn, there was a somber mood. It appeared that war would become a reality. Heretofore, the hours of drilling, marching and target practice had been somewhat of a lark. The fact that they would now be leaving their homes, their wives and their children began to sink in and with that reality, the men and those families, who had gathered, were quiet and tearful.

Harriet Owen came to the Courthouse to see her husband off. At 30 years of age, with his sandy colored hair, well-trimmed beard and blue-gray eyes, he was a handsome figure in his light, gray, uniform with the gold braid of a Captain's rank.

After the brief prayer service held in "Old Brick", the men once again assembled on the Courthouse lawn. Henry, seeing the distress on the face of his beloved Harriet, took her aside and promised he would take care of himself, her brothers, and cousins. The Robertsons of Nottoway County made up a large part of Henry's Company.

Henry and his company boarded the next train for Richmond. After a few hours, they reached the Capitol City of Virginia and disembarked. The next three days were, no doubt, three of the worst days in Henry's life. His "Nottoway Rifle Guards", were assigned as Company C of the 18th Virginia Infantry Regiment. Commanding the 18th was Colonel Robert Enoch Withers, a physician, originally from Campbell County, who had moved to Danville sometime in the 1850's. Withers had received no formal military training, but was a strict disciplinarian by nature. His assistants were Lt. Colonel Henry A. Carrington, a Richmond attorney and Major George C. Cabell. Major Cabell was from Danville and was both an attorney and a newspaper publisher.

From Danville, Colonel Withers had accompanied the spiffy "Danville Blues." This unit was made up of men who were predominantly city residents. Their blue uniforms were of the best material and they were an impressive sight when marching to the beat of their drummer.

10

Nottoway Courthouse

(Photo by Graham C. Owen)

The Nottoway Courthouse, a Roman Revival style brick structure was completed in 1843. It was here, on the morning of April 23, 1861, that the Nottoway Rifle Guards were mustered and then departed for the the "camp of instruction" at Fort Lee.

Colonel Withers housed the Danville Blues in good quarters and placed most of the rest of his command, including Henry T. Owen's Company C, in a warehouse for three days. The Company was not furnished any rations and thus the first of Henry Owen's confrontations with Colonel Withers took place. Protesting heavily that his men were not properly housed or fed, a heated exchange took place between Henry and Withers.

Eventually the men were furnished rations, but were then transferred to cattle stalls at the camp of instruction.

After training near Richmond, the 18th Virginia was ordered on May 25, 1861, to proceed to Manassas. They camped near Manassas Junction and were under orders to guard the important railroads. Manassas Junction was the junction point of the Orange & Alexandria Railroad and the Manassas Gap Railroad. With only a few tents available, the troops were ordered to encamp in an open field. The saplings and brush, used to construct lean-tos, had gone to the first men to arrive and Henry T. Owen could not find proper shelter for his men. In another confrontation with Withers, Henry stated his men would perform no military duties until they had proper shelter. Withers placed Henry T. Owen under house arrest and this incident, together with others led to the eventual court-martial of Henry.

The 18th remained in camp at Manassas, to guard the rail junction, until they were sent to a camp near Centreville. Food and water was more abundant at this site and by then there were more tents available. At Centreville, the 18th was one of the first units in the line of fire when the Federals moved toward Manassas. The unit clashed with the Federals at Fairfax Court House on Wednesday, July 17, 1861.

Drawing back to Manassas, the 18th was engaged on July 21, 1861, in the First Battle of Manassas. Following that battle, in which the Federals were routed and retreated back to Washington, D.C., the 18th was left at Manassas Junction as rear guard to the rest of the army. After a few weeks at Manassas, the 18th was moved to a camp near Centreville. They remained at this camp through most of the winter.

It was from Centreville that Henry wrote to his wife, Harriet on August 28, 1861. Many of the men in that engagement had become very ill from contaminated water at the Manassas battle site. Harriet apparently had heard that there were fourteen sick men at

12

Lynchburg in the home of the Cabell family. She apparently was very upset at this news and in the letter of August 28, 1861, Henry tries to re-assure her that all is well.

This letter indicates Henry's concern with his family. The education of their oldest daughter, "Millie", is mentioned as well as his concern for his brother, Sandy.

****

Camp Near Centreville
August 28, 1861
My dear Wife,

Your kind and very interesting letter of 24th from Moore's Ordinary has just reached me and I hasten to reply. I waited since the 22nd in doubts whether to direct my letters to the C.H. (Court House) or Meherrin. I presume you are now at home as your letter has been four days dated and you spoke of a hasty leave you intended making within a couple of days.

Mr. Irving still abides with me and we are very considerable friends. I was a little sick a few days ago and sat moping about my tent and he sat around all the time and would have me in a good humor in spite of my life. I said to Tom Cousins that I wanted to have an onion if the Dr. would let me have it, but nobody could find one. Mr. Irving got up and went off, presently came back with five of the largest I ever saw except those we once raised at Mrs. Smith's, and told Tom to fry them up for Capt. Owen, but the Dr. would not let Tom fix them up, so we laid them away for future use.

The Dr. said that evening that he thought if I had some good nice ripe peaches they would help me, but nobody could get them. After awhile, Mr. Irving took his hat and walked off again without saying a word to anybody and was gone awhile. He found a man who had a flour barrel full of nice peaches giving them to his company. He got ten large nice ones and came back with both hands full. I would not have but five and he ate two and gave three to Lieut. Gibbs.

He wanted me to have all, but I would not take them and he finally disposed of them as above.

Our Regiment marched to Fairfax C.H. (Court House) today but came back tonight. It was raining and as I have been taking a little medicine night before last and felt weak, I condescended not to walk so far for nothing, so I remained behind. Mr. Irving told me he would stay too and we remained here chatting all day. Some times we would get in high argument but he always gets me a little.

13

I am quite well now and most of my company are very well, some few are sick and they make a great fuss because they are scared and low spirited too I reckon. When there are so many people together there is obliged to be sickness, but it is all humbug about our army being bad off. I am satisfied we have the healthiest army ever seen and don't let any news from any body deceive you about it. We have now two hundred thousand men in the army and if one in every ten was sick we would have still one hundred and eighty thousand well men and only twenty thousand sick. This would give Richmond say one third, six thousand. Petersburg half that number, three thousand, Lynchburg three thousand, Norfolk five thousand, and still leave three thousand for other places.

Now don't you know at once that if there were three thousand sick at Lynchburg that more than fourteen would be at the Cabell house.

The fact is if one sick soldier passes along the road in a wagon or through a village, directly somebody says half the army is dead and the other half so near dead that our cause is hopeless. I have not lost a man out of fifty four I took from home and when I loose by actual sickness eighteen, one third of my number, people may say we are a little complaining, in war some companies never send home a man to tell the tale of their deaths and here with just one in about two hundred dead, people stare as if they never read of war or heard of death. But I have already said more than I expected when I mentioned this subject.

I am sorry you got fretted with old Irving and think you ought to have kissed him instead of getting mad with the old cuss as you seem to think him. I do not think brother Sandy (See Note #1) ought to come to war as it will not suit him at all. The exposure does not suit middle aged men and young men seem to stand it. Last and besides, a married man unless he has an office ought to be at home with his wife. Whenever I get up a company for war again, I shall object to all married men. They make the best soldiers in every way and are more orderly, but then if one is killed perhaps his whole family will suffer. I saw Pat Sunday and he was well. He has been sick but has gotten well. Tony is now sick and has a very sore throat.

We go to Fairfax tomorrow. Still direct your letters to Manassas. No pay yet but it will be a pile when it does come and do us the more good. Live as close as you can and don't go in debt. If we do not pay out now some way, when the war is over we shall be ruined completely. Now or never is the time to save.

Taxes are going to be tremendous for years and common yardage about 40 cents a yard, sugar fifty and coffee a dollar, with salt ten dollars a sack and every thing else high in proportion. If Milly is not learning fast better keep her at home, tho' I am sure if you made her attend to her books at home just five minutes after school, she would learn. People who depend so much on teachers don't have smart children. When I taught school I found Mrs. Smith made her boys get their lessons at home and therefore they knew how to study at school and are now businessmen worth all the other children in the neighborhood. Write soon.

Most truly yrs, Henry

****

Note #1: "Sandy" was Alexander Macon Owen, born April 14, 1816. He was 45 years of age at the time of this letter. Alexander had been married for several years and had children.

****

In his letter to Harriet of October 9, 1861, Henry again shows his concern for his family and his devotion to Harriet. As the winter months wore on, the 18th, encamped near Centreville and at Fairfax Court House, found little to keep them occupied. During this period of time, visitors from the various towns and hamlets began coming to the camp. The passing back and forth of relatives of some of the men from Nottoway afforded a good way to send letters to and from the home front. Henry took advantage of these couriers whenever he could.

In this letter, Henry also mentions that he is expecting to be court-martialed. The trial was not held until late in 1864.

****

Fairfax C.H. Va
Oct 9th 1861
My dear Wife,

I wrote you on the 4th or 5th and expect you have recd the letter but I have not gotten a reply, yet, I write again as I have an opportunity of sending a letter by a gentleman going to Danville.

We are all well and my men's health is improving rapidly since the weather became cool. It is very cold here and I thought this morning it was going to snow but it turned out a cold rain.

I sent you a little bag of chestnuts that I picked up yesterday. There are thousands upon thousands of them up here and I reckon I shall get fat on them. I had worn out my white pants so I fixed up the chestnuts in them.

I have no news to write. When I saw Pat he was well. That was Sunday.

I am expecting Tom Cousins from what he wrote last week. Write me all about the Orders and accounts I sent you as I may keep my book straight. If I send you an order and somebody else collects the money I can't help it unless I know in time to present its collection. Mr. Harper is ready to start and I must close. My respects to Dr. and Mrs. D. J. Tell Clay I wish he was here to help me get chestnuts. He could fill his hat soon.

I have not had a trial yet nor can I tell when it will come off. Gen. Cocke is our friend and will do all he can for us but he says he can't tell when the court martial can meet.

It seems hard for the men at home to get well. We are expecting a fight now every day but I myself cannot see what is to bring it on more than usual. Everything stands just as it did two months ago and there is no new sign of battle to me. There is some talk that we shall go to Aquia Creek soon but I doubt this too. Heavy cannon firing every day down on the Potomac but nobody hurt that we know of.

In great haste I am
Most truly and faithfully
Yrs, Henry

****

Note #2:   "Clay" was Henry Clay Owen, born on May 15, 1853, Henry Clay was the oldest son of Henry T. and Harriet Owen.

****

In a letter to Harriet on November 6, 1861, Henry replies to Harriet's question posed in her recent letter, regarding the lending of one of the slaves to neighbors, Mr. and Mrs. Clarke. The Clarke's owned a bad bull named, "Meckleface". Henry was concerned that the bull might gore the children of his slave, Martha.

Henry again mentions his pending court-martial that was again postponed. Despite the hardships of war and camp life, Henry was concerned for the welfare of his family.

****

Centreville (VA)
Nov 6th 1861
My dear Harriet,

Yrs of yesterday came to hand today making a quicker trip than letters usually make. I shall send this off tomorrow but you will not get it in two days for one day from here to Manassas and one day on the Road will take up the time.

I am truly sorry for Mr. Smith and trust he will bear up under his afflictions for he is truly unfortunate. I wrote to Mr. Jackson this morning before I began your letter and he will get his letter one day before you will I presume.

Tell Mr. Clarke he can get Martha if you think "Meckleface won't pull the little negroe's eyes. I am really afraid "Meckleface" might get after them and kill some of them. There is no better people than Mr. and Mrs. Clarke and I will leave the bargain to you. Do just as you think best about it and I will be satisfied. You can take Catherine if you want her. In making the bargain tell Mr. Clarke to clothe the little negroes and Martha best he can and don't charge him any hire provided he will do so. Or you can leave it to Dr. Jackson to say what she is worth and we will clothe her ourselves. Better wait until Christmas before making the bargain with Mr. Clarke. There will be time enough and we can tell better then what negroes will hire for.

You had better buy some corn if you think you will stay there another year. If you have any hogs buy about fifteen barrels and get somebody to haul it to you. Buy it from Mr. Dalton if he has it to spare or from somebody that will bring it to you. Get the best, for corn is cheap and the best should be bought. Dr. Jackson or Mr. Southall will tell you what to pay for it and I will send you the money to pay for it by Mr. Richard Irby. He will come home in a few days and I will send by him the little books and a pipe for Dr. Jackson. One of my men made the pipe and I made the books.

My books were not quite finished when Jas. Robertson (See Note #3) left so I could not send them. I forgot the chestnuts and felt like I had forgot something. I went in and out of my tent forty times and looked about but I could not think what else it was that I wanted to send by Jas. After he was gone I remembered the chestnuts and as they began to get wormy I ate them up. I will try and get some more before Mr. Irby leaves.

You did right to keep the flannel for I have no earthly use for any more clothing now and have already so much I am greatly troubled when we go to move.

I have my trial postponed for a few days on account of the absence of Major George C. Cabell who is an important witness for me. He is sick in Danville but I expect him on here in a few days.

Capt. White of the Tigers is my lawyer and he is a capital hand on such things. Mr. Irving has left our Regiment and gone to Winchester with Gen. Jackson.

Governor Letcher appointed him Aide to Gen. Jackson with commission and pay of Captain. Irving and myself had made up our difficulty and I was truly sorry to see him leave. When he got ready to leave he came around to bid me good bye and I felt truly melancholy after he was gone. He told me just as he was leaving if I wanted him to stay and attend to my case he would do so and give up his commission. Of course I would not allow him to lose his commission to save mine so I told him "no." He then said he did not see any danger to me and Capt. White would attend to it all right for me but if any danger there attended me I must telegraph him and he would come on here at all hazards. He would not let me pay him for his services before at Manassas and I offered him money twice. The last time he told me "he had no use for money and did not attend to that case for my money." When I drew my money before, Irving told me not to keep any more than I had a use for then, for if I did I would spend it foolishly. He is a glorious friend. In speaking of our difficulty he said he had enemies who had misrepresented him and he hoped the time would come when their injustices would be apparent to his friends.

On the 6th we had an election and all the Nottoway boys voted for Pryor. Everything passes off quietly and pleasantly more so than is usual for election days.

The soldiers are all very uneasy, afraid that Gen. Beauregard is going to resign. They all prefer B. to Davis because Beauregard is here with them and they have all been with him in battle.

My men are all well and hearty. Looking for a few more from home. Give my best respects to Dr. Jackson and family and Mr. Southall.

We have had some very wet weather up here lately and the ground is very muddy. Today is of 6th inst and I will say a word in the morning.

Nov. 8th: Our company will be paid off today and I will send you some money by Mr. Irby. Let me know how much you will need and I will send it to you.

Kiss the children and respects to the negroes. Write soon and write a long letter. Give my best regards to Sis Helen and Cousin Carey and that to their sister too.

Most truly Yrs,
Henry

****

Note #3: Jas. Robertson, was probably James A. Robertson, a cousin to Harriet, who later joined Company C on March 10, 1862. James A. Robertson died on May 10, 1862 from wounds received at Williamsburg on May 5, 1862.

****

After going through the early battles in Northern Virginia, Henry was not discouraged. Some of the civilians, left at home, began to panic and fear that the war would come to their doorstep. Harriet had written Henry that she felt she should move from Nottoway to a safer location. Henry suggested she might be safer at his mother's plantation in Prince Edward County. In a letter to Harriet, dated May 21, 1862, Henry instructs her as to the move and expresses little patience with some of his neighbors whom he says are "easily frightened."

****

Laurel Hill Church
Below Richmond
May 21st 1862
My dear Harriet,

I have just recd yours of the 19th inst. and it furnishes me items of good news as well as some of painful interest. I wrote you yesterday but the arrival of yr' letter today furnished me the plausible and gratifying excuse to write you again in reply.

While I think of it, I must say, I forgot to ask you yesterday to send Mr. Temple's Bond by Lieut. Watkins when he returns. Also my clothes if you have not already sent them and if any body else brings them I think I shall hardly get them as the orders are very rigid in camp and no visiting allowed from camp to camp. I might not see Mr. Slaughter in several months tho' in five miles of him. Still you can ask them if you see a better opportunity to forward them here. I wrote you yesterday how many clothes I had on hand

and they are amply sufficient for all my needs at this time. Don't make me any more yet and save your flannel for hard times.

In your letter you seem to be in a speck of trouble and I really think you give way to grief too much and from too simple causes. Since I got your letter I feel in fine spirits because you are still well and I am living. I do not think you have any cause to be despondent and think you must cheer up. Remember there are many chances in favor of my escaping the enemy's bullets and I will be prudent in my diet so as to avoid as far as possible camp fever and diseases.

We are expecting each day to be paid off and I hope it will be done before need have occasion to move to Pr. Edwd. As soon as I get my money I will send it to you and you can then move everything of value to Pr. Edwd that you may need. Prove yourself sufficient for the times and don't stop and cry and grieve when reason teaches that time is precious and nerve of the utmost importance.

Send your things – chairs, beds, bureau, etc. to some of your friends or neighbors and just take such things along as you are unwilling to trust out. But all this may be unnecessary and I hope it will not be required that you should leave home at all. Some of your neighbors are weak minded and so easily frightened that they cut rare shines I expect but don't catch their hasty fever and get scared before there is some real danger. Women are not asked to take the Oath of Allegiance and you will be safe from invasion at my mother's. I can see the dangers from where I am better than those at a distance and if I was at home I should neither leave or take the Yankee Oath and think I should have nothing to fear. I would like to see who of my ancient neighbors would take the Oath and just witness their shame and degradation when our cause finally triumphs. You will have ample time to move after Petersburg falls and so don't be in any hurry or haste nor let people frighten you who never have been near the Yankees nor smelt powder.

I hope Tom Ives may yet recover and join me again. He was one of my messmates and altogether a nice clever fellow – besides he is a very brave boy and fought well upon the 5th inst. until wounded.

Sam Morton is in my mess and Pete Temple. We three get along very well. Sam is now well and hearty again. Pryor and Archer are both well and send their best wishes and respects to all.

Pryor is one of the best soldiers and never stopped for his toe. He is well now and does duty up to any soldier.

Some of my men get off on any slight excuse but I don't care much as we have not needed them and besides they wanted to see their friends whom they parted with more than a year ago. Our surgeon who remained at Williamsburg has returned to our Reg and informed me that little Jimmy and Davis will die but Allen may recover. He says that Jeffreys too will not get well. Jimmy had never been conscious of his condition since the Battle and fever on his brain would soon end him. He saw all our prisoners but Verser was not among them so I fear the worst befell him and that he was killed among the thick bushes where we were fighting.

If Lieut. Sorey stops when returning give him my best love but I fear his trip will end in his capture by the vandals. I am glad he called on you and it proves his <u>friendship</u> for me. I have heard from Bill once since coming to the Peninsula but his letter was so old I did not know where to answer it. I got it the 25th of April written the 12th and he was moving. If you know where he is write to him that I am well and will write as soon as I hear where he is.

Nothing of importance going on here and we are expecting a great fight but it may not come off for several weeks or even months.

Tell your neighbors that I shall fight to the last and go with the army for if we separate then we will be all conquered at once. If we keep together we can carry on the War for a hundred years.

It will not do to give up just because a few battles go against us. Keep in good spirits and if you stop the children from school employ yourself in teaching them. It will help your head and their minds. Write when you can and I say again don't be low spirited at anything.

(Direct to Richmond)   Most devotedly etc.

Henry T. Owen

****

Encamped near Richmond in June of 1862, Henry arranged for a visit by his oldest son, Henry Clay Owen. Again, concerned for the education of his children, Henry requested that Clay bring his book so that Henry could hear him spell and read.

****

My Dear Harriet,

I seems I am not to get a letter until the mail becomes steady again. I understand that every coach and box on the Danville RR is busily occupied carrying troops up to the Great Jackson and therefore no mail passes up or down that Road.

At first I was a little uneasy and feared that perhaps you were sick but I can now see why I have not recd a letter from you for ten days and shall submit patiently especially since I am so because our Government is reinforcing Jackson. If he is furnished with twenty of thirty thousand more men we should see McClellan obliged to fall back to defend Washington or Jackson will capture their capital. We have plenty of men here and can spare Jackson as many as he wants.

Lieut. Lowery is down on a visit to see his Danville friends and we came near taking a good hug – but then I knew he was hard and bony and it would make my mouth water for something better than one of his cruel squeezes. I saw Col. Wm S. Guy yesterday – he was to see me and looked sad and melancholy. I tried to cheer him up but don't think I succeeded in making a change in his feelings. I shall send you a small box this evening or tomorrow with your jars and two others that belong to Mrs. Leuth. She will send for hers. I packed them as best I could and know they will hardly break. If I could have gotten to Richmond I would have sent you something nice but we can't go there at all although we are in sight. I expect that Peter La Neve will come down to see us in some week or ten days and if you can fix Clay up a little I should like for him to come down and stay a week or two. Peter is a good boy and can take care of him, and says he will let Clay know when he is ready to come. Caution Clay that when he gets on the cars to keep his seat and make him promise not to move from coach to coach. Fix him up as genteel as possible as he is a Captain's Boy and I would like to see him appear well in Camp. Let his clothes be nice and fit him. If he brings any luggage a shirt is all that is needed and he can just put on one over the other as one may get dirty. Don't let his clothes be too light as they will show dirt if so and if too thin he may take cold. If he can bring his <u>Book</u> I would like to hear him spell and read and if he will study hard I will keep him until he gets tired and wants to go home.

Peter will see my Box to the Express Office but it may be some time before you get it as the Road is so blocked up. Don't trouble Clay with luggage as he will have enough to get along without bundles.

When you can do so – please send us some of that splendid butter that we love so well. Send it to E. H. Stokes again for me – and write soon. I am sorry to hear that Lieut. Vaughan will probably die from his wound. He was a noble fellow.

Most Dutifully Yrs &c

Henry

****

Despite his efforts to try and keep Harriet's spirits up, Henry, on occasion, related some of the sadder events of the war. In a letter of June 21, 1862, he relates the fate of a deserter.

****

June 21st, 1862

My dear Wife,

Since writing you yesterday Lieut. Watkins has come in and informed us of the death of Mrs. Dalton. I am very sorry for I set a great deal by her she was always so kind and neighborly and she took such good care of the little children. I expect Mr. Dalton is broken up.

I saw yesterday on dress parade a Deserter have his head shaved and today he will have a large letter D burned into his leg and placed in the Penitentiary. He was a substitute in the Charlotte Company and ran away and went to Richmond several weeks ago. Sam Spencer was in the same company and one day when walking down the street by himself he overtook two officers with this man. He immediately recognized him and attempted to grab him but the man knocked him down and tried to escape. Sam was at him again and called for help saying the man was a Deserter. The two men dressed like officers said he belonged to their company and tried to get off with him but Sam hung to this fellow and the Police came up and carried all the party to the Provost Marshal's office. Sam was sent after his Captain and returned with several members of the company who were sent into a room separately where several hundred prisoners were confined and told to find the man. As each one picked him out and left the room another was brought in and each one fixed upon that man. His name is Burns and he was brought to Camp and tried by C Martial and condemned as I have said above. I thought it was right to punish him as he was but I felt sorry for the poor fellow as he bowed down with shame and said not a word while the barber took off his long black locks and left his head white and bald. The Regiment was drawn up in line and the prisoner placed in front under guard while sentinels paced to and fro back behind to keep off a large crowd who pressed up to see the sight. He was an Irishman and a large, strong, desperate looking man.

We look for Lyons today and I hope Clay will come down with him. If Clay can come send him and if Mr. Mann is at the C House tell him to come and see me. I wrote to him but have had no answer.

For such I am as ever
Yrs devotedly – Henry
****

Following the Battles of Gaines Mill, Williamsburg and Seven Pines, Henry was again encamped near Richmond. His letter to Harriet of July 16, 1862, included an expression of his hope to buy a small farm.
****

Camp below Richmond
Darby Town Road July 16th 1862

My dear Harriet,

Yrs of the 14th now rcd last night and I have an opportunity of mailing a letter at once. I write you in reply. If you can purchase the bacon from Archer even 5 cents. Take it and pay on the bonds if he will settle in that manner. There is some interest due on the notes and uncle Boggy (?) will settle that or see to it for you. I would rather settle that way than have to bring cash for the bacon as anyone else. You can purchase the whole amt in bacon or any thing else he has to spare. I wish I could get Archer to settle up our matters as this is the third season that our machine has threshed without my receiving a cent. We are expecting to be paid off in a few days and I shall wish to use the money in paying some of my old debts, unless you need it.

As soon as we get before hand, if ever, I want to buy a home some where that has good land, I should like of all things to possess a small rich farm where I would not have to work from land so hard and get nothing for my labor as I seem to be obliged to do.

I am sorry for Archer (See Note #4) and feel even on his account. I wrote a long letter to Lyons and insisted that he should act prudently but suppose he has been confined to camp so long that he now feels like a bird and can't constrain the inclination to travel around among his friends. I am well again but a little home sick yet if I come home soon I would not perhaps live a month as a soldier means a great risk of taking typhoid fever by change of life. It is decidedly more dangerous going home that it is coming to camp – because we can not get good things enough here to bring on fever and at home our friends will say "eat this-eat a little of that" and so on until we are taken with fever and they then say we acted very wrong to eat so much fruit and cake. I would eat enough anyhow without persuasion but how much would I eat if you set by and fed me like a young crow? Where would I stop?

Henry Dyson has deserted and will probably be shot unless he escapes. You need not say anything of it to anyone for I have failed to tell you before because I don't want to hear people saying they heard Mrs. Owen say this and that. If they say anything to you just keep silent about this matter. Henry ran off to Richmond and remained there for several days upon a forged pass he then, after being caught, escaped from the guard and it is thought left the city by way of the canal. He will have a hard road to travel and will have to be quite shrewd to escape the police on all the roads.

No more now

Yrs devotedly

Henry

Send in a box by the
first one passing or by Express

****

Note #4: Archer was Archer Robertson, brother of Harriet Robertson Owen. He was badly wounded on June 27, 1862 at the Battle of Gaines Mill and lost a leg by amputation soon thereafter. Following the war, Archer moved to Georgia and died there in 1890.

****

After the visit to camp by Clay, a group of boys evidently visited the camp. Henry showed them the battlefield. In his letter to Harriet of July 27, 1862, he mentions this incident.

****

In Camp 18th Reg. Va July 27th 1862

My dear Harriet,

Mr. Dalton expects to leave for home tomorrow and I avail myself of the opportunity to send you a few things and write a letter also which he will take up to you.

I sent a blanket which I bought for 4.00 from Giles Miller. I rather think an officer is out of place strolling a crop or battle field in search of plunder, and I would rather pay for what I get – but it is different with the privates and they should be allowed to have all they can carry along.

My blanket has a small slip of white cloth sewed on the corner with my name roughly marked with black thread. The other blanket and oil cloth is Pete Temple's and he wants them saved until the winter. We have plenty of covering for the present but will need our blankets next winter if we still have to battle the Yankees.

I send two shirts which have gotten torn and if you can sew them up I would like to have them again after awhile. I send two newspapers one is the Dixie with Genl Johnston's report of the Seven Pines Battle and Henry Dyson's card in reply to Col. Carrington. Save the paper as I shall perhaps have to refer to it in future times. The other paper is the Bn. Johnathan which I found upon the battle field and send you to read because it is a little interesting. You will also find the life of Jas. W. Jackson who killed Ellsworth in Alexandria. I send too a little string of buttons and a Yankee cap for one of the children.

If Leo Hawkes wants any of my papers let him have them as I shall write to him to try and settle some business and besides Mr. Dalton paid me fifty dollars today and will pay more I expect in a few days.

I wish Clay could have come down with these little boys as he would have enjoyed himself much more in their company. We all went down on the Battle field and I spent a day showing them every thing about the place. If you send me a box any time soon send me some pepper if you can procure any in the neighborhood. I have no news of interest and must close my hasty letter.

I hope the sick ones are better now and may mend soon – My respects to all who inquire after me at any time.
Most devotedly yrs
H. T. Owen
I hope I shall be fortunate enough to come up soon though so far I have failed in all attempts to get off – yet there is some chance still that I may get a furlough in a week or so.
Yrs truly
Henry

****

Henry, apparently, enjoyed corresponding with his ten-year-old son, Henry Clay Owen. In a letter to Clay, dated September 7, 1863, Henry tells Clay of his some of his own experiences with one of his tutors.

****

Camp 18tg Regt. Va. Inft.
Orange Co. Va. Sept. 7th 1863

H. Clay Owen
My dear Son,

Your letter of the 24th of August came duly to house and I was glad to learn that you had enjoyed yourself so much upon your trip and visit to your Grand Ma's.

I would have liked to had some of the good water melons you spoke of as I have not eaten one since I was at Manassas two years ago. I have eaten only three peaches this summer and the season will soon be over. We sometimes get a few little, sour, apples but I expect we enjoy better health than if we had an abundance of fruit and vegetables.

You spoke of a visit to old Mr. Medleys. When I was eleven years old I went to school at Mr. Medleys to Mrs. Gallion. She taught school upstairs and had a large number of scholars. There were four of us little boys and all the others were girls.

One of the boys is dead now and I have not seen the others for ten years. Mr. Medley was always very kind to us and so was Cousin Polly but she would make us hop sometimes when she caught us in mischief about her chicken coops.

Mrs. Gallion was a very fine teacher and I learned very fast under her instruction. I remember she bought one Paisley's Geography and I learned all I ever learned at school about Geography under her. Study hard and don't waste your time at play. I want to see when I get home if you can point out on the map all the places I have been to in Virginia, North Carolina, Maryland and Pennsylvania. Kiss you Ma and the children for me.

Your affectionate father
H. T. Owen

****

In mid September 1863, Henry requested a leave to visit the family.

****

Camp 18th Regt Va. Inft.
Sept. 17, 1863
Capt. Linthicum,

I respectfully ask for seven (7) days "leave of absence" to visit my family in the County of Nottoway.

I was at home on a twenty day leave of absence last Feb. last and rejoined my command one day before my leave expired. I will again return on time unless prevented by insurmountable obstacles.

I have present for duty eighteen men in my company and Lieut. Fowlkes Co. F who has command will continue in command until I return.

> Very respectfully Yr obt
> humble Srvt
> H.T. Owen Capt C. Co.
> 18th Regt. Va.

****

Henry, again, demonstrated his love and concern for his family, in a letter to his son, Henry Clay Owen, dated April 18, 1864. In the letter, he also demonstrates the value he places on education. In this letter, Henry also relates to Clay a lesson in abstaining from liquor.

****

Barracks 7th & Clay Streets
Richmond Va Apl 18th 1864
My dear Son,

Your letter of the 11th instant came duly to hand Saturday night and I was pleased to see your improvement in letter writing as well as hear from my family and get the news it embraces. I hope you will apply yourself closely to your studies and will not loll away a single precious hour. Remember that your first letter was written a little over a year ago and since then you have improved very much but there is still a great deal to learn. If you wish to be a wise man. You must not waste your time and neglect your books while you are young, I hope you will soon begin the study of Latin. When Mr. Irving was ten years old he had gone through his English Grammar and commenced studying Latin. He had the White Swelling and could not run about and play with the other little boys but had to remain in the house or get a negroe man to carry him wherever he went. The other little boys went fishing and hunting and climbed fruit trees or ran and skipped across the green lawns through the beautiful fields and shady woods in search of wild flowers and fruits

28

while the poor little cripple was forgotten and left behind in the lonely school room until they came back laughing and cheering with their cheeks flushed with the glow of health and exercise. He could not join in their sports upon the green grass and as he looked out and saw them playing and leaping and could hear their merry laughter he often sighed and felt lonely to think he never should walk and run like they did, but he spent his time in study as he had no one to keep him company and cheer him in his solitude. So as he kept learning book after book and studied very hard he soon became a smart boy and grew up a very wise man. When he was about fifteen he got well of the White Swelling and went to College where he found very few boys that knew more than he did. You know he is now a wise man and I consider him one of the smartest men I ever saw. Twenty years ago he was a lawyer in Memphis Tennessee and the Mexican War commenced. A company of Cavalry was raised in Memphis and he was elected Lieutenant and went to Mexico. The Cavalry did not have much fighting to do but he was in one desperate fight at Madeline Bridge where our troops whipped the Mexicans. Mr. Irving ruined himself by drinking liquor and could have been a General now but for this ruinous habit. Genl Pickett, Genl Jackson and Genl Longstreet were all Lieutenants in Mexico and Genl Wheat was a Lieut in the same company with Mr. Irving. Wheat was 1st Lieut and Mr. Irving 2nd Lieut and all those officers who let liquor alone have made great Generals.

An education will do more for a man than all the wealth in the world and no robber or king or person on Earth can steal it or rob a man of the possession. I have a man in my company who can travel among the Spaniards and talk to them in their language and I wish you to learn all you can and if I am able I will give you an education that will help you more than any other property or possession.

I would like to have you visit me and bring your Grammar with you.

Mr. Talley had his little boy here from Petersburg last week and he is a smart little fellow about ten years old and very well behaved indeed. He wants to know when you come down to see me and he will come to see you. His father told him you had been down and he came over and stayed several days. He is a curly headed little fellow and is named William Henry Talley. You can come down whenever your Ma and cousin Bettie will permit you to do so

29

and if you will bring your Grammar I will keep you so as to help in your lessons.

Give my love to Mrs., Cousin B and all the children. Write to me often and tell Mich I expect to get a letter from him soon.

Genl Lee is preparing for a great Battle with the Yankees. Genl Longstreet has come up from Bristol with his entire Corp and Genl Loring is coming on with fourteen thousand men from the far South. In a week or two at most, the great conflict will begin and thousands upon thousands will go down upon the bloody fields or come out maimed for life. War is a terrible thing and all men should love Peace and hate strife.

I am in haste
Yr affectionate father
H T Owen
****

From the battle front, Henry writes regarding bank notes (currency) issued during the war. Henry advises Harriet as to the value of certain currency and requests that she send him some apples, potatoes, peas and muskmelons.

****

Chester Station Va
August 22, 1864

Dear Wife,

Yrs of the 20th was received today and I hasten to reply. The old $10 note is worth $6 and the 15 is worth 5 but people don't like to take them. You must send me all you get and I will pass them off for you. I send you a N.C. State note, Bank of Commerce at Newbern worth 5 for one. Don't spend it till the War is over. It will then be worth as much as gold.

I will write to Mr. Brown about the flour and to Dr. Thaxton about your teeth.

You can send me a box or bunch of eatables such as you can spare. Apples, potatoes and some peas in the hull and some muskmelons if you will gather them before they get too ripe. Direct your box to "Capt. H. T. Owen 18th Regt Va Infty Hunton's Brigade, Chester Care of A. S. Buford Richmond." Don't fix up your box 'till the day you intend to send it or the things will spoil. All the boys are getting boxes and we live splendidly.

There is no firing in front of us and we can walk upon the breastworks in full view of the Yankees. We can hear the fighting at Petersburg very plainly and there has been some fighting on the other side of James River. We are about six or seven miles from Petersburg and four miles from Bermuda Hundred which we could see up the river from City Point last fall.

All the boys are well except a few whom you do not know. Ben is as fat as a bear and has grown very much. Pryor is quite well but looks thin. Gilliam is still at Chester Hospital and Kendrick is at home. He is better. I am in good health and fattening fast but crave some good action.

Charley and Joe can go home every week.

Give my love to the children and Mother. When did you hear from Bill and Wm Henry?

Yrs truly

Henry

****

A fragment of a letter from Henry to Harriet, probably written soon after August 22, of 1864, states that he has enjoyed a mess of peas for dinner and praise for the apples. Henry also warns that the "old issue" will go out on January 1, and advises that Clay should not take any more than Harriet can spend before that date

****

(?) 1864

My dear wife,

The --- appears to---day and night and thankfully----had a fine mess of peas for dinner and the boys say the apples are the best in the world. A great many soldiers to beg some but I told them I none to sell. Some of the -- get a box every day or two and we live very well. I have written --- hope to hear from him in a few days. I forgot to tell you that the old issue goes out of date on the 1st January, so Clay must not take any more than you can rid of easily. Pryor and Ben are both very well. Capt. is with the Co. again. Our boys frequently get a chance to talk with the Yankees and they say they are all---is quiet in the front of us and no firing between the pickets.

Give my love to Mother & Bob and Cousin Matthew. Also to W. Henry, Mr. Ewing and sister Ann.

Mr. Temple has just returned and he is well but looks thin.

Let me know how the corn looks and how many good ears are on the stalks. Let me know if Mr. Johnson has paid you. How is cousin Bettie. I hope we shall all be back before Christmas to eat a good dinner at home, but God will end this strife in his own good time. Yankee deserters all say the Yankees are tired of fighting and that a peace President will be elected.

I am truly yrs

Henry

****

In early October of 1864, Henry tells Harriet he has received apples and peaches from home. He also writes of Harriet's brother, Pryor, and then expresses concern that Grant (General U.S. Grant), will take Petersburg and Richmond.

****

Chester Station

Oct 1st 1864

Dear Wife,

Yrs of 27th inst. reached me yesterday. I am at the hospital at this place but have gotten well and would go to my company today but it is raining and the surgeon advises me to wait till Monday.

I intended to say in my last that the apples were as fine as I ever saw and decidedly better than any about camp. The peaches were beginning to spoil but most of them were not hurt. I gave Pryor a fair chance at this box and explained to him how he had missed getting his dues in the band. Pryor is helping Stephen Scott in the settler's tent and makes a good deal of money. He is litter bearer and has nothing to do except in time of battle so that he is at liberty to assist the settlers in selling.

Ken passed here a few days ago going to the Company. He is a great deal better but does not appear to me as fully recovered.

I do not know what advice to give Cousin Bettie about falling back with the army. I am not able to advise her in this matter.

There has been very heavy fighting on the north side of James River near Chaffin's Farm about six or eight miles from here and it appears that the Yankees got the best of the fight. Our troops were driven back day before yesterday and there was some heavy firing in that direction last night and yesterday but I can't hear the result. Thousands of troops passed here going over there on Thursday and I expect the Yanks have been repulsed. I think Grant will certainly get Petersburg and Richmond in less than a month. Some of these mornings you will find Grant's Army between you and Richmond and all communication with me cut off. But don't despair. If he gets between me and home you must still do all you can to make a living and I will be as cheerful as I can under such circumstances.

32

I send you obituary of Col Carter written by Capt Palmer of the 3rd Va Cavalry. Put it away so it will be preserved.

I will send your box back as soon as I can get some old shoes to put in it. This I can do when the boys draw new shoes again.

I am glad to hear that Bill was not hurt in the late fight in the Valley.

Give my love to all. Write soon.

Yrs truly

Henry

I can get about $50 per barrel for the apples. If you send them down at once I will sell them for you.

****

Always concerned with the affairs of his family, Henry writes that he is saddened by bad news about his brother, William J. Owen. William J. Owen was born in Prince Edward County November 14, 1825. He was five years older than Henry. He served the Confederacy in Battery B, 13th Virginia Artillery.

****

Trenches near Chester
Sunday Oct 9th 1864

My dear Wife,

I recd yrs if 5th this morning and feel sad at the news it contains about my brother. I hope he is not killed and will take every step, likely to avail, to find out if he is a prisoner. Write me at once whether Calvin stated the name of the Battle or where it was fought. You said it took place on the 22nd but did not name the Battle ground. This is important and let me know all the particulars, whose Brigade and whose Division he belonged to. I wrote about ten days ago and have been very busy ever since besides I have waited for a letter from you and I had nothing worth writing. Ben had a letter from you a few days that stated all well. Our duties are heavy and important here so we have very little spare time and see nothing around us worth writing.

Abner's wife is staying at Chester Depot about two and half miles from here and Abner is up there. She came down yesterday and will go back today. I have gotten well and the boys are well. Fighting is going on to our right at Petersburg and our left across James River but none just here. We are still working and strengthening our fortifications and are preparing for the enemy if he intends to attack us. They may do so but we don't much expect it here. There are great many chestnuts about here but they will not get ripe good 'till after the first big frost. Some few faulty ones are getting ripe and the soldiers are beating out the green ones and selling them. My company is the largest in the whole Brigade and looks like a Battalion.

The men are well behaved and I have no trouble with them.

Give my best regards to Cousin Bettie, Sister Ann, Mother H Rob and the children.

I will write as often as I can as so without neglecting my duties and find anything to write.

I am truly Yrs

Henry

****

In November 1864, Henry received a care package from Harriet and she had apparently shipped some apples. He evidently had sold the apples for a good price.

Always concerned for the kin and neighbors at home, Henry mentions a medal won in a card game by Pryor. This Pryor was Theodorick Pryor Robertson, another of Harriet's brothers who served in Company C. Named for the famous Nottoway preacher, Pryor Robertson apparently thought an occasional gambling game was no sin.

****

Near Chester Station Va

Nov 3rd 1864

My dear Wife,

Yrs of the 31st came to hand this morning and I recd the box and barrel of apples a few hours after. Weldon sold the barrel of apples for me by the time they were set on the ground for one hundred dollars. He told me that was as much as they were worth and I hope you will be satisfied with the price. I left the matter to him entirely and told him to do as he thought best so he fixed his price and sold them in two minutes. The box is a real treat to us and we had a real slew of turnips today for dinner.

I sent you fifty dollars a few days ago and will send you one hundred dollars in this letter. I will send your box back and the jar and will try to get you some clothes and shoes if I can but the weather is getting cold now and the men use their old garments for bedding.

I was so glad Mother has heard from brother Bill. I could not help from a hearty cry when I read your letter. When I first heard he was missing I tried not to mind it and no one saw any

34

change in my conduct. I went to work to find out where he was and I intended to do everything possible to learn of his fate. Now when I heard he was safe my feelings were overcome and I could not help crying heartily. I had tried not to mind it and worked hard for him.

You wrote that Pryor had won at cards a medal from Junins Lipscomb that he got from Miss Sallie Hardaway which was the property of Luther Rowlett. Now I should advise Pryor to keep it. Miss Sallie ought to know better than to give one gentleman's property to another and if she gave Junins the medal or lent it to him she did wrong. Junins and Pryor set down to play a game of cards and if Pryor wins fifty dollars loser Lipscomb may claim it but if Pryor loses his money it is all right. If Miss Hardaway has such associates as Junins Lipscomb she is unfortunate and must expect to suffer. Pryor is expected back today from furlough and I will deliver the message you send from Miss H. but if he asks my advice or sense of right in the matter I shall tell him that he is clearly entitled to the medal and can do as he likes. I hope I am not expected to use my influence or authority in the matter.

I wish you to let me know how much Cousin Bettie has taught and how much she charges. I am willing to pay for all the time she has taught but not for any time she has not.

Anything you wish to sell then tell me and I will sell it for you if you are satisfied with the price of the apples.

Let me hear from you and give my love to Mother and family.

I am Yrs truly
Henry
****

In late 1864, Henry was confined to the hospital for a few days and he wrote a brief letter Harriet, requesting that she visit him before he re-joined his company.
****

Saturday Morning
(1864)

My dear Wife,

My company left for Lee's Army this morning. I am sick at the hospital and will remain perhaps for five or six days but I can't get home.

Meet your Pa at the Junction Monday and he will come with you down to see me before I leave. I just have time to say these lines.

Yours as ever
Henry

I will meet you at the Depot.

****

In 1881, Henry was in Richmond and the family was at Green Bay. In a letter to his five year old daughter, Mary Eliza (Mamie), Henry shows his love of family, cloaking it with his humor.

****

Second Auditor's Office
Richmond Va Feb 2nd 1881

Dear Mamee,

I received on yesterday your very precious little letter and called together my friends Mr. Cross, member of the Legislature from Nansemond County, Dr. Wing and Mr. Morrisson and all together we made it out to read:

"Dear Pa, write to me Mame." Then there are six A's and then comes Mame again, followed by nineteen A's and the letter closes with a picture of that dog Mich sent to your Ma. She wrote to me and described him very well so that when I saw your picture of him I recognised him at a glance. Dr. Wing thought it was a cat and Mr. Cross said it was a cow with the feet going the wrong way and Mr. Morrisson said it was a horse, but all agreed it was well done and a good nice letter for a little girl to write.

You must take pains and try to improve and write me another letter. You must slip up on your Ma and kiss her for me sometimes and be a good girl and don't let her freeze during this cold spell. You must hug Helen and Sallie for me and kiss the whole family all around but if it is too much for a little girl to do all at once you can kiss half of the lot and then rest awhile or get Helen to help you but you and Helen must both kiss your Ma and tell her Pa is coming home Friday night if he can get off and if not the he will come as soon as he can.

I will write to Helen tomorrow.

Your affectionate father,
H. T. Owen

****

Ever the family man, after the war, Henry corresponded with several members of the family. On March 21, 1900, a cousin, B.T. Medley wrote Henry the following:

****

March 21st, 1900

Capt. H. T. Owen
Dear cousin Henry,

Your kind letter lies before me. I am always glad to hear from you. I want you to keep that dear old Bible till I call for it. If you live longer than I, then it will be safe in your hands, and you must name the one you think will appreciate it the most when you are done with it. If it were in my possession when I die it might be lost or go in the hands of strangers so you might keep it for me. -- -- rather have his love than his money. I have no idea why he has to pen this position against me and still look after my welfare and at times he writes me very kindly. I let him do as he likes and I do as I can. I never say anything to him that is unkind. I love him and try to look over all his faults. He has never been to see me since my father's burial. Willie and Pinkie are very kind. Emmett wants to pay my board but they will not accept it but I gave them all the crop raised at my old home and I dare say this makes us equal. They will not let me leave them. I wish I could see you and will do so if it is ever in my power. It seems that we never meet at G. Bay at the same time. I will be glad to hear from you occasionally as you go on down life's journey. With much love for you and your wife and children believe me

Yr cousin
B. T. Medley
****

As an after-thought, B.T. Medley enclosed with his above letter, a letter written by Henry T. Owen to B.T. Medley. Henry was a young boy when he wrote the letter to Medley.
****

Sir,

I am very sorry I had to disappoint you last Sunday. I expect Mr Thomas will teach nex Sunday also you must come and see me for I am by my self. Ma is goan half of the time cousin A. H. is gone over to see Miss Mary and I am in hopes he will bring her home before long and depart no more.

When you go up home holy day you must come by and tell B--- he must come by for I expect I will walk up home. You must excuse the bad riting for Mr. Thomas has made me change the holding of my pen so it looks now. I am at the riting bench and Mr. Thomas has the eye of a halk. I have to rite a few and then hide my paper as the saying is he is one of em. Give my best respects to cousin Jane and Mr. Gallion and cousin Betty. You may have them too but I would rather you would come after them.

Yours forever
Henry T. Owen

Cousin Henry I send you this letter.
It will remind you of your youth.
You must keep it.

With love
Your cousin
B. T. Medley

****

In a letter to one of his grandsons dated July 16, 1901, Henry again exhibits, his love of family.

****

2601 E. Franklin
Richmond Va. July 16, 1901

Master Kenneth C. Johnson
Bruceville, Va,
My dear Grand-son,

I received your letter last week and was very glad to hear from you. I miss you and Bernard very much and lose things just as bad as when you were here. I lose the hatchet, the hammer, the forked iron and everything here and have no one to lay it on but your grandma but I don't dare tell her so. Mr. Corson brought your grandma a beautiful black kitten, white breast and white stripe around the neck and she stands to set a store by that kitten for she had him in her arms sixteen times a day carrying him out to get fresh air. She did not want to separate the kitten from its mother and I heard her ask Mr. Corson to carry it back to its mother. She told me she would rather have a rat or two than deprive that pretty little kitten of its mother. We got the fleas off of Flossy and Scott so they are getting to be great big fat dogs.

Your Grand-father
H. T. Owen

Kiss Bernard for me.

****

After the death of his beloved, Harriet in 1918, Henry lived with one of his daughters in Richmond. His youngest daughter, Mary Eliza (Mamie), born on April 10, 1875 had married a

38

prominent Richmond Attorney, Harry Halstead Styll. Harry Styll later became the head patent attorney for the American Optical Company in Southbridge, Massachusetts. The following three letters, written to Mamie Owen Styll, are additional examples of Henry's love of family and his good sense of humor.

****

2601 E. Franklin St.
Richmond Va. 12 Nov. 1913

My dear daughter,

Your kind letter received a few days ago and your Ma and Sally have seized it and you know them well enough to cipher out, it, like all else, will not return my way. I hardly know what to say about The Saturday Evening Post and the Outlook. Both are interesting and I have enjoyed the articles very much, but I do not see how I could expect to tax Mr. Styll for my Reading Matter. However am said to favor Genl Grant. Judge Walter Watson, now in Congress, spent the evening with me two months ago and said I reminded him of Genl Grant's picture very much. I know I am like him in one respect. He would accept all the presents offered him from a pen knife, or carriage and horses, to an Island in the West Indies, and gave as excuse "I never like to disoblige any friends." So he took everything coming his way to please his friends. We are having a bitter cold spell down here but nothing like the blizzard along the lake shores as the papers report. I am afraid this cold snap will ruin the oranges and kill the orange trees in Florida. We had a letter from Ruth (See Note #5) two weeks ago and Mr. Watkins' trees were loaded with fruit. Some of his neighbors had sold their crops of oranges, on the trees for a good price and Ruth was elated at the prospect of big profits.

This leaves us all in usual good health. We are looking for Jaque and Hattie soon. Wish you and Mr. Styll could be here at the barn dance for they will be sure to have one. When you can be sure to bring Mr. Styll. People here wear eye glasses and spectacles as well as elsewhere and he ought to know it. Best regards to you both.

Affectionately,
H. T. Owen

****

Note #5: Ruth was one of Henry's granddaughters. Ruth Owen Watkins. She and her husband, W.T. Watkins, lived in Hillsborough County, Florida.

39

****

2601 Franklin St.
Richmond Va.
March 12th 1918

Dear Mamie,

    Your two letters have been duly received with a box of candy by parcel post and all duly appreciated. I have been sick with a very bad cold and cough ever since you left and, only been out when the day was warm, two or three times to the bank or P. Office. While your mother was sick I did not take off my clothes at night for weeks and often kept on my overcoat as I had to jump up a dozen times during the night to warm the salt or give medicine and the weather was bitter cold. Besides contracting a severe cold, my eyesight has almost entirely failed. With spectacles containing large lens I have to hold a magnifying glass in my left hand to read or see the lines on the paper as I write.

    I am not in a condition to go anywhere at this time and doubt if I ever will be able again. I wish I could write a more cheerful letter but my head aches and I cough so that my very ideas are weak and sick.

Very truly Yr Pap
H. T. Owen

CHAPTER 4 - THE WAR WITHIN THE WAR - A COURT MARTIAL

"You can tell all your neighbors that the sentence of Cashier has been revoked and that is what I have been fighting for." *Henry T. Owen - June 21, 1863*

Henry T. Owen, having read military books on the ancient armies of Rome and Greece, as well as some of the books on the later wars of Europe, understood that discipline was necessary to the operation of an army. As a young officer in the Confederacy, he apparently felt that other matters, especially those matters affecting the welfare of his Company C, were more important.

On three occasions, Henry put the welfare of Harriet's relatives and other members of Company C, above good judgment. In confrontations with the Commanding Officer of the 18th Virginia Infantry Regiment, Colonel Robert Enoch Withers, Henry, apparently, lost his usual calm.

The first incident took place during those first few days in Richmond, where Henry had brought his company of men from Nottoway to report for duty. Col. Withers housed Henry's troops in a warehouse for three days without rations. Henry's loud protests to Withers accomplished naught, but to have Henry placed under house arrest.

The second incident took place when the 18th completed training and was sent to Manassas Junction and Centreville. Henry's troops, having no shelters, were placed in an open field. Henry again protested to Withers, stating his men would perform no military duties until they were provided proper shelter.

The third, and apparently final incident took place in 1862 after the Battle of First Manassas. Many men in the 18th were ill from drinking contaminated water and Henry wanted to move two of his men to a hospital or at the least to a dryer, warmer place. Withers and the Assistant Regimental Surgeon refused this request and apparently a heated argument took place. Henry may have taken action on his own to have the sick men removed from camp. He alludes to this in a letter to Withers.

Although we have been unable to find the records of a court martial, apparently Withers entered charges against Henry. We believe those charges were insubordination to a superior officer.

The trial, for various reasons, was delayed in 1862 and 1863. Henry mentions his pending trial in several letters to Harriet.

Letters in 1862, 1863 and 1864 show that Henry was still in command of his Company and was present at the battles and movements of his troops. On Nov. 22, 1864, his letter is headed "Castle Thunder", which leads us to believe that Withers had him incarcerated there sometime in late 1864. A letter from Henry to Harriet dated December 1, 1864, also shows he is at Castle Thunder. Apparently the matter was eventually resolved. The charges or the trial were reviewed by the Secretary of War of the Confederacy and apparently erased from the records.

****

Culpepper C H Va
June 13th 1863

My Dear Wife:

We are now at this place where we arrived on yesterday and may remain here for a week or more tho' everything is unreliable in the army and no certainty about anything. I am rested and doing very well. We are in the woods about 3 ½ miles from the C. Ho. and again in sight of lofty blue mountains that I love so well. We think when we move that we may go in the direction of Maryland or perhaps Manassas and since our army is so much larger and better disciplined than ever before I am quite willing to advance upon Yankeedom. When Lee moves this time I think the Yankees will pitch fits.

You can still direct your letters to Richmond and I will get them all safely. I am glad you found the Genl Order of the C Martial and I have sent it to Mr. Campbell who is attending to my business with the Sec of War.

Clay wrote me a good very good letter and I felt really proud of it – He is ahead of Millie and you must induce her to take more pains in her studies. Whenever I write to them don't read their letters to them until they have exhausted their patience trying to make all out - and don't copy a letter for them to write me. I am afraid you helped Clay on his last letter as it read very much like your dictating – now I would rather see their scribbling with all their mistakes than see one they copied without a blot or scribble.

But you must not praise them too much nor spoil them.

42

I will write to Millie soon but I must say that I was surprised and mortified at her negligent manner of writing – I am afraid she begins to consider herself grown and smart enough. You must not allow them to have their own way too much nor spoil Millie because she is the oldest. Let me know if you can fix Clay up for a short tramp with me. I would like for him to bring one extra shirt and pair of pants and socks and have a pair of shoes that will not be too small or too large so as to hurt his feet and if not too much trouble to fix him up for a visit I will write for him soon after hearing from you. He will learn a great deal here in a few weeks and something then he will never forget.

There is no news in Camp - everything quiet. I have not seen Pat yet but reckon he is at home.

Write soon and give my love to all. Let the children study Arithmetic, Geography, Reading and Spelling but not Grammar as they are too young.

Yrs faithfully and devotedly
Henry
****

Bivouac near Berryville, Clarke Co. Va
June 21st, 1863

My dear Harriet,

I wrote you a letter yesterday while in the pass at Snicker's Gap and did not expect to cross the Shenandoah until this morning, but orders were sent for us to move, soon after finishing that letter and moved over or rather through, the river just before night and marched to this place, some four miles from the Gap and three from the C House of Clarke Co. which is at Berryville.

The Shenandoah is one of the prettiest rivers I have ever seen. It flows along at the Western base of the Blue Ridge, with lofty, blue mountains banks overhanging its clean water on our side while upon the other side are spread out extensive plains and gentle declivities, a kind of elevated table land, covered for mile upon miles with clover and Blue Grass waist high and some of the most beautiful residences I have ever seen anywhere.

The river had risen by reason of several recent heavy thunder showers and took us up to our armpits and vest pockets, the men having to carry their cartridge boxes around their necks to prevent their ammunition being wetted. The stream was very swift and cold but the boys made a great frolic of the crossing and took the water

43

like otters. Where we crossed it was some two hundred yards wide I suppose, and ordinarily about knee deep to a man. I wrote you that Lin Jackson had been needed and after crossing the river we passed the Cavalry camp so I saw Lin and found him well and hearty. I asked him if he had written to his Ma about being wounded and he said he had not had an opportunity to mail a letter since his fight and did not suppose his family would hear of so slight a scratch and therefore he would wait for a chance of sending off a letter. I told him to write by all means as his mother would be very uneasy if she heard of his being wounded and he did not write. So he wrote and gave me a letter which I mailed today. If Dr. Jackson does not get it tell him I saw Lin and his wound is so slight as hardly to leave a scar. He acted very gallantly and killed two Yankees in the fight. I heard from Mr. Slaughter also and he is quite well. Give my respects to Dr's family and Mrs. Jackson. I saw John Ewing today. He paid us a visit and he tells me that Uncle Henry is yet safe and with his Regiment near Leesburg. John is a strapping fellow and full of life and fun. I had a dream while at Hanover Junction and thought I saw a Yankee shoot W. Henry and I saw him fall from his horse with his face all bloody and though I do not believe in dreams at all and never tell them, yet this one has troubled me no little. I saw him plainly. I thought and it was upon a battle field but I did not see anyone else on either side. The Yankee was dressed in a blue uniform and stepped out raised his rifle and fired at a horseman. I knew the Yankee by his dress and when I turned to see the other man it was W. Henry tumbling from his horse as I have related. I could not sleep well any more that night and ever since when I run upon a Calvary fight I become totally nervous until I know it is only a dream. I merely mention it so that you know why I am so anxious to hear from him and mention him so often.

I have at last heard from the Sec. Of War and he has commuted the sentence of Cashier and allows me to hold rank from the date of reorganization of the company. In plain language there is now no obstacle in my way to promotion and the way is open if a vacancy should occur, but before I could be Major, there are several senior officers who will have to rise ahead of me. I did not <u>expect</u> <u>promotion</u> but merely stated, that all obstacles would be removed from my future promotion whenever a vacancy occurred and without a removal of the sentence of Cashier I could not be promoted. As to the rumors and reports circulated by gossiping neighbors they are hardly noticeable and if you do not mention them neighbors they are hardly noticeable and if you do not mention them I should not know anything of them. You can tell all of your neighbors that the sentence of Cashier has been revoked and that is what I have been fighting for.

The Boys have recovered from their fatigue and are rested for a long march again soon. We expect to go to Harper's Ferry tomorrow and if so I will write you an account of the kind of place it is. I have now been all around the place and begin to wish to see it. We have been in sight of the place a dozen times but a long distance off. We should hereafter get our letters from Winchester but you can continue to mail mine to Richmond until I order elsewhere. I can tell as soon as we see Thackary, our mail carrier.

I heard a fine sermon today. I hope you will attend preaching more frequently and remember that we are poor and ought not to be proud. If we were rich we might go in fashionable style but as it is we must not lose the chance of Heaven because we are poor.

I would send you some money if I had some safe way and reckon I shall have to trust it in my letters in small sums but if you let anybody know that I send money in a letter or even allow the children to see you take it out a letter they will be obliged to mention it and then somebody might rob them on their way to you.

It is raining and I must quit.

Yrs truly and devotedly,

Henry

****

Castle Thunder
Nov 22nd 1864

My dear Wife,

I recd your letter of the 6th inst and was glad to hear that you were all well. Hope you will not distress yourself on my account. Am fighting a good battle and hope I shall soon return to my company.

The charges against me appear somewhat grave but I can ---- -- ----- ----- only I am very disappointed. I expect a trial at an early date and would have had it before this but for the military movement of my Division which prevented the attention of the witnesses.

I wrote Mr. Clifford Anderson to come see me and should have -- --- ----- counsel but for business that took him to Georgia about the

45

time I ----- him. If he returns I may get him to attend the trial with me though I truly think counsel will be unnecessary.

Mr. Campbell and Judge Gholson both visited me having heard of my imprisonment. They came in friendly visits and I felt flattered to find I have not been cut by all my friends at once.

I hope my mother's health is good and that she will not grieve at my imprisonment. I am confined in the best room and among the best company in the prison. We are restricted from buying anything and have no communication with the outside. I received a kind letter from Mr. Smith since getting here.

Tell Clay I will reply to his letter soon.

The socks were mine that you found in the box. I sent then for the Negroes. The clothes are all for the children.

Before leaving camp I sent you $200 in three separate letters. A hundred in one and fifty apiece in two others. Let me know if you recd it. A letter will reach me if you address it: Capt H. T. Owen, Care of Capt Richardson 1st Provost Marshal, Richmond. It will be opened and read before I get it.

I am truly Yrs,

Henry

****

Castle Thunder

Dec. 1st 1864

My dear Wife,

Send me my camp chest as soon as possible with the following articles:
My checked brown shirt and some colors, my new uniform coat and a pair of socks. Send the roll of court martial papers and a letter from Capt. Bentley respecting some commissary stores. You will find this letter among the papers sent home in the last box. Send me some paper and pens. You can send me some apples, walnuts, potatoes and some peas and corn meal. Put my clothes up in papers so that they will not get much on them. Send me "The Lives of the Apostles." Send the volume that has not the children's
Baptism in it. We have two copies, you know.

I am very well and doing as well as I can expect in prison. Expected to have a trial before this but presume operations on the line prevents it. Try and send my box early next week. Send me corn bread or any sort that is convenient. Send the key by some one who will bring it to me at the Castle or leave it with Major Buford at the "Old Columbian Hotel." Give them the name so there will be no mistake. My love to all,

Yrs truly etc.
H. T. Owen

Send me some red pepper.

****

On March 29, 1902, thirty-seven years after the war, Henry wrote a letter to Colonel Robert Enoch Withers. Apparently the two had met briefly, on one occasion, a few years after the war. In the letter, Henry reminds Col. Withers of two of the incidents, during the war, when they disagreed.

****

2601 E. Franklin St
Richmond City Va
March 29th 1902

Colonel R. E. Withers
Wytheville Va
Dear Sir,

Your favor of 25 inst duly received next day and I assure you that I am truly glad to find we have no cause of quarrel between us. I remember our meeting at Meherrin Station soon after the war and that made me more surprised at Mr. Boswell's statement, as I could not see how you could have forgotten that interview and my expressions of good will and friendship for you. I cannot recall the exact words I used when we met a Meherrin, but I know the idea I meant to convey was taken from a letter of yours to me, written two years before the war ended, in which occurs this sentence: "What I did then was done from a sense of my duty as commanding officer and few would be better pleased than myself if your subsequent good conduct would be deemed sufficient to wipe out all stain caused by the unfortunate occurrence of Sept. 1861" and in your letter to the Sec. of War, inclosed for my use, you were kind enough to attribute my conduct "to want of experience and not to any wish to subvert military discipline."

When I decided to appeal to the Sec. of War for a revocation of the sentence of Cashier, I felt it my duty to notify you of my intention and give you the opportunity to say whatever you thought proper on the subject. I stated in my letter that I felt I had no claim upon you but if you could say anything to assist me I should be grateful. I knew full well the Sec. of War would not act on the case

47

at all, unless he heard from you. I had no hope that either you or any other officer connected with the case, or 18th Regt would endorse my petition favorably. So confident did I feel at the time of their disapproval and consequently of the failure of my application and reduction to rank that I wrote to my brother-in-law, Mr. Dean, who at that time kept the Cabell House in Lynchburg, to get me a substitute and hold him in readiness to take my place in case I should need him. He succeeded in finding a man, a little over conscript age, who had already served in our army with credit, was highly praised by his officers, and was willing to go in again provided he could make thereby a couple of thousand.

When your reply came, with your letter to the Sec. of War inclosed, I was greatly and very agreeably surprised and saw at once if I accepted your assistance and made use of your kind letters, then I could never again go behind them to reopen and renew any complaint growing out of previous difficulties.

I did not mean to say to you at Meherrin, nor do I mean now to say that I am sorry for anything I did during the war, or that I want to be forgiven for what anybody may consider great crimes and heinous offences against law and order. I do deeply and sincerely regret the untoward circumstances that forced me to pursue the course I did on several occasions, so much so, that if I had to begin again the same war, or something similar, and some genie would hold before me a kaleidoscope, unveiling the events as they afterwards occurred, I would refuse to go, but if once enlisted, beyond favorable recall, I would meet the issues and fight them as I did before.

What else could I have done at Manassas than I did in June 1861? We had no tents. More than fifty men were furnished with twenty-five planks, sixteen feet long and eight inches wide, to build shelter. By placing the planks end to end there were three lengths of eight planks, and the lap and slope made a roof about five feet wide without front, back or sides and this located upon a slope or inclined surface, where the water had fair sweep for three or four hundred yards.

On the 5th of June 1861, two of my Company were excused from duty. They had high fever, eyes red, back and head ache and continued to grow worse. Sent for the Surgeon of the Regt. His assistant came, looked at them and departed. Showers all day and the shelter not wide enough to cover the men much below the knees if they stretched out. Very heavy rains during the following night and next morning. The clothing on the sick men was thoroughly saturated and the water had flowed under and around them, according to the testimony addressed on the trial, "deep enough to swim a duck." On the second day, the rain pouring down in torrents, no man able to build a fire to cook rations, one of the sick men now broken out with measles, the other delirious; no Surgeon appearing, I went out to hunt him down and found Dr. Richard B. Walton, who was ditching around his tent that had been flooded by the showers still pouring down. I told him the condition of the sick men and asked him to send them to the hospital. He answered that the hospital was crowded and there was no room for my men. I asked him to send them to Culpeper C.H. or Charlottesville. He replied that he was only the Assistant Surgeon of the Regt and did not have the authority to send sick men away to other hospitals. I asked him where the Surgeon of the Regt was. He replied that he was in Culpeper, Charlottesville or Richmond, he had been gone a week, had been expected back for several days, might come that day or the next, no certainty about it. I asked him to allow me to telegraph in his name and find the surgeon and get his permission to move the men to some other hospital. This request he refused. I then asked him to permit me to move the men to the hotel at the Junction or to an unoccupied house within half a mile of the Regt and I would furnish a physician and nurses from my Company. This he also refused. I then walked up to your tent and asked you to go with me and hear the propositions I had made to Dr. Walton in regard to some sick men. You very readily went with me and I repeated my different requests to Dr. Walton, which he again refused as before. I then appealed to you and asked the privilege of moving the men to the hotel or to the unoccupied house nearby. Your answer was that when the men were reported sick they were in the hands of the Surgeon and you had no authority in the matter. I called on you to witness what I had proposed to Dr. Walton and called on Dr. Walton to witness what had been proposed to you. I then started back to the shed where my men were, with the determination to do something to remove the sick men and not allow them to lie there and die in the mud. I had but little time to think, for the distance was not much over one hundred yards, but I thought rapidly. My first impulse was to make my Company carry the sick men to the unoccupied house near the Regt but then I knew you would interfere to prevent it, or if you did not and the men should

49

die after I removed them, I would be held responsible and charged
with causing their deaths.

****

NOTE #6: We believe the above letter from Henry T. Owen to
Col. R.E. Withers contained an additional page or pages. To
complete this episode in the life of Henry T. Owen, we must reach
our own conclusions. It is our belief that Henry took some action to
have the sick men removed from camp and that Withers then filed
charges.

CHAPTER 5 - THE WAR OVER HISTORICAL PRESPECTIVE - FIRST MANASSAS

"Behind the Henry house, we found four artillery pieces abandoned in haste by the Union forces. We turned them on the enemy."
Henry T. Owen, November 11, 1878

Henry, like many other Southerners did not, until the very end, lose confidence that the South would win the costly and bitter struggle. It began in a glorious display of the Virginia Flag, a marching band and the cheers of the masses.

We do not know when Henry wrote his description of the 18th Virginia Infantry as they left the camp of instruction and paraded through the City of Richmond on the way to their first assignment.

****

Richmond Parade of 18th Virginia Infantry
(By Henry T. Owen)

On the 26th of May 1861, the 18th Regiment of Virginia, numbering 762 and commanded by Colonel Robert E. Withers, left the Camp of Instruction at the Old Fairgrounds above Richmond, and about 5 o'clock in the afternoon, marched out in all the "pomp and circumstance of war' in open order by platoons down Broad Street. The muffled roar of the tramping feet kept time with martial strains of Southern airs that stirred the soldier's breast and the flag of the Old Dominion fluttered and flauntered proudly over them, while loud and long prolonged cheers greeted them at every step from the dense masses thronging the sidewalks, crowding the doors and windows, and gathered upon the housetops.

Glittering buttons and braid on unsoiled uniforms flashed in rivalry with the dazzling sheen of the bright finished muskets and sparkling bayonets.

****

By the 26th of May 1861, when the 18th Virginia Infantry Regiment made its grand march out of Richmond, several important events had already taken place.

A special convention of the South Carolina Legislature had voted to secede from the Union on December 20, 1860. Between

January 9, 1861 and February 1, 1861, the States of Mississippi, Florida, Alabama, Georgia, Louisiana and Texas had also seceded.

In February of 1861, delegates from six of the seceded states met in Montgomery, Alabama to form a government. They elected Jefferson Davis as President of the Confederate States of America. Davis had served previously as United States Secretary of War.

A showman, Harry Macarthy, wrote the song "The Bonnie Blue Flag", which celebrated the growth of the Confederacy:

"First, gallant South Carolina nobly made the stand;
Then came Alabama, who took her by the hand;
Next quickly Mississippi, Georgia and Florida,
All rais'd on high the Bonnie Blue Flag that bears a Single Star.
"Ye men of valor, gather round the Banner of Right,
Texas and fair Louisiana, join us in the fight....."

The song, though never as popular of "Dixie," became an inspiration for Southerners to join the new nation. A new flag was quickly devised and Confederate stamps for a Confederate postal service printed. Confederate currency replaced United States money, and patriotic Southerners invested heavily in Confederate bonds.

Abraham Lincoln was inaugurated as President of the United States on March 4, 1861, and immediately after taking office, began preparations for war. His strategy included blockading the Southern ports and as part of this plan, he sent troops to occupy Fort Sumter in Charleston Harbor.

On April 12th and 13th, South Carolina responded by bombarding Fort Sumter and the garrison at Fort Sumter surrendered to South Carolina General, P.G.T. Beauregard. On April 15, 1861, Lincoln declared a state of insurrection existed in the South and called for 75,000 volunteers to enlist for three months of service.

Between April 17 and May 20, 1861, the States of Virginia, Tennessee and North Carolina seceded from the Union. On April 19th, Lincoln ordered a blockade of all Confederate ports.

Soon after these events, Robert E. Lee, a graduate of West Point and a resident of Alexandria, Virginia, was asked to head up the Union Army. Lee, then a Colonel in the U.S. Army, refused, stating he could not take up arms against his native state. He resigned his commission on April 20, 1861.

Two days before the 18th Virginia Infantry Regiment paraded through Richmond, on May 24, 1861, Union troops crossed the Potomac River from Washington, D.C., and captured the city of Alexandria, Virginia. They invaded the vicinity around Alexandria and, during this conflict, a local innkeeper killed Colonel Elmer E. Ellsworth. Ellsworth was the first officer to die in the war and he became a martyr for the North.

Jefferson Davis, no doubt missed the grand parade of the 18th Virginia. The Confederate government was moved to Richmond three days later on May 29, 1861.

Henry's Company C, were then encamped near Manassas where they were under orders to protect an important railroad junction. In June 1861, Henry's Company C suffered its first casualty when John Reese died of disease.

Following several marches to and from Fairfax Courthouse, Centreville and other locations, the 18th Virginia was ordered to return to Manassas and there they became a part of General Phillip St. George Cocke's brigade. The Confederate army, under the command of General P.G.T. Beauregard, met the Union forces on July 21, 1861 at Manassas. During the battle, the 18th Virginia was ordered to close a gap in the Confederate lines, during this charge, they captured several cannons and then turned them on the charging enemy. General Beauregard was very impressed with the performance of the 18th.

Late in the afternoon of July 21, 1861, the Union forces were routed and began fleeing back to Washington, D.C. Several hundred civilians, who had accompanied the army, rushed back to the Capitol city also. With the Union army in retreat, the 18th was ordered back to the railroad junction. It was anticipated that the Union forces might attempt a night attack. The first of many land battles had been won by the South.

****

In several of his letters, Henry mentions, briefly, the Battle of First Manassas or Bull Run, as it was called by the North. His letters after the war however, are more descriptive. In a letter to Captain Richard Irby of Company G of the 18th Virginia, Henry notes some of the incidents at First Manassas.

****

Capt. Irby:

Dear Sir,

I have just finished reading, with much interest, your "Historical Sketch of the Nottoway Grays" and noting several mistakes in dates and of facts, no doubt unintentionally made, I felt it a duty to call your attention to one at least of the more important errors that you may make, in some public manner, the necessary corrections, which I confidently believe you will do, lest injustice be done the memory of some brave men who no longer live to speak for themselves.

On page 13 of your Sketch appears this remarkable sentence in connection with your description of the First Battle of Manassas.

"When the line was fully formed, the Brigade swept up the hill, in full charge, on both sides of the Henry house, capturing a battery of artillery stationed on the crest of the ridge. This was the last charge of the day, for then commenced the rout of the enemy made more complete by the turning of their own guns upon them, which was effected by Lieut Shields, of Company E, of the 18th Regiment, and others. Forbidden to pursue we could only exalt and cheer as the great victory of the day was consummated."

As corrected this sentence would read thus.

When the line was fully formed the Brigade swept <u>down</u> the hill in full charge on both sides of the Henry house and halted abruptly at the country road, in the bottom, back of the Henry house where four pieces of artillery, which the enemy had attempted to carry off the field by hand, had been abandoned and left on the roadside in the bottom.

This charge by Cocke's Brigade made upon the enemy in front was most timely and of the greatest importance in controlling the fortunes of the battle and turning the tide of victory into the hands of the Southern troops, for at this particular crisis Early struck the hitherto victorious Federals in flank, coming as he did most opportunely to the support of Kershaw and Kirby Smith. The enemy thus taken simultaneously in flank and front immediately gave way and retreated rapidly their repulse becoming a tumultuous rout before they reached Centreville.

Cocke's Brigade having halted along the road, as before stated, remained in action for fifteen or twenty minutes during which time the enemy had entirely disappeared from the front and a fresh body of the enemy appeared in an open field near a farm house about a mile to the right of this position and exhibited signs of preparing for an advance upon the right of Cocke's Brigade.

Attention being called to this fresh body of the enemy, the thought occurred to Capt. H. T. Owen commanding Company C, (the other Company from Nottoway) who was at the time leaning upon one of the pieces, to turn the enemy's guns upon them. Giving the order at once the men seized the gun and attempted to turn it and were assisted by a portion of Company A. While doing this Capt. Owen asked if any body there knew how to shoot a cannon and seeing a soldier dressed in artillery uniform going to the rear called to him to come back and as the soldier did not seem to hear two men were sent after him and brought him back. Capt. Claiborne then came up and Capt. Owen said "Capt. Claiborne take charge of the gun and fire it as I don't know what to do with it." Capt. Claiborne, assisted by his own men and part of Company C, loaded and fired the gun three times at the enemy's line, striking the line with the second shot as we could see from the commotion created and as we afterwards learned from one of the men wounded and left at the house where the line was forming.

There were only three shots fired before the enemy broke and fled precipitately toward Centreville. Capt. Claiborne sighted and fired all three shots and I never before heard that Lieut Shields had any thing to do with his incident and if he was present at the gun at all I have no recollection of the fact. I am confident the foregoing statement can be substantially verified by affidavit (if necessary) from Lieut Samuel Burke, T. Pryor Robertson, Wm J. Downs, H. H. Dyson and others of Company D who aided in turning the gun as also by every surviving member of Company B who was present in the battle.

I regret the necessity of having to allude to any part taken by myself in the transaction and but for the importance of connecting the links of incidents would not do so.

With Capt. Thos. D. Claiborne, however, the case is different. He deserves the credit of loading, sighting and firing the gun with accuracy at the enemy. His previous military training at Lexington had fitted him for such work and he did it well.

You will remember he afterwards fell in battle upon Nottoway soil, leading his regiment against a body of raiders approaching the court house and although he lost his life in the charge he yet succeeded in breaking the ranks of the enemy and scattered their forces and no doubt saved the County from pillage.

I will call your attention to one other mistake as to dates in your Sketch.

The Battle of Williamsburg was fought on the 5th of May instead of the 6th as you have it. The retreat from Yorktown began on the night of the 3rd instead of on the morning of the 5th as stated. We reached Williamsburg on the afternoon of the 4th, a clear sunshiny day and passing through the town took the river road which we followed some three or four miles and then retracing our steps camped for the night just outside the village or town where we remained all night of the 4th. The 5th was a rainy day and was the day on which the battle was fought.

(No closing or signature.)
****

On November 25, 1878, Captain Irby responded to Henry's letter.
****

Ashland Va.
Nov. 25th 1878

Capt. H. T. Owen
Meherrin Va.
Dear Sir,

Absence from home and consequent pressure of business on my return have caused my apparent negligence in answering you letter.

I take occasion now to say that I certainly had no intention nor object in giving a wrong version of the incident you claim as incorrect. Inasmuch neither I nor any of my Company ever claimed to have participated in the matter of turning the Federal gun on the routed foe. I gave the only version I have ever received, and if I have given the wrong one I have been led into the error by others. I submitted my manuscript to Col. Withers and also sent him one of the first copies, requesting him if he discovered any omissions or errors to report the same to me so that I might correct, but he made no correction of this point. Should you deem it of sufficient importance to procure a certified statement of eyewitnesses, as you suggested, I will lay it before Col. Withers, along with certified statement of others who did claim the credit viz. Lt. Shields, etc. and let the credit be given to whom it belongs.

I do not know what more I could do. Whatever the verdict may be I will have it published more widely than the little sketch only intended to reach the members of my old Co. and the friends who felt enough interest in the Co. to read it.

Col. Withers is anxious to have a history of the Regiment prepared, and if that be done, I trust full justice will be done to any and all who deserve credit.

Most resp.
Rich. Irby

****

Captain Richard Irby of Company G, the Nottoway Grays, was a First Lt. at muster and was elected Captain in 1862. He was wounded at the Second Battle of Manassas. He died in 1902.

Henry, ever determined in his quest to "get at the truth" of the various battles, apparently had also written to Abner Anderson of Company G. The reply from Anderson came on December 11, 1878.

****

Office of
The Danville Register
Danville, Va., 11th Dec. 1878

Capt. H. T. Owen:

Dear Sir,

I have taken time to reply to your letter of the 27th ulti. in order that I might confer with some members of the old Blues and Grays, as I did not happen to be an eyewitness of the affair at Manassas to which you allude.

Cpl. Green, Capt. Harry Wooding, Jno. Enright and others think your version is correct. Green says you are right in your description of the charge of the Brigade over the hill. He also says that Claiborne was the man who directed the firing of the cannon upon the retreating enemy though he is not willing to say that Shields was not also present. It was the accepted opinion from that time forward in the regiment, that Claiborne was due the credit. The fact as to Shields, I suppose, could be readily ascertained from him if he is living.

My recollection is that you are correct as to the dates and the weather while on the retreat from Yorktown and during the battle at Williamsburg. I have a vivid remembrance of seeing Gen. Johnston in the rain for several hours while the fight was progressing.

Very respectfully yours,
Abner Anderson

****

To further verify certain events of the Battle of First Manassas, Henry secured an affidavit from E.B. Coleman of Company F, 18th Virginia Infantry Regiment.
****

"When the line was fully formed the brigade swept up the field in full charge on both sides of the Henry house capturing a battery of artillery stationed on the crest of the ridge. This was the last charge of the day, for then commenced the rout of the enemy, made more complete in our front by the turning of their own guns on them which was effected by Lieut. Shields of Company E of the 18th Regiment and others."

My attention having been pointed to the foregoing paragraph which appears in a recent "Historical Sketch of the Nottoway Grays Co G of the 18th Regiment and others written by Capt. Richard Irby" and being requested to give my version of the incidents alluded to, I hereby certify that according to my recollection of the circumstances the facts were these. That when the line was fully formed upon the crest of the ridge, where the horses attached to the enemy's artillery had been killed by some other troops before our arrival upon the field, the Brigade swept forward down the hill and halted abruptly upon a line along the country road in the bottom where several pieces of the enemy's artillery, which we had seen them trying to carry off the field by hand, were run together and abandoned, that after the enemy, then in full retreat, had disappeared entirely from the front a large body of them suddenly appeared upon a hill to the right of our position, about a mile off, and showed sign of preparing to advance when some members of the Regiment turned one of the enemy's abandoned guns upon them and it was loaded, sighted and fired three times at the enemy by Capt. Thomas D. Claiborne of Co. B 18th Regt. I never heard before that Lieut Shields had any part in the circumstance and remember that during the war whenever the matter was spoken of, the credit was given to Claiborne.

Given under my hand this 14th of Dec 1878

(signed) E. B. Coleman Co F 18th Va Regt. afterward Co. H.

58

CHAPTER 6 - THE TALK OF SOLDIERS

"We have had our elections and the Company is organized with the following officers; I am captain, Tyree G. Leath is 1st Lieut., M.P. Vaughan 2nd Lieut., and Watkins 3rd Lieut. Gibbs got one vote for Capt. and then three for 1st Lieut. He is mad as a wounded tiger and will join some other company."

Henry T. Owen, April 27, 1862.

Following the Battle of First Manassas, Lincoln appointed, on November 1, 1861, George B. McClellan, age thirty-four to replace the aging General Winfield Scott as Commanding General of the Army of the Potomac.

General McClellan kept most of his army sitting in Washington, D.C. through the winter of 1861 and during the first few months of 1862. In the meantime, General Ulysses S. Grant, commanding the Western Division of the Union Army, won victories in Tennessee.

On December 20, 1861, a portion of the Army of the Potomac, under the command of Brigadier General E.O.C. Ord moved toward Dranesville, Virginia. Brigadier General J.E.B. Stuart, with a brigade-sized mixed force of cavalry, infantry and artillery met Ord and his forces on the Georgetown Pike. The 18th Virginia was a part of Stuart's Confederate force. Henry seemed to feel the Battle of Dranesville was never given the recognition that it deserved.

****

The Battle of Dranesville
(Notes by Henry T. Owen)

The recent visit of the survivors of the 6th Regt. of South Carolina veterans to the battle fields of Fair Oaks and Seven Pines recalls to mind some incidents connected with the Battle of Dranesville in which that regiment played a conspicuous part and suffered very severely.

Some of the War histories are completely silent in regard to this battle while others make a bare mention of the fight as a very small affair; none enter into details or the particulars and give the number of casualties, the officers present or in command of the

Departments made few and very brief reports and therefore, we have to rely almost wholly upon letters of army correspondents of newspapers, written hastily at the time, but however, in the immediate neighborhood for much of the material for this article.

Possibly there may be some errors or some omissions, some facts overlooked in the difficult research necessary after the lapse of so many years to collect accurate information concerning the data, the exact number of troops and their movements upon this occasion, or at any occasion of the war, but if this is so, now is the time and the Annals of the War the medium where disputed or doubtful questions should debated, explained and scttlcd whilc the participants and eye witnesses of the occasion are still living.

We often hear it said the time has not yet come when a correct and truthful history of the Civil War can be written, that too much sectional prejudice still prevails, too many bitter heartaches still remain unhealed, and too many sad, bitter, memories still exist for our people to tolerate the facts and realities of the War. We are frequently requested and encouraged to wait for that period when all the sectional animosities and hate engendered by the War and all painful recollections of the cruel strife are forgotten, but then shall come, as it soon will, soon it must, a time when the Jacket of Blue and the Jacket of Gray, both alike faded and moth eaten, shall hang mouldering with all the other trappings of the soldier, no longer prized and burnished by familiar hands, but lying rusting, corroding and wasting away together in the dust and rubbish of some neglected garret or cellar where children fear to tread at twilight; a time when the last heroic soldier on either side shall sleep beneath the sod and then no martial note of the bugle blast nor of rolling drum and fife shall arouse him again to arms. And then, another generation of aliens and strangers to the history we helped to make, shall pander to the public taste and write our history to suit the prejudices of their day.

About 3 o'clock on the morning of the 20th day of December 1861, General J. E. B. Stuart started from Centreville with about two hundred wagons on a foraging expedition into the southeastern part of the County of Loudoun. The distance to travel was about twenty five miles, and he took as an escort to protect his wagon train four regiments of infantry, namely, the 1st Kentucky commanded by Colonel Tom Taylor, the 6th South Carolina under Lieut. Col. A. J. Secrest, the 10th Alabama under Col. John H. Forney, and the 11th Virginia under Col. Saml. Garland, being in all about seventeen hundred infantry besides the Sumter Battery of four guns under Capt. Cutts with sixty men, and detachments from Ransom's N. Carolina and from Radford's Virginia Cavalry, making a total available force of about two thousand men.

The weather was extremely cold and frosty, the sky bright and clear without a speck of a cloud to mar the beauty of its boundless depths while the stars twinkled brilliantly and the waning moon, just past the zenith of its course, sank slowly down the western arch of heaven shedding broad fields of light on lawns and meadows where little drops and spangles of ice on frosted grass and weeds reflected ever changing, ever shifting, scintillations of sparkling gems. There were broad patches, long lanes and wide avenues of light flecked with dark shadows leading away into the gloomy forests.

The tramp of infantry, the clatter of cavalry, the rumbling artillery and the rattling of a long train of empty wagons jolting over the rough, hard frozen, roads in the early dawn echoed through the dark forests, down the gloomy bottoms and over the hills for miles away arousing restless house dogs that barked and howled by turns, thus helping to spread from village to hamlet, from hamlet to farmhouse for miles around in ever widening circles away from the line of march the information that troops were on the move. Soon after leaving Centreville, there was seen to shoot up in the northern sky, a blazing rocket that went skimming along just above the horizon leaving a long, comet like tail behind for a few seconds and then suddenly disappear in darkness and gloom. This was supposed to be a signal between different camps of the enemy stationed along the Potomac, apprising them of Stuart's advance in that direction. The column moved rapidly and by daybreak was many miles away from Centreville.

On arriving at Dranesville, Stuart posted his troops so as to guard the approaches from the direction of Washington while his train of wagons was sent out to collect corn and hay from the neighboring farmers.

It appears that on the same morning, Genl McCall, with a large number of wagons escorted by three brigades of infantry, a regiment of cavalry and a battery of six guns, started upon a foraging expedition into the same section selected by Stuart, and placing two brigades at Difficult Run under Genl Reynolds, he sent Genl Ord up to Dranesville with one brigade of five regiments, also the First Regt. Penn Rifles and Eastern's battery of six guns.

Being notified of the approach of Genl Ord, Stuart at once began to collect his wagons as fast as possible and hurried them to the rear while he made disposition of his forces to protect his train. Taking the road that leads from Dranesville towards Fairfax C. House, Stuart fell back about half a mile from the village where he selected a position in the road for his artillery and aligned his infantry, one each side of the road, facing toward Dranesville. It was now 12 o'clock and Stuart had scarcely time to complete his defensive arrangements before Genl Ord's troops appeared in full view advancing through Dranesville in line of battle, while his battery, posted upon a little knoll just at the edge of the village, opened fire at point blank range straight up the road upon Stuart's position. The artillery of the combatants, firing at each other rapidly and constantly, created a line of fire so hot along the road that all communication was cut off from the wings of both of both armies operating on each side.

Stuart at once threw forward the 11th Va. Regt on his right and the 6th South Carolina upon the left of the road while his battery fired straight from his center along the road, the Federals line of battle now advancing through Dranesville. The enemy also moved their infantry into the battle on the right and left of the road. Advancing through the thick brush, the 6th South Carolina became engaged and appeared to be doing very well until the 1st Kentucky, coming to their support, and intending to form on their left, became entangled in the thick underbrush, and mistaking their direction, came up directly behind the 6th South Carolina, and mistaking them for the enemy, fired a heavy volley into their friends at close quarters. In the confusion which followed, it was hard to restore order and both regiments were soon afterwards retreated from the field, the 6th Regiment having lost more men from the volley fired into them by their friends than in the battle with their enemy. While these things were taking place on the left of the road, the 11th Va. Regt. and 10th Alabama were fighting desperately and falling rapidly on the right of the road. Stuart had first thrown forward the 11th Va. on the right of the road which drove the enemy back for some distance, but meeting reinforcements, they soon rallied, and in turn, drove back the 11th Va. when Stuart pushed forward the 10th Alabama to support the 11th Va. The 10th Alabama soon reached the hottest part of the field and within a very short time had its Colonel wounded, its Lieut Col. Martin killed and seven Captains killed and the other three wounded, besides losing nearly fifty men killed or wounded.

The battle had lasted about forty five minutes when Stuart, knowing his wagons had reached a safe distance and expecting the enemy to be reinforced at any moment, left the field in possession of the Federals and retreated rapidly.

Stuart's loss is set down as forty three killed and about one hundred and fifty wounded and that he lost twenty artillery horses. It was reported that the Federals lost over three hundred killed and wounded.

Genl McCall reached the field while the battle was going on and after its close sent the following dispatch to Washington, which does not seem to magnify his own merits or prowess nor exaggerate the forces engaged.

"We have found 40 killed of the enemy and ten wounded on the field. Our loss is two killed and three wounded. We have taken two caissons with the harness, the horses having been killed. The regiment of rifles behaved finely. Lieut. Col Kane was very slightly wounded, but is still in the field.

I have collected the dead and wounded and am about to move back to camp.

Geo. A. McCall
Brig. Genl Commanding"

The reporter of the N. York Herald who was present, stated to his paper that "there were 40 dead and 15 wounded. The latter were taken and placed in the houses at Dranesville."

A letter to the Richmond Dispatch dated Centreville Dec 23, 1861 (three days after) states "The Confederates loss much less than at first reported being now ascertained to be 50 killed, 150 wounded and 40 missing."

****

Henry wrote of rumors among the troops. He also mentioned in several letters that they had camped in a location sometime before. The rations of the soldiers consisted of bacon and biscuits. In the first stages of the war, Henry asks Harriet to send him recruits several times.

****

Camp Wise Richmond Va
March 12th 1862

My dear Harriet,

We arrived in Richmond safely and procured Passports and Transportation but before we got off, orders were recd from Gen. Johnson that no more troops must be sent on until he got matters a little settled around Manassas. We hear many rumors that our troops are hastily falling back from Manassas to Gordonsville and that Centreville was burned before evacuating it. We are now in camp about two miles from Richmond waiting for orders to join our Reg. There are a great many volunteers and recruits here situated like ourselves and some of them exhibit considerable impatience to hasten on to the scene of battle – Manassas.

We are all really well satisfied and it looks to me very much like old times when were here at the Heritage F. Grounds last spring. We borrow pans and eat fried meat (good old bacon) and that same light bread we used to have. We may stay here for several days and you can write to me here or wait until I stop again.

If any letters come for me mail them to me at Richmond Camp Wise Care of Col. Bain. Tell Dr. Jackson to send me all the recruits he can and let the people know that I will still have recruits.

A gentleman is waiting for me to finish my letter and as I have no news will close with good wishes and much love.

Yrs most devotedly etc.,
H. T. Owen

****

In a letter of March 14, 1862, Henry states Mr. Morton is on a recruitment mission. Henry tells Harriet that he must stay with his company.

****

Camp Wise near Richmond
March 14th 1862

My dear Harriet,

Mr. Morton goes up to Nottoway today and I take the opportunity of writing a letter to you which he will take.

We are all well and enjoying ourselves here very well. Plenty to eat and a good straw bed that suits me first rate.

Mr. Morton goes on a furlough of ten days to recruit for our company. I could not leave as it is entirely necessary for me to remain with the Boys and prevent disturbances and dissatisfaction. Don't know how long we may remain here but expect to go off soon, say a day or two.

Let Mr. Morton have as many of the oil cloth's as he calls for. One roll is cut into pieces of two yards. Let him have them.

There are some shorter pieces and some longer that you must pick out and lay aside. We just want the 2 yd. pieces.

Kiss the children and write to me. Leath gave me this pretty paper and Mr. Charley Mottley lent me ink.

I have gotten two recruits since I got to Richmond and hope Samuel may bring me a dozen. Tell Dr's Jackson and Jones to send me all the men they can.

No news and Sam is in a hurry so I must close.

Most truly Yr Husband,
H. T. Owen

****

In his letter of March 18, 1862 to Harriet, Henry is in Gordonsville but does not seem to have his company with him. He says some of the soldiers are afraid of the Yankees. Many times he mentions they have nothing to eat, but adds the soldiers do not complain.

****

Gordonsville Va
Mar. 18th 1862

My dear Harriet,

We were hurried off from Richmond Sunday evening at ½ past 5 o'clock with only a few minutes notice and left Archer and Joe Leath behind but they followed us by the next train and are here with us.

I heard yesterday that our Regiment was at Rapidan Station some thirty miles from this place coming on slowly. General Johnson with his whole army is in full retreat pressured by the Yankees. It is thought we may fall back to Richmond before fighting but I think not and I hope not. It is 76 miles to Richmond and I hope we may at least summon a force sufficient to give the enemy battle before retreating so far. Our men are fighting as they fall back and I am distracted not to be with my old company in their difficulties. I am afraid they may lack confidence in their officers and perhaps fail to do their duty. If I was only with them all would go right and no cause for complaint against their courage.

Tom Cockman came to Richmond and joined my company and then left me. He was not bound to stay but I fully expected him to remain but many of our people are afraid of the Yankees and if our Independence rested with them we never would be free.

There is no news of interest and my letter must be short. We were stopped here and could not go on as our Regiments are expected daily. Some six or seven hundred of us are here in the woods some half a mile back of Gordonsville without tents and hardly anything to eat. I am perfectly satisfied and had some sweet dreams about you last night.

Some of the boys think our life a little hard but they don't grumble. I heard yesterday that our Regiment had to burn all their tents and baggage except what they take upon their backs. We shall suffer a little if the weather is cold but it will soon be warm and then we shall not need tents. Napoleon never had any tents and with plenty of will nothing can hurt us.

Send your letters to me at this place but I might never get them. You must just write as you hear where we are.

Most truly Yr dearest husband,
Henry T. Owen
****

From a camp near Yorktown, Henry pens a letter to his wife quickly as he is sending it by someone leaving for home. He says the company has voted and reorganized. He asks Harriet to send him some clothes. In many letters there are requests for oil cloth.
****

Camp near Yorktown
Apr 27th 62

My dear Harriet,

I write hastily and must send you a very short letter. Know here and now we are not able to get a letter off until somebody is about to leave for home and then we are able to scribble off a few hasty lines.

We have had our elections and the Company is organized with the following officers. I am Captain, Tyree G. Leath is 1st Lieut., M. P. Vaughan 2nd Lieut. and Watkins 3rd. Gibbs got one vote for Capt and then three for 1st Lieut. He is mad as a wounded tiger and will join some other company. His promotion required him that he attend more in battle.

I want you to send my coat and those gray trousers. Don't send my trunk as we have no wagons here to carry baggage. If you will fold up my coat and pants in a small bundle Branch Leath or Tuck Fowlkes will bring it to me. Let any of the men have an oil cloth that belongs to this company or they may bring the whole roll if they will. You can pick out the short remnants as we will need them here often and they are in use here now.

66

The boys are all well and no news of interest but a general organization has taken place. Write often and send your letters by the boys whenever you have one. Affectionately my love to all.

Most truly and devotedly Yours etc.

H. T. Owen

****

Henry writes Harriet a lengthy letter on the march from Williamsburg on May 6, 1862. He describes a battle and tells of those killed and wounded. He says some men deserted the fight in the beginning, but most fought bravely in the battle which he states was worse than Manassas.

****

On March From Williamsburg
May 6th 1862

My dear Wife,

We had a severe fight and I thank God I am alive thru' a terrible battle as the Yankees surrounded us. My Company suffered significant loss but stood up gallantly and fought bravely to the last.

Upson Robertson and Otis Watson both killed, Lieut Watkins lost a thumb, Sergt. Wilkinson shot in the hand, Frank Dalton shot in the arm, Tom Jones in the side, Pryor lost one big toe, Mr. Allen shot in the knee, Mr. Davis shot through both legs and little Jimmy Robertson expected to have been killed as he was shot badly in the side of the head.

Some few of my men acted most shamefully and deserted me early in the action, but a larger portion of the company stood manfully up and fought desperately. Three times the companies on my right were forced back but my men bounced along with the tide but each time I succeeded in rallying them without trouble and held our ground against heavy odds for two hours and twenty minutes when we were relieved by another Regiment. Manassas did not come half up to this and the balls rattled against the trees around us like hail upon window panes.

The fight commenced at daybreak but nothing much was done until about 11 o'clock and lasted until eight o'clock at night. It rained hard all day and we were drenched to the skin. Our ammunition gave out and the cartridge boxes of the dead men searched and all the ammunition was used. It was a hard fight and we pushed the Yankees back for two miles but it was a dense thicket where no line could be kept long together.

It is thought we lost in our Regiment some dozen killed and sixty wounded. Mr. Davis and Allen had just joined my company a few days before the battle and were two really once clever men. I regret their being wounded and fear they will fall into the hands of the Yankees.

Upson was killed in the first fire and shot through the heart died without a groan or struggle. Watson also shot through the breast and he fell and died instantly. They were both splendid soldiers and Watson fought very bravely until shot down.

We managed to get our wounded up to the hospital in Williamsburg but our dead were left upon the field and as soon as dark we fell back and commenced retreating. Our whole loss is thought to be some eight or nine hundred. We got some four hundred prisoners.

The Yankees are following us up but we expect another fight in a day or two perhaps this evening. We marched all night in the mud knee deep and just stopped to eat a few crackers here at 2 o'clock. It will soon be too late for a fight today and during the night we shall make good time as we want to reach the Chickhominy Swamp before another fight.

Tom Jones is not much hurt so I hear from some of my men.

Keep good spirits and thank God for my protection. I will write soon.

Truly and Hopefully yrs,

Henry

I got your letter in reply to mine of 23rd yrs dated 28th but I have not had time to reply.

****

Henry writes from Front Royal, Virginia. The Confederates attempt to secure a gap on the Shenandoah River and they "race" to do so.

****

Front Royal
July 22nd 1863

My dear Harriet :

Yours of 16th (a week old) just recd by me and altho' in a hurry I want to write you a few hasty lines. You have not yet sent a letter that said you got one I wrote you from Berryville about the 28th of June and enclosed $10 in it. Please say in your next letter if you did receive it or not.

We had a race with the Yankees for Snicker's Gap from Bunker Hill and then from Harper's Ferry but the enemy got the gap first then we took up the Shenandoah for Ashby's Gap and when we arrived there found the Yankees had that gap too and we still followed up the Shenandoah and found them in possession of this gap – Chester's but after crossing the river we were placed in front and have been driving the Yankees ahead of us yesterday and today.

I had to deploy the 18th Reg on the right of the road as skirmishers and tho' we had only 63 men they did very well. There was a large Cavalry force of Yankees forming up in line of Battle in front – prancing about on a hill and I was ordered to advance and drive them off the hill. Before we started I told the boys they knew as much about fighting and their duty in battle as I could tell them, that I regretted that they had no more experienced leader and I feared that some of them would not behave well because not accustomed to my command, but the said that they would fight as well under me as under any body and that they knew the importance of driving the Yankees off from the gap. We moved on steadily in a long line of skirmishing men five paces apart and began to expect a little fight but when the Yankees saw us coming over hill and bottom through brush and briers they took out and would not let us come near them. We followed them till night then waited for daylight. Major Simpson had been fighting the Yankees for several hours with the 17th and we united just before night. He killed six and had one man slightly hurt. The enemy kept a long distance off. Today other Regiments took our places and still pushed the Yankees back. God is great and I have placed myself in his hands. You need not be worried but must pray constantly for me and be thankful for his blessings.

I wonder if Tyne will let Joe and George Anderson stay at home and not arrest them at once. Mr. Hudgins says he saw Mrs. Bettie Varner's brother Algy yesterday and he was not hurt. He did not speak of his brother and Mr. Hudgins says he would have told him if he had been. He sends his respects to Mrs. Slaughter and wife Bettie. He saw Franklin and he was not in the fight. I heard a few days ago that Len was not captured as I wrote. Please tell Dr. and Mrs. Jackson. No news.

Yrs truly and lovingly

Henry

Some of Henry's letters to Harriet and to others included descriptions of battles. In July of 1863, he writes of the losses in his Company and the Regiment.

Culpepper C Ho Va
July 24th 1863

My dear Harriet,

We have just reached our old camping ground at this place that we left on the 15th of June and I have rested about an hour so will write a letter as our mail carrier will take it tomorrow morning.

It is 4 o'clock PM and very hot and sultry but I am have put my oil cloth in the shade of a large tree and can write without suffering much from the sun. What a change has taken place in our Reg and Brigade since the march of 15th of June! When we were here last the wood was white with tents and filled with men laughing and talking, sometimes so many as to be boisterous –Alas what a change!

Everyone has lost friends and comrades and did not fully appreciate the misfortune until they reached this camp. I came to the familiar spot where my tent stood when we were here in June and how sad and lonely it made me feel to look around and miss so many friendly and familiar faces. Six stared on my tent then and now I am only left to visit the scene of our resting place. Near me stood Lt Watkins's tent with six inmates and not one is left to reclaim the spot. On another side of my tent a few yards off was the shanty of two other of my men – both gone, one killed the other a prisoner wounded. Thus it is all over the woods in all the companies but the saddest sight I have witnessed was that of one of my men who had camped near me when we came in awhile ago. He went over, sat down all alone and resting his jaws between his hands presented the most incongruous picture of distress I ever beheld. The only companion he had for a long time and was with him here was his brother and he is reported killed. There are three brothers: Burke, in my Company, one dead of small pox in Richmond, one as I said reported killed and this one is alone left. Some squads are all gone and many gaps are left between the tents.

As my letter from Front Royal stated that we were driving the Yankees ahead and saw a fight. The enemy held a lofty mountain peak and soon our boys drove off the Yankees. We were not in the fighting and have not been engaged since. We marched all night that night and will move in the morning towards Racoon Ford and perhaps Orange C H. I expect some hard fighting before long but hope they may not require our services and don't think we shall be employed unless a great need for us arises as we are so cut up and have so few officers.

I wrote to Mr. Watson concerning Lt. W._ . Tell Miss Mary Eckolls that Joe Holt is missing and we think he is a prisoner, I sympathize deeply with her as Joe made me a confidante. This much you need not tell here though. The five or six boys here are well but foot sore. It will be a pleasure to you to know I have been riding ever since I left Gettysburg. Am riding our Adjutant's horse who was missing.

I will not close my letter till the morning.

Yrs truly and devotedly

Henry

****

From Soldier House in Richmond, Henry pens the next two letters to Harriet. He explains in the first letter that as the Yankees secure the railroads, it is harder to get mail to her. Many railroads were captured by the Yankees who then tore up the tracks and burned the depots. Henry mentions a significant battle is going on between Richmond and Petersburg in the first letter.

Again, Henry mentions the difficulty of getting mail to Harriet in the second letter. He has sent a letter by packet boat. He mentions the battle fought on the Petersburg railroad about eight miles from Soldier House. His need for care from his wife is evident as he feels poorly and wishes her to be there.

****

Soldier House

Richmond Va

May 16th 1864

My dear Wife,

I wrote to you several days ago but as the mail has been detained I suspect you have not received my letter.

The Yankees seized the Danville R.R. at Coal Field last week and no mail has passed up the line since. They burnt the depot and wood sheds at Coal Field and tore up the track for several miles then turned on the Powhatan Station where they also burnt the depot and did considerable damage to the public buildings. From thence they passed to Chula and burnt the depot and did great damage to everything in their course. When they arrived at Mattox or the

71

Appomattox, they were repulsed by a small guard at the bridge under the command of a Lieut who had two small pieces of cannon but no horses to draw the pieces. Have being driven from the R. R. bridge they turned up the river and crossed about four miles higher up at Country Bridge and pressed on towards Amelia C. H. They were met by a small force of cavalry from S. Carolina and some little infantry who gave them a severe battle on Mr. Louis Harvey's plantation but the only turned their course and one source says they are gone toward the High Bridge and another says towards Blacks and Whites.

Λ great fight is going on between here and Petersburg and has been progressing for five or six days. The great battle began this morning at 5 o'clock between Beast Butler the Yankee and Genl Beauregard. We are getting the best of the fight and Genl Heck and five hundred prisoners have just arrived from the field. My company has not been ordered out yet and we expect to remain here.

Bill left this morning for his company in Genl Lee's army. He has been around Richmond on the fortifications for several days and did not get into any fighting.

I will write whenever I can do so with any surety that my letter can go thro'. I will send this up by boat to Lynchburg and hope you will get it. Don't be uneasy about me. All is well.

Yrs truly as ever,

Henry

****

Va Soldier House

Richmond May 20, 1864

My dear Harriet,

I have written two letters to you and one to Clay since my return from Lynchburg and as the mail has been detained by rains I fear you did not receive either. The first letter was mailed in Richmond and second a day or two before the enemy cut the Danville Road at Coal Field and no mail passed out for a week so if my letters don't go off the day before I doubt whether you got it at all or not. My next letter mailed on the Packet Boat from Lynchburg so you will get that unless the canal on S. Side Road is cut somewhere so that he mail is stopped.

A great battle was fought between Beauregard and Butler on the Petersburg R. R. about eight miles from this city on Monday. The Yankees were driven back two miles and we took more than two thousand prisoners. The 18th Regt was in the fight and covered itself with glory.   Everybody says they fought with terrible desperation and drove the Yankees back further than any other Regt did. Major Cabell was shot through the face and it is thought he is mortally wounded. He passed through the city and is gone home. He had just mounted the breastworks and shouted to the 18th to "charge" when one of the enemy's sharpshooters shot him. He fell but the men rushed on upon the enemy determined to avenge his death. It is said they fought like demons.

I hear that the Yankees have burnt Blacks and Whites (bridge). Genl Lee has been fighting for fifteen days and the Yankees have lost over fifty thousand men. We have lost about twenty thousand.

I wish the strife was over or was quick so you could visit me. I would give a great deal to see you now. I have been sick ever since I got back and feel very weak. I have not had any "chills" since the one in Lynchburg.

Bill has gone to his company in Guinea Station. I want to get him a transfer to my company if possible. Major Cabell tried to get us back with the Regt but Genl Winston would not give us up. I don't think we will have to go out to the field any more during the year and as soon as everything is quiet I want you to visit me.

You never said whether you read all the letters in Lynchburg or not. Let me know in your next. My love to all.

I am devotedly Yrs

Henry

****

A letter from Henry's nephew, W.H.H. Ewing of Coleraine Plantation, Prince Edward County, Virginia was written to Henry on July 28, 1864. W.H.H. Ewing was one of the sons of Henry's sister, Ann Owen Ewing.

****

July 28, 1864
Dear Uncle,

Your favor of the 26th inst was gladly received on the afternoon of yesterday. I hasten to reply though I have nothing new to write. Everything in the way of war news or campaigning is still unchanged with the usual shelling of our Calvary Corps has been quiet now for three weeks or more lying about in the flat marshy pines of Dinwiddie doing nothing living hard. No vegetables or anything of the sort can be had in this section not because the army has eaten them out but because they had nothing before the war.

Col. Carter's loss is severely felt in this Regiment and throughout the whole Brigade. I was always struck with his accurate memory and that rare facility of his mind which never failed him in forming an accurate idea of a man's disposition, honesty, at first sight. On the evening of his misfortune Gen Fitz Lee saw me standing on the road and knowing that I staid as ?? asked me the particulars of his command & c. I told him the circumstances and he remarked "I am sorry for Carter, he was a good one to have along in a fight."

I heartily sympathize with you in your scratch afflictions. I have had it for more than four months but have never used any remedy. It is a great annoyance and keeps me hard at work with both hands many nights while tired and fatigued by a long march. Seven different kind of Confeds would not pester me much more. I do not now think that I can get home time enough to meet you there. I will come to see you however when you get in the trenches provided Grant stops his shelling. At any rate I will pass you soon where as the march for as the Examiner says "the cavalry is a rowing race." I wish you could see our Division now on a Brigade mounted parade. We have as fine body of light cavalry as was ever mustered an excellent Band. A fancy General Major who is a soldier by profession cares for nothing but his cavalry the ladies and good whiskey .. His mother, sister and little brother was out to inspect us on a grand review or dress parade a few evenings ago and it is said the old lady was delighted to see her Fitz in command of so large an army thoughts Gen Bob had as many as that. Have you eaten many vegetables yet? I want some raw potatoes and salt above all things believe I had rather have them than a Brunswick stew. I am missing you with my tit tat and with stop sight short.

The weather is so warm I can't write. Give my love to all and accept for yourself the kindest regards your
Nephew
W. H. H. Ewing
3rd Va Calvary
Fitz Lee's Divis Va
****

Both the North and the South had men who deserted the fight. Men who felt they were needed more at home than at the battle front and others who simply tired of the fighting, left the ranks to slip away. Although the records show that Henry had only a few men desert his Company C, he apparently made an effort to get them back in the ranks. Soon after the Battle of Seven Pines, he put the following Military Notice in at least one newspaper.

****

Both the North and South had men who deserted the fight. Men who felt they were needed more at home than at the battle front and others who simply tired of the fighting, left the ranks to slip away. Although the records show that Henry had only a few men desert his Company C, he apparently had some. Soon after the Battle of Seven Pines, he put the following Military Notice in at least one newspaper.

****

MILITARY NOTICES

ATTENTION! All absentees from my company, who do not report in person, or furnish at the headquarters of this regiment a certificate of disability from some regularly appointed surgeon, before the 22nd of June, will then be advertised as deserters, and a reward offered for their immediate apprehension.

It is hoped that there is no member of this company so lost to a sense of honor and manly pride, as to bring disgrace to himself and be a reproach forever to his family and friends. But appeals to patriotism, in some instances, have been made in vain; kind words have failed to produce their intended effect; moderation has ceased to be a virtue; and duty to our country, duty to the brave men who are still at their post of danger, and who have boldly confronted the foe at Manassas, Williamsburg, and Seven Pines, and duty to the friends and relatives of the brave men who have fallen in defense of their homes and their liberties, requires and demands that some sterner steps should be taken, and that the cowards who have ever deserted us in the hour of peril should be brought to justice and punished as they deserve.

H..T. Owen
Capt. Co. C - 18th Regt. Va. Vols.

Owen Family Papers

****

In the years following the war, Henry wrote several articles that were published in various newspapers including The Philadelphia Weekly Times, The Farmville Journal and the Charlotte Gazette. One such article is included below.

****

FARMVILLE JOURNAL - THURSDAY, APRIL 26, 1883

AN INTERESTING ARTICLE. - We publish on the first page of this issue of the Journal, a very interesting article by Capt. H.T. Owen, of this county, relating several reminiscences of the war. The article was written by Capt. Owen for the Philadelphia Weekly Times, and we copied it from that paper. This article is well written and will well repay perusal.

SOME STIRRING INCIDENTS
A Feat of Unsurpassed Daring By a Federal Cannonier at the Second Manassas

---

By Captain H.T. Owen,
Formerly of Pickett's Division,
A. N. V.   (Army of Northern Virginia)

The most conspicuous act of reckless courage I ever saw displayed on any battle-field during our great Civil War occurred at the second battle of Manassas on the 30th of August, 1862. It was performed by a Federal artillerist in the presence of both armies and was witnessed by at least a thousand men, many of whom are still living and can readily recall the incident when reminded of the circumstances. There had been a great battle on Friday between the Federals under General Pope and the corps of Stonewall Jackson, in which the Federals were repulsed. During this battle, Longstreet had come upon the field and taken a part in the fight just at nightfall. On Saturday morning the 30th of August, General Pope's army occupied a position stretching along the plateau about the already famous Henry house while the Confederate forces were concealed in the woods and bottoms behind the Chin house. The whole forenoon wore quietly away except an occasional slight skirmish along the advanced picket lines of the two great armies, where any movement of troops or change of position would cause a rattle of musketry to break out at times and spread along the lines for five or ten minutes, but this would gradually die away into profound stillness that would reign for an hour at a time.

FORWARD AT DOUBLE-QUICK.
Thus the day passed on until about 2 o'clock, when General Lee suddenly put his whole army in motion and advanced rapidly to attack the Federals. Moving forward at double-quick across bottoms and fields for a mile or more, we passed through a body of woods and entered the large open field around the Chin house. Here we came in sight of three separate lines of Federal troops drawn up in line of battle along the bottom just below the dwelling. There was a

76

ditch about four feet wide and three or four feet deep, dug along this valley to drain it for half a mile and the Federal lines were formed parallel with this ditch - two on the side next to the Henry house and one line over across on the side next the Chin house. There was a battery of artillery with the front line which the Federals had moved around the head of the ditch a half mile up the bottom. The Confederate lines on entering the field were not exactly parallel with that of the Federals and the left, under Hood, being advanced became engaged just below the Chin house, while the right of our line was still several hundred yards from the ditch, up the valley, but was swinging around rapidly to take part in the action.

SUCCESS OF GENERAL HOOD.

Hood's headlong charge had taken the enemy in his front completely by surprise, and hearing the heavy volleys of musketry and fire of artillery on our left, our attention was drawn in that direction, and although moving at a double-quick we could plainly see across the open field the bloody work going on and observe distinctly the rapid movements and changes taking place there. Hood's men had come upon the field on a run, yelling and firing as they advanced, and soon came to close quarters with the first line of Federals, which outnumbered them greatly and extended beyond both his flanks. Here, then, began a fierce conflict that raged for a short time with uncertain results and the State flag of Texas (a large blue silk ground with a single star in the center) was seen to go down and up several times. But the Federal line finally gave way and fell back across the ditch in great disorder, and Hood, following up this advantage, led his men over the ditch and charging the other two lines before they could recover from the confusion caused by their first line breaking into them, he very soon drove back the whole Federal force in his front towards the Henry house.

A DARING ARTILLERY MAN.

But just as Hood's men charged down the hill upon the first line, as already stated, and it became evident he would capture the battery stationed there, a Federal artillerist determined to save one of the cannon, if possible, and to do so he had to take it up the side of the ditch in front of the Confederates for a half mile. How he got his horses hitched or whether they had really ever been taken from the piece I never have known, but the first I saw of him he was coming up our front in a sweeping gallop from the cloud of smoke and Hood's men were firing at him. As soon as he escaped from that volley he came in front of our brigade and under range of our muskets on the left, as he swept on up the line a file fire was opened upon him. Our line was approaching the ditch rapidly at a double-quick and the lane between us and the ditch was getting narrower each second, but the artilleryman seemed determined to save his gun from capture and he flew along his course at a tremendous rate of speed. He had four large gray or white horses to the cannon and they came up the valley in splendid style. The man sat erect and kept his team well in hand while his whip seemed to play upon the flanks of the leaders and all four horses appeared to leap together in regular time. The ground was very dry and a cloud of dust rolled out from under the horses' feet and from the wheels of the cannon as they came thundering along.

A GRAND DASH

Three regiments of our brigade had already fired at him as he rushed along their front and as he approached the left of another I ran down the rear ranks shouting to the men: "Shoot at the horses! Let the man alone and shoot at the horses! You are firing to high." At this I saw a noted marksman in Company F drop upon one knee and sight along the barrel of his musket and fire, but on came the man and the gallop of his team was unbroken. Ramming in another cartridge, the marksman was ready again in a minute and just as the cannonier swept across his front within a hundred yards he kneeled down and taking deliberate aim at the foremost horse fired again, but on went the team unharmed as before. Thus he passed along the whole front of our regiment and then along another on our right and escaped around the head of the ditch and across the field and up the hill beyond. As far off as we could see him his team was still going in a gallop, but when out of range on the hill beyond the ditch he turned in his saddle and taking off his hat waved it around his head several times and some of the Confederates cheered him. At least five hundred men fired at that Yankee gunner and I have often wondered if he escaped death in the subsequent battles of the war and lives to tell of the fearful gauntlet he ran along the front of a whole brigade of Confederates firing at him.

ARCHER AT CHANCELLORSVILLE.

When General Jackson made his sudden attack on Hooker's right at Chancellorsville, General Archer led his brigade through a thick-set undergrowth of bushes and in face of a storm of shot and shell tearing the limbs of the trees overhead and mangling his men around him. It was impossible to keep a line of men in regular order under such a fire and where a man could not see through the bushes twenty feet from him, so the line soon became tangled, overlapped and mixed up, but still the men all advanced bravely through the storm of shot and Minies. General Archer was on foot in front of his men, leading the charge, and being of small statute, the end of his scabbard touched the ground and went bobbling along over the bushes. General ---- came galloping up, and seeing Archer's men advancing in great disorder he shouted out: "Halt your men, General Archer, and form them in line. Form your men in line." Archer, without stopping, looked back over his shoulder and replied: "Halt, hell! They won't go more than a hundred yards further before they will halt themselves." He saw the impropriety of trying to reform a line under a heavy fire, especially while the line was doing well enough and advancing bravely. So he pressed on and captured the earthworks in front of his men.

NOT MUCH OF A DRILL MASTER

Colonel P---- was a very wealthy and highly educated gentleman, belonging to a very distinguished family of our State, but he had no turn for military tactics and looked upon the various complicated maneuvers of troops on drill with contempt, as all nonsense and unnecessary. His lieutenant colonel and major, both well drilled officers, did the training of his regiment, but when Colonel P--- took command on a march or to change camp he was at a dead loss what orders to give, so if the regiment was in the woods where he could not see both ends of the line he usually gave his command in this manner: "Come out in the road, boys; now get in two rows" (double ranks). "Put on your stickers" (bayonets). "Now face up this way and follow me." The men always cheered him after receiving these orders and followed wherever he thought proper to lead, for they idolized him and he was as brave as any man in the army.

HOW LIPSCOMB HAD FUN.

There was a soldier in the Eighteenth Virginia Regiment by the name of Lipscomb, noted for his droll wit and prompt replies. He lost his right hand in the charge at Gettysburg and was disabled for active service. Being at home after the surrender of Lee's army he caused great fun and merriment among the old soldiers of both armies by going among the Federal troops whenever they passed through or stopped at Burkeville, his native place. Having only one hand and being very small, not weighing over ninety pounds, a sallow, sickly-looking boy, no one ever got angry with him, and he was considered a sort of privileged character and went wherever he pleased. One day a train load of troops was delayed at Burkeville and a lot of a dozen or more officers were out upon the platform at the depot, smoking and talking, when Lipscomb came along and tried to get into conversation with some of them. For some time none of them paid any attention to him. Then Lipscomb pretended to get angry and to speak of the war, and wished another war would break out so he could kill some more Yankees. A proud-looking lieutenant stood this for awhile, and then losing patience turned to Lipscomb and asked him;

"Mister, can you tell me what you fought for?"

"Yes, " said Lipscomb, "I fought for eleven dollars a month. What did you fight for?"

"I," said the lieutenant, "fought for a principle."

"Well, " replied Lipscomb, looking surprised, "I always thought both sides were right in the war and were fighting for what they needed most; I lacked money and you wanted principle."

This caused a great laugh, and the Colonel, slapping Lipscomb on the back, said;

"Young man, you must take something with me on that." Then he had to join the other officers in taking something more until they all tried to carry him along with them.

TURKEY HUNTERS UNDER FIRE.

There was an old blacksmith here named Carwiles, who was conscripted in 1862 and sent to Jackson's army in the Valley of Virginia. Arriving in camp at night he was assigned and enrolled. The next morning, just before day, a brisk fire opened on the picket line, stationed two or three miles from camp. The drums beat the long roll, the bugles sounded, and soon Jackson's whole force was hurrying to the front. Reinforcements were sent forward to sustain the picket line, which had fallen back to a strong position, and Carwiles was coming on in rear with a body of troops held in reserve. He had been a noted turkey hunter in his past life, but had never heard a cannon fire nor heard the whistle of the shell. Just before sunrise the Yankees brought up a piece of artillery and fired a shot over a wooded hill where they supposed some of Jackson's men were concealed. Just at this time the troops to which Carwiles belonged was about entering the woods on the opposite side and the shell overhead, very high in the air, passed over Carwiles with that peculiar fluttering sound, which induced all old soldiers to call them "wet geese." As the shell went over Carwiles' head --flut! flut! flut! he threw up his head and said; "Good God, boys, what a gobbler!"

80

The line moved forward and took a position in the woods where they were safe from danger except an occasional stray Mini ball or a few shells that crashed through the tree tops and tore off some large limbs. The men were ordered to lie down, and as they were unemployed and in sound of the battle, the sight of the wounded carried to the rear and of couriers galloping about with orders, made a severe ordeal for the raw conscripts. Pretty soon Carwiles began to pray and prayed loud. The Colonel came walking along the line and seeing Carwiles on his knees praying, said to him; "Take your d- ---d head down before it gets shot off, " and down went his head. A little while after a wounded pheasant, with a broken wing, came along the line trying to find an opening to the rear and passed a few inches or Carwiles' nose. This bird is rarely seen in Eastern Virginia, and some of the men on the line said; "Lor! look yonder, what sort of bird is that?" Another said; "Catch that thing Carwiles!" Carwiles looked at the bird just then within two feet of him and kept on praying: "The Lord will please have mercy on us today, boys; this is no time to be catching fowls."

Green Bay, Prince Edward County, Va.

- Philadelphia Times-

Owen Family Papers

****

CHAPTER 7 - THE BATTLES OF WILLIAMSBURG AND SEVEN PINES

"I am so sorry for my company I can hardly write about it." *Henry T. Owen - June 1, 1862*

The long winter of 1861 was over. Compared to some of the other Confederate units, the casualties suffered by the 18th Virginia Infantry Regiment had been light. On the day after Christmas, the commander of the brigade, Brigadier General Cocke, unable to cope with a host of personal problems, committed suicide. In February 1862, General Cocke was replaced with General George E. Pickett. Pickett was a Virginian, a graduate of West Point, and the commanders of the 8th, 18th, 19th and 28th Virginia felt that he was an excellent choice.

In late March of 1862, the Army left their encampment at Centreville. It was learned that General George B. McClellan, Commander of the Army of the Potomac, had moved his army from around Washington D.C. and was disembarking on the Virginia peninsula. Henry's Company C, and the remainder of the 18th VA Inf. Regt. were left behind at Centreville to destroy all remaining supplies and to destroy sections of the Orange & Alexander Railroad. It took the 18th ten days to accomplish this task The 18th then began a march toward Richmond and joined parts of the other Confederate forces at Yorktown.

McClellan, true to his past history of hesitation, refused to move his army for awhile. This delay gave the Confederates time to re-organize. The 18th recruited additional men and with approximately 700 officers and soldiers became the largest of the regiments in General Pickett's Brigade.

On May 4, just over one hundred thousand Federals of the Army of the Potomac, began moving from Yorktown toward Richmond. General Joseph E. Johnston, with a force of about forty one thousand Confederates, was forced to give ground. On May 5, at Williamsburg, the leading forces of the Army of the Potomac struck the rear guard of Johnston's army.

The Commander of the 18th, Col. Withers, was at home in Danville recuperating from illness and the 18th was under the command of Lt. Col. Carrington.

Carrington moved the 18th up to the center of the line. General Pickett placed the 19th Virginia and the 28th Virginia on the flanks and a fierce battle took place. The 18th sustained the highest losses in the brigade with 14 killed and 21 wounded or captured. With the massive Federal army close behind them, the Confederate army moved westward in a heavy downpour of rain. The westward movement, frequent halts to dig the wagons and casements out of the mud and the unrelenting firing of arms by the Federals, caused long delays. On May 31, the 18th, temporarily encamped near Seven Pines, broke camp and marched the several miles to a position just outside of Seven Pines. Their orders were to guard a section of the York River Railroad.

At dawn on June 1, Pickett moved his brigade out at dawn. Near Seven Pines they encountered the Federal forces. The Federals were well entrenched and the 18th, exposed in an open field, took heavy fire for over two hours. Around one o'clock in the afternoon, Confederate reinforcements arrived and the Federals drew back into the woods.

Henry Owen had fourteen casualties in his company. In a letter to Harriet, written that night, on June 1, 1862, he wrote of the losses.

****

6 Miles Below Richmond
June 1st, 1862

My Dear Wife,

In great hurry I drop you a few lines to inform you God has protected me again most signally in a great fight.

We had a fight yesterday and tremendous casualties reported on both sides. We were near the Battle field but not actually engaged. Today the fight commenced again and we were led into the hottest of the Battle where our Regiment behaved nobly and stood up admirably for 3 hours and nearly four hours.

My company suffered again severely and on this night confirmed losses more than all the others combined. We were more exposed to the enemy's fire and Col. Withers speaks in the highest words of the courage and bravery displayed by our boys.

June 1st

We had killed these - L. Taze. Robertson (Littleton Tazewell), Jos. L Jenkins and A. Sydney Foster. These were some of my best men and I am deeply grieved at their loss.

84

Mortally wounded - James C. Baughan and Charles V. Vaughan dangerously.

Wounded - Lieut. Madison P. Vaughan severely, T. Pryor Robertson slightly, R. Hudgens slightly, Hiram O. Fowlkes slightly, Jos. H. Phaup slightly, Jacob T. Osborne slightly.

Missing -- N. A. Mottley and Samuel H. Morton

I am so sorry for my company I can hardly write about it. We were in a terribly bushy thick place and fear Sam and Mottley are killed, as poor Dick Verser was perhaps at Williamsburg. I hope they will yet come up. My company had today 13) thirteen as you will see by counting them up.

I sent you $80 dollars by Lieut Watkins yesterday and when I collect the balance I will send you more. I hope you will not want for anything.

I must say both yesterday and today we have beaten the Yankees back several miles so our Brigade is resting and unless the Yankees come in any large numbers we will not have to go in the fight anymore today. Col Withers says that in the next fight our three companies that suffered so much shall be held in Reserve and not get into the fight unless we are actually needed to beat of the Yankees.

So you may rest easy about the next fight as we will not be in much danger I hope and thank God for our preservation in this fight and pray him to spare us in future battles.

I never want to see such work again if possible to preserve our rights without. Yet it is now all we can do under these circumstances. Send word to all your neighbors as they are all uneasy on our account.

I hope you will get this safely and early. I may not have a chance to write again in several days but don't be uneasy as it is hard to get a letter off and we are in the bushes, wading mires and swamps night and day.

My Love to all
Most devotedly yrs
H. T. Owen
****

Littleton Tazewell Robertson, a cousin to Harriet Robertson Owen, was killed. Her brother, Theodorick Pryor Robertson was wounded.

Although the Federals were repulsed and their losses were heavy, the Confederate Army suffered the greatest losses. General

Joseph Johnston was wounded in this battle and it was at this point, that Jefferson Davis appointed General Robert E. Lee, Commander of the Army of Northern Virginia.

With the loss of General Joseph Johnston and the loss of General Albert S. Johnston at the Battle of Shiloh, the South, from this point in time, began to lose hope that the war would end before year's end.

The Confederate forces in Northern Virginia moved slowly from Williamsburg,
pausing to fight the pursuing Federals at every opportunity. On the Williamsburg Road, Henry writes that his company is so depleted he finds it difficult to attend Roll Call.

****

C Company 18th Reg Va Vols.
On Wmsburg Road Below Richmond Va
June 16th 1862

My Dear Harriet,

I have had a hard time of honesty between duty on one side and inclinations on the other. There is a detail of one officer from each company sent home after stragglers and I could have gotten the detail but when I continued to think this matter over I thought Lyons was entitled to it so with many sighs I gave up and sent him to get the stragglers. I would have given him two hundred dollars for his detail now, but he will not take a thousand. He has never been home since he left with me more than a year ago. When I found I could get off or one of us could go I could not sleep after everybody else was snoring away. I sat up chewing tobacco and thinking whether I should go or let Lyons go. He was sleeping soundly and did not know any such thing was going on. I thought I was best to go but then I was best to stay and if a Battle took place I ought to be here, Lyons turned over and waked up. I told him what I had been thinking of and that while I hated to give away my chance still he was entitled to it and I would succumb. I then lay down and slept soundly all night. He now goes and I am left without a single officer but in case a Battle comes on I will lean on the Brave Boys that still answer at Roll Call in this once fine company. I seldom attend Roll Call and feel sorry when I see the small squad upon drill. I am thinking and thinking all the while of the brave boys that followed me to end and now lie unburied on the bloody fields of Williamsburg and Seven Pines. I have seen today where one of my men left wounded at Williamsburg Hospital died at

Washington on the 18th of May 1862. It was John A. Allen a tall fine handsome man and as brave as M ------. He had only been in my company eleven days and joined the day after I was elected. He had a brother killed at Rich. mountains last July and they were from Cumberland Co.

If you can send us some more good butter by any body, please as so as our mouths are all the time watering.

I heard to-day that Lieut. Watkins ----- ----- starts here tomorrow and if he does I hope he has since found you in time to prepare us something, Lyons will stay 5 days and bring back the stragglers who are now at S -----.

I am here and can't get to Richmond to eat any vegetables or pies or cherries or anything good. I know if I was at home you would fix me a good dinner.

Write soon and kiss the children.

I am most dutifully your Husband,
Henry T. Owen
****

Following the war, Henry did extensive writing, including several articles for the Philadelphia Times and for several Virginia newspapers. The following is a draft of an article he apparently was writing. The notes describe Henry's recollections of the battle.
****

Notes on the Battle of Seven Pines
By Capt. Henry T. Owen

Saturday morning Armistead's Brigade was surprised by the enemy between Fair Oaks and Seven Pines and Pickett's advancing drove the enemy back into a R.R. cut ½ mile east of the station. Here Pryor came up with his Brigade and Hill sent two Regiments of Colston's Brigade and these troops fought for three hours.

The Federals were driven back 6 or 7 miles on the Willamsburg Road. The Federals had six Divisions in the battle at 7 Pines. The Confederates had in Saturday's battle 9 Brigades and whipped 3 of the Federal Divisions. Johnston puts the troops on the Field at about 40,000 Federals. His own 23 Brigades must have exceeded this force by at least 3 to 1. The loss in Longstreet's Division was about 500, in Hill's Division about 2,500 in Smith's Division 1,233. Col. Jones, Lomax and Moore of Alabama were killed and Genl. Hatton of Tennessee killed.

The Feds lost 350 prisoners, (10) ten pieces of artillery, 6,700 muskets and four Regimental Colors. Their killed and wounded about 10 or 12,000.

On Sunday morning there were 6 fresh Brigades in Smith's and Magruder's Divisions ready for action, only 4 or the 10 being engaged the day before.

There were five Brigades under Hill and Longstreet engaged on Saturday and 8 fresh Brigades on Sunday morning.

A gap of 6 miles between Sumner at Fair Oaks and Heintzelman and Keyes at Bottom's Bridge existed on Sunday morning. Making $6 + 8 = 14$ Brigades fresh and 9 Brigades used in Saturday's fight. Federals had at Fair Oaks 2 Divisions and 1 Brigade troops Sunday. Richardson's Division came up at dark Saturday
bringing attack upon the Fed left by Genl Rhodes in front and Rains on flank were finally successful and the enemy abandoned their entrenchments. Just then reinforcements were received from their second lines and they turned to recover their lost position but to no purpose. They were driven back fighting upon their second line (Couch's Div at 7 Pines). R. H. Anderson being transferred to the front line by Longstreet bore a part in this second contest. Casey's position taken, his Div fell back to the second line and was reinforced by Kearney's Div of Heintzelman's Corps but the Confederate troops still advancing and fighting courageously, the Federals were driven from their ground and fell back to Heintzelman's entrenched line two miles from Bottoms Bridge two brigades being separated and driven southeast into the White Oak Swamp.

Genl D. H. Hill pursued the enemy more than a mile along the Williamsburg Road then about dark reformed this troops with the center and right facing east and his left thrown back facing north and the position of Sumner's Corps at Fair Oaks. In an hour or two Longstreet's and Huger's Divisions came up to this new line. This is the fight on the right of Johnston's lines. His left under G.W. Smith advancing along the 9 mile road came upon the enemy drawn up in line across the angle made by the 9 mile and Y.R.R.R. at 4 o'clock and a spirited battle ensued. Hood was thrown across the R.R. and united with Longstreet's left. An obstinate contest ensued which lasted until dark. At seven o'clock Johnston was wounded, first by a musket ball and then by a fragment of shell thrown from the field. Davis and Lee both on the field. The fighting ceased at dark. Genl Smith in commencing by the right flank, to fall on the enemy's left flank as soon as our troops became engaged with them in front. It was understood that abatis and earthworks that might be encountered should be timed. Genl Smith was to engage any troops that might cross the river to assist Heintzelman and Keyes Corps and if none came he was to fall upon the right of those troops engaged with Longstreet.

The rain fell ardently in the afternoon and the little streams were swollen and the river overflowing so as to cut off the Feds on the west side from aid on the east side of the river. The Divisions of Longstreet and Smith were in position early enough but Huger was delayed by swollen streams and after waiting until 2 o'clock Longstreet put his own and Hill's Division in motion and advanced upon the enemy. Hill's formed the first line with it's center upon the Williamsburg Road. Three of Longstreet's Brigades formed the second line – two on the Ch's City Road and one along the Y. River R. R. on the left.

At 3 o'clock the Federal advanced troops were encountered – a long line of skirmishes supported by 5 or 6 Regiments of infantry covered by abatis. The ardor and greatly superior numbers of Confederates soon overcame their resistance and drove them back to the main line of Keyes Corps (Casey's Div). It occupied a line of rifle pits, strengthened by a redoubt, and covered by a redoubt on the right of the road and covered by an abatis. Here the resistance was obstinate for the Fed troops commanded by an officer of tried courage fought as soldiers usually do under good leaders and true and rigorous efforts were required to drive them from their position. But the resolution of Garland's and Genl Anderson's brigades that pressed forward on the left thru an open field under a destructive fire the admirable service of Carter's batteries.

Genl Johnston says (narrative pp 129) Heintzelman and Keyes Corps crossed the Chickahominy at Bottoms Bridge (Williamsburg Road) on 22nd May and were stationary, apparently for several days constructing a line of entrenchments two miles in advance of the Bridge. They then advanced step by step , forming four lines, each of a Div. in advancing. There was a sharp skirmish on the 24th between the Confed Hatton's Tennessee Brigade, Smiths's Div with the leading troops of the Federal troops 3 miles below 7 Pines and the enemy were driven back upon their main body. On the same day (24th) the Federals drove our Cavalry out of Mechanicsville and occupied the village.

89

Near Hanover C. Ho. On 27th Branch's Brigade was attacked by Porter's Corps and suffered severely in the encounter. R--- Div. now reduced to 3 Brigades ordered from Petersburg numbered 9,000 men on the morning of the 30th and reconnaissances were made under Genl. D. H. Hill's direction on Ch's City Road by Brig. Genl Rhodes and on Williamsburg Road by Brig. Genl Garland. No enemy found by Rhodes but Genl Garland encountered General Ro---- more than two miles west of 7 Pines in such strength as to indicate the presence of a Corps at least. This fact was reported to Johnston soon after noon. An hour or two afterwards orders were given for the concentration of 23 of 27 Brigades against McClellan's left wing (about two fifths of his army). Longstreet and Huger were directed to conduct their Divisions to D. H. Hill's location as early as they could next morning. Smith to advance to the fork of 9 Mile Road with the New Bridge Road.

Longstreet (ranking officer of the 3 Div.) Huger, Hill and his own, was instructed to form his own and Hill's in two lines crossing the Williamsburg Road at right angles and to advance in this manner while Hayes Div. marching along the Ch City Road.

Note 7: Swinton was William Swinton, a reporter for the New York Times. Apparently Henry included some information from Swinton in these notes. General Longstreet provided Swinton some information on Gettysburg when Swinton was writing a book on the Federal Army of the Potomac. Some passages of the book came across as being critical of General Lee's strategy at Gettysburg.

Swinton

Passage of the Chickahominy at Bottoms Bridge on 20th May by Casey's Div. and by the 25th the two Corps of Heintzelman and Keyes even had crossed and began to entrench. Sumner, Porter and Franklin were left on the east side of the river. By the 28th Sumner had constructed 2 bridges known as "Sumner's Upper and Lower Bridges."

The river flows through a belt of heavily timbered swamp for a mile to two miles from the river. The country is flat and marshy with pools of water throughout the winter and spring. Johnston took advantage of McClellan's grave mistake in thus dividing his army to plan an attack on the two Corps on the right or west side of the stream.

On the night of the 30th there was a severe storm and the next morning the river was in places a mile wide. A reconnaissance by the Confed disclosed the fact that Casey's Div. (Keye's Corps) held and advanced position on the Williamsburg Road ¾ mile above 7 Pines or 6 miles from R. Couch's Div (K Corps) was stationed at 7 Pines on both sides of the Williamsburg Road and along the 9 Mile Road his sight resting at Fair Oaks Station. Kearney's Div (H Corps) was on the Williamsburg Road and the R. R. ¾ mile above Savage Station and Hooker's (of H Corps) was guarding the approaches to the White Oak Swamp. Huger was to advance along the Chs City Road and attack the enemy in flank which Hill and Longstreet attacked in front. The troops were to advance at daybreak.

The Divs of Hill, Longstreet and Smith were in place by 8 o'clock but Huger, delayed by swollen streams, bad roads and tangled swamps, caused a long delay of opening battle. For hour after hour Longstreet and Hill awaited the signal gun that was to announce the arrival of Huger in his proper position. At length at 10 o'clock Hill went forward on the Williamsburg Road and struck Casey's Div one mile west of 7 Pines drove back the skirmish line to their main line protected by a redoubt, rifle pits and abatis. The first blow fell on Nagle's Brigade which held a position in advance of the breastworks where it fought gallantly for a time but finally gave way and fell back to the breastworks. While fighting in the breastworks the Federals were reinforced by Peck's Brigade, sent forward by Genl Couch. While Rhodes was advancing in front Rains turned the flank of the redoubt and appeared on the rear and left of the Fed breastworks and they were carried. Casey had two Brigades at the breastworks, Nagle's in front, Wessels' in the breastworks and Palmer's in rear of Wessels'. One battery in front of Nagle's, one in rear of rifle pits to the right of the redoubt, a third in rear of the redoubt and a fourth in the redoubt. When the troops gave way the guns in the redoubt and a portion of those in front were captured. The troops were rallied by Couch at 7 Pines. Early in the action Keyes had sent to Heintzelman for aid and Kearney's Div was sent up at 4 ½ o'clock and the leading Brigade (Berry's) was thrown forward on the left of the Williamsburg Road where his rifles commanded the camp occupied by Casey in the morning. Casey's Div was struggling to hold its ground. Smith's Div was thrown forward at 4 o'clock and attacked the enemy at Fair Oaks. Thus when Casey's had fallen back on Couch at 7 Pines and Couch advanced with a Regt to relieve the pressure on Casey's left flank he was met by large masses of the enemy bursting on his right by the rear of the 9 Mile Road and another heavy column moving toward Fair Oaks Station. This was Smith's column. Couch was reinforced by 2 Regts but was thrown off to the right and the Confederates penetrated between Couch's 4 Regts and his Div on the Williamsburg Road. And now between 5 and 6 o'clock the whole left wing of McClellan's army appeared doomed to capture or destruction. Couch's forces bisected while the 2 Brigades of and Jameson (of Kearney's Div) which had gone up on the left had been drawn off to the left of the Williamsburg Road into the White Oak Swamp and only regained the main body under cover of night while the center was struggling hard to maintain its ground after being driven from 2 positions. But just at this critical moment Genl Sumner with his Corps from the other side came upon the field. The lower bridge had been swept away and the other floated on the surface of the angry waters with its end tied by ropes to the trees on either bank. The men waded across the flats to the bridge and their weight held the frail structure while they crossed rapidly to the west side and being directed by the sound of cannon to the course of Fair Oaks. Sedgwick's Div arrived on the field about 6 o'clock and Richardson's arrived about sunset. Sedgwick came up in time to support Couch who had made a stand at Fair Oaks. They were just in time to meet the advance of Smith's Div. Several gallant charges were made by Smith's troops but the Federals held this position till dark when Sumner ordered a counter charge by 5 Regts into the woods held by the confederates and they were driven back at the point of the bayonets in great confusion. Sumner was the hero of the day.

The Confederates lost nearly 7,000 and the Union Army upwards of 5,000, Genl Johnston wounded, Hatton killed.

The 5 Regts that charged just at nightfall were 24th N.Y., 82nd N.Y., 15th Mass. of Gorman's Brigade, 20th Mass. and 7th Mich. Of Dana's Brigade.

Preparations for withdrawal were actively pushed forward during the night but through some accidental circumstances a portion of Sumner's Corp turning, became engaged on the morning of the 1st June. There ensued a battle which lasted for 2 or 3 hours. It ended however, after some brisk battles in the withdrawal of the Confederate forces to the lines around R.

Johnston, in his report, says "Genl Smith was prevented from resuming his attack on the enemy's position next morning by the discovery of hard entrenchments not seen on the previous evening."

On the morning of June 1st the enemy attacked the Brigade of Genl Pickett which was supported by that of Genl Pryor, the attack was vigorously repelled by these 2 Brigades, the brunt of the fighting falling on Pickett.

On the Williamsburg (Road) the Federals had 4 Divisions 3 of which had been beaten the day before and one of them, Casey's about destroyed. At night fall Saturday McClellans's army was placed so that two of his Corps were on the east side of the Chickahominy separated by the swollen river from the troops on the west side and these latter were distant from each within six miles with a vicious enemy threatening to attack both at dawn next day.

Huger's Div had 3 Brigades present at 7 Pines Saturday 31st. One of his Brigades had been left at Drury's Bluff. His force is put at 9,000.

Hill's Div seems to have been composed of Garland, Rhode, Rains, Genl B. Anderson and Colston Brigades.

Longstreet's Div seems composed of Pickett, Pryor, R. H. Anderson and two others.

Smith's Div seems composed of Hatton, Hood.Sumner's Corps, Keyes' Corps, Heintzelman's Corps, Sedgwick's Div, Couch's Div, Hooker's Div, Casey's Div.

Johnston says there were 6 Fed Div on the Field.

Keyes' Corps = Casey's Div, Nagle's Brigade, Peck's Brigade, Wessels' and Palmer's Brigades.

Couch's Div Heintzelman's Corps, Kearney's Div = Berry's Brigade – Jameson

Hooker's Div Sumner's Corp, Sedgwick's Div, Dana's Brigade

Richardson's Div

****

Author's notes:
1. The railroad mentioned was the Richmond & York River.
2. The abbreviation "Chs City" Road refers to Charles City Road.
3. Henry abbreviated Williamsburg Road in several ways. We spelled it out.
4. Henry did not finish his description of the Federal forces or there may be a page missing.

CHAPTER 8 - OTHER BATTLES OF THE WAR

"I hope the war will be ended now very speedily and I may once more embrace my sweet little wife."
Henry T. Owen, June 30, 1862.

The Union army made several attempts to take Petersburg, Virginia. As segments of the Confederate forces moved to block their advances, the 18th Virginia was involved in several battles and skirmishes. During these marches from place to place, Henry's letters to Harriet became shorter.

****

Louisa C.H. Va.
April 11th 1862

My dear Harriet,

We start tomorrow on a long march for Richmond and it is supposed we will reach the place by Tuesday night. It was first intended to take us on the cars but there is a want of trains and the Generals drew lots to see who should walk. Our General was unfortunate enough to get the lot to walk and so we shall have to tramp it through. It seems nobody has any idea where we are going but it is generally thought to be the Peninsula to help Genl Magruder.

I can't tell when we shall arrive in Richmond or how long we may stay there. I will write to you again before we get there and if you can possibly come down and see me I shall be rejoiced to see you. Uncle Bogy will let you have the money and come with you too. I will manage to pay him back in Richmond. Come to Mrs. Mottley's on Main St. above the American Hotel. Uncle Bogy can find the place but if I find that we should stop in Richmond then I will let you know for we may go straight through without stopping an hour. I do wish I knew or I could be certain now but make your arrangements so you can take the first train if I write or telegraph for you.

No news. Writing on my knee by firelight late at night. Tom Jones sends his love to Capt Jones and says he us satisfied now and thinks the service first rate. The Boys all well and they and Archer send their best love. I heard from Pat a few days ago but his letter was several days old being of the 24th March. He was then at

Warrenton. Morton is very sick with measles at Orange C.H. and I fear he suffers for attention.

In haste I am
Most devotedly Yrs etc.,
Henry

****

Harriet's brother, Theodorick Pryor Robertson, (Pryor) received a slight wound. Henry mentions this in his letter to Harriet of May 11, 1862.

****

Sunday morning
May the 11th 1862

My dear Harriet,

I have already written you some account of our Great Battle and do not know anything else I could say repeating it would be interesting.

Tom Jones started to Richmond Friday morning and will be home in a few days I hope. His wound is a bad one but he is not in danger. Lieut. Watkins started Tuesday and I expect is now in Richmond or at home. I miss them both very much. Pryor is well and again in ranks. He would not leave the company and his wound is light.

Our health is good and we are on the banks of the Chickahominy where we get plenty of provisions but no mail yet. You must write often and direct to the 18th Va. Vols. A man is waiting for us to finish our letters.

Send my coat by the first one coming to this company but don't rush it by anybody else. Some of my men at home will be coming on here nearly every week and Uncle Boygy can send my things by one of them.

Do the best you can and don't be uneasy as I should take the best care I can of myself. Kiss the children and write soon.

Yrs devotedly etc.,
Henry

We never know when any body is going to town until they fix up and then we have to hurry up so we can hardly think how to write or what to say.

Yrs etc.
H.

****

In a letter of June 28, 1862, Henry mentions to Harriet that he has heard that Col. Withers has been mortally wounded. Henry later learns this rumor was not true.

****

Jun 28th, 1862

My dear Wife,

I was a little sick with rheumatism and not in the battles of the last two days. Mr. Gill goes home wounded in the arm. He left the Regiment last night about 5 o'clock some sixteen miles from here and they are then still fighting and the Yankees running.

He reports Col. Withers mortally wounded and perhaps dead. I am truly sorry since he has been very kind and friendly to me of late. Archer severely wounded and Carter and Bob Holloway. He could not tell any more as he was wounded early in the fight.

Our Reg suffered severely. Capt Lyle from Charlotte killed. Four of Capt Irby's men killed and several wounded.

In Great haste
I am most devotedly yours
Henry

****

Two days later, Henry writes Harriet again stating that he has not heard from her in half a week. As the war drags on, he becomes more homesick and in a rare moment, expresses in a letter that he wishes the war would end speedily so that he might embrace "his sweet little wife."

****

Camp 3rd Brigade
On Williamsburg Road
June 30th 1862

My dear Harriet,

I have not recd my mail for several days as no one from Camp visits the Office so I have not heard from you in half a week. It really looks like a long time.

Mr La Neve came down yesterday and goes up today. I shall take the chance of writing this letter for you and he will either send it to you or mail it at the Junction. I have no stamps so am forced to make you pay both your own and my postage. I am still in Camp but tolerably well – my leg hurts a little sometimes and I do not think I could go on a long march since I was so tired on the march of last Monday which I wrote you of.

The Brigade has rafted down the Chickahominy to cut off McClellan's retreat to James river and it is thought his whole army will have to surrender. Won't this be a grand victory. His army is beaten already and God has blessed us again and should return him thanks for such signal evidence of his continuous care and guidance.

McClellan is trying to escape but we have got him hemmed in and even if he breaks through his giant army is destroyed. We have taken up to last night some five thousand prisoners and it is thought killed and wounded twenty five or thirty thousand. I will send you a list of the members of my company engaged in the different battles we have been in and I want you to save them for future reference. You can see that while some of my men have been in all the Battles others whom you know have taken care to avoid every danger and of course deserve no credit for independence.

I hope the War will be ended now very speedily and I may once more embrace my sweet little wife. Mr. LaNeve said he saw Clay and Pryor and Archer all on the road to your Pass and I expect Clay got home all safe. I sent some Muster Rolls which I want you to keep for me where the mice can't bite them. Mr. Morton has returned to camp worn down with fatigue and is quite feeble but in no danger. Pete is well and still keeping after the enemy. A great Battle is expected today but very little cannon has been heard this morning. The enemy is giving away everywhere and our boys don't stop for breastworks and embankments. The Yankee prisoners say our men fight like devils and nothing can stand before such men.

Write soon.   Yrs most truly and
                            Devotedly
                              Henry
                ****

Following the second Battle of Manassas, Henry wrote Harriet a short account of that engagement. He stated that several officers of the 18th had been wounded.
                ****

Manassas Plains
August 31st 1862

My dear Harriet,

We are on the previous Battle field of the 21st of July and yesterday gained a great victory on the same ground. God has again been merciful to me and spared my life where thousands went back home. Capt Holland wounded also Capt Irby and Capt Booker, Col Carrington also, and Lieut Watkins, Lieut Jackson and Lieut Mc Culloch, Lieut Glenn and one Sgt Major. This was nine officers and we had a great many more at muster. I got your letter of the 27th and was rejoiced to find that you were not uneasy about me as I have not heard from you so long. My last letter from you was on the 14th (I think). I will write whenever I can and you must not be uneasy if you do not hear from me as often as usual for we have no Rail Road to Manassas from Gordonsville and have to send a man on horseback sixty miles after the mail. The Yankees fought very hard but we drove through at last, and pushed them across Bull Run. Col Crump was killed late yesterday evening. Our men are in fine spirits and we expect to be after the Yankees again today, Gen D. H. Hill is here and will do the next fighting. He came up to our help last night with about thirty thousand men. The Yankees are falling back on Washington. I do not know which side holds the works at Manassas as we are five miles from there.

I will write again soon.

Yrs forever and truly
Henry
My love to all
(Direct to Gordonville)

****

On November 7, 1862, Henry wrote Harriet from a camp near Culpeper Court House. As the weather was turning colder, he asked her to send him his new blanket.

****

Camp Near Culpeper C House
Nov 7th 1862

My dear Harriet,

I have not recd a letter from you for thirteen or fourteen days but I believe you have written several times and that it is owing to the delivery state of the mail why I do not receive them. Our mail was sent to Winchester after our departure from that place and has not been returned and assorted for the different Brigades and Divisions. I will console myself with the hope that you are all well at home and think I shall soon hear from you.

It is snowing rapidly here and the ground is already white, the wind howls and sweeps the chilly blasts around us, while the thick shower of snowflakes insure a shroud upon the wood and plains, through the dark swamp and over the blank hills.

Bill and myself were industrious when we first arrived here and built us a close brush tent or bower open on ones side and then we built a rousing log fire and sit far back snug as bugs in a rug. We have the best shanty in the brigade and are quite comfortable while hundreds are entirely out doors stooping over their smoking log heaps and taking the weather. We had some few tents issued to the Regiment a few days ago but my little shelter is far better than a tent and is much warmer as we can have a fire in front while none can be built near a tent. A little fine sand occasionally penetrates the bushes and sifts in fine drops upon my letter but not enough to hurt.

Bill is sewing buttons on an overcoat that belongs to some of the absent men and several boys come near our fire and warm themselves while speaking of the War, weather and women.

Upon the whole the soldier is a "devil may care" jovial kind of a fellow and takes things as they come.

I wish I had my new blanket and if you find a chance please send it to me. I would like for you to cut a slit in it about the middle for me to put over my head as I shall make it answer for an overcoat this winter. Cut the hole a little from the middle towards one edge but not far from the middle and not too long. You will have to put a binding around the hole to prevent raveling. The hole must be a little larger than your head so I can put it on and off easy.

If the snow gets deep I think the War will close for the winter as the roads will become miry and the army can't travel and scramble about much. I then hope to get a furlough for ten or twenty days and come home to get stragglers. I shall try at any rate but don't want to build up your hopes and then disappoint you. But when I expect anything of the kind I like to tell you however small the chance of success.

Cannon are firing a long way north of us and as the heavy reports come booming upon the bosom of the breeze the boys through camp here now and then raise a yell. We heard them yesterday and day before and expect to hear from Jackson in a few days and get a good report from him. No music in the world is so solemn or grand or as beautiful to my ear as the far off, dull, sullen muttering of the deep mouthed cannon. Its sublime and heavy distant peals seem like a voice calling from the far off battle field for brave men to marshal themselves in battle array and rush onward to the strife. The battle is fiercely raging and perhaps gallant men are charging through carnage and destruction and almost feel like being there and one of them.

(Closing & Signature Missing)

****

On December 13, 1862 the 18th was near Fredericksburg but was not engaged in the battle that raged most of the day. December 14, 1862, Henry penned a short letter to Harriet from camp saying "thank God, they were not needed."

****

Camp near Fredericksburg Va
December 14th 1862

My Dear Harriet,

We have had some desperate fighting and this is the first chance I have had to write you. I shall only have time to say a few word as the sun is setting. We are all safe so far and have not been engaged at all yet but within sight of some of the bloodiest work I have seen. We could see both sides charging on each other all day yesterday and expected to be sent in every minute but thank God we were not needed as our men finally drove the enemy off before them with the greatest slaughter that has happened during the whole war. The prisoners we took say we cut them up terribly. They had over a hundred cannon firing upon us at once and did not appear to have hurt us much. I can see over the flat country below Fredericksburg where the valley is four or five miles wide and the whole space is full of the Yankee Army moving about in the flat low ground. The Yankees fought on our right and we saw that part of the battle but I understand that the fight far off on or left above Fredericksburg was much heavier and the losses in proportion. We have held them back for four days and I am nearly worn out with anxiety and suspense expecting every minute to be called on to go into the fight. I trust in God and hope you will remember me in your prayers. I will write again as soon as I get time. Genl Lee says we can stop the enemy here easy if the men will only do as they have done so far. My love to the children –

I am truly yrs
Henry

****

In early 1863, the 18th was detached from General Pickett's Division and sent South into North Carolina. Henry wrote Harriet on March 14, 1863.

****

Pitt County N. Carolina
Saturday March 14th 1863

My dear Harriet,

I will commence a letter this morning before we begin to march and will mail it if I see an opportunity but fear very much that I will not have a chance of doing so for several days as no one is expecting to leave for the rear. However I will add something each day and mail it when I can and you may rest assured my sweet wife that you are too dear to me to allow a chance of sending a letter to pass.

We left Tarboro Thursday morning at 7 o'clock and marched twenty miles camping just before night within 5 miles of Greenville. The next day (yesterday) we resumed our journey at an early hour and took the road towards Washington, leaving Greenville 2½ miles to the right. We do not exactly know what our object is but I think that we will get near Washington and let our wagons get forage and corn from all the country behind us while we keep the Yankees back. Or we may attack the town as there are only some thousand Yankees there now and we have about three times their number. They have six gunboats and have also a large number of runaway negroes dwelling in the place. I would like to fall upon them and give them a genteel thrashing. It is reported that we will return to Petersburg in about fifteen days, and I rather think so, but there is no certainty in such reports and we never rely upon them much.

We encamped here last night, at "Great Swamp Church" and it is truly deserving this title. Just around the church the ground is sandy and a little bit elevated but fifty yards from the road a swamp begins that stretches away for miles upon miles – filled with reeds, briers, brushwood, cypress and pines. Yesterday after we halted I went out into the swamp to see what sort of a place it was – and had to get along upon fallen logs to keep up out of the water that was about a foot deep. The place looked like it ought to be filled with game but I saw no living creature except two little birds – a pair – that had sought this deep recess to build and rear their young. There was no sound except the breeze as it sighed in the tops of the lofty pines and the whole place was most solemn and gloomy I ever saw.

This whole country up to Tarboro is filled with such swamps and houses are scarce and mostly in on the road that has to wind and turn in a thousand tortuous ways to miss these bogs.

6 o'clock P.M. We have not moved today but waited for our wagons with provisions to come up and will not get off now till tomorrow morning. We have heard all day at intervals, distant cannons firing and suppose it is the Yankee gunboats at Washington that is some twenty miles off yet, but I can't see what they are firing at.

I understand that Genl Pickett was very much fretted when we were taken from him and sent south and that he said "if they took away (us) his old Brigade - the rest of his Division might go to hell."

He had five Brigades and we were the first and gained him all his credit as a General. We are now under General D. H. Hill and while the Boys have a good opinion of him they regret the change. I prefer Pickett and we hope the transfer is not permanent but will only last a few weeks and that we may return to Virginia and to Pickett.

We have just recd orders to march a 7 o'clock tomorrow morning. I will write again as soon as we stop.

(No closing and unsigned)
****

In September of 1863, the 18th was again encamped near Petersburg. Clothing was becoming scarce and Henry suggests ways Harriet might recycle one of his coats.

****

Camp 18th Va Regt Petersburg
Sept 27th 1863

My dear Wife,

Yrs of yesterday with the carpet sack was recd this morning and I have had some of the potatoes for dinner. I will send my coat back home and if I need it hereafter will send for it. The sleeves are too small and if my blue pants will be enough for another set of sleeves let me know and I will have it fixed up at once unless you have already made Clay a pair of pants of them. I want you to fix him up and send him down some day with Joe Leath. Joe will go up on the train twice a week and you can find out from Mr. Irving when he goes up so Clay may come down with him.

My company and the Farmville Guard (Co. F) are ordered to City Point tomorrow or next day and I am very well pleased with the post as the work will be light and the quarters first rate. Then we shall likely remain there during the winter and see all the prisoners passing North or South. I want Clay with me and all his books and will teach him myself. Michael must also pay me a visit soon and see some of the world. The more they see and learn the better as they may have to work their way in the world and I want them to know how to start right. If you box up Henry's books I shall want some dozen or two of mine to come along and will let you know which I want as soon as you have him ready. Or you can send him along as soon as he is ready and I will afterwards send for such books as I want.

Have your trust in God. He is still blessing us and we must continue to serve him faithfully and truly. I think of making both of our boys preachers. What do you think of it ? Write to Petersburg until I direct otherwise.

Most truly and devotedly yrs, Henry

****

Henry's idea to "make both of their boys a preachers" never materialized. Both Henry Clay Owen and Michael M. Owen became railroad men like their father.
****

CHAPTER 9 - THE SPIRITUALITY OF HENRY T. OWEN

"God is great and I have placed myself in his hands. You must not be worried but must pray constantly for me and be thankful for his blessings."
Henry T. Owen - July 22, 1863

Spirituality is a broad term encompassing many meanings. The spirituality of Henry Thweatt Owen probably reflects the spirituality of his era. From his letters the essence of a profound belief in an omnipotent God is felt by the reader.

The first example we notice of Henry's beliefs is in a letter to his wife where he mentions the death of Sarah's baby. Henry lost a child of his own. He never mentioned this loss in his letters that are archived. Perhaps he didn't because he truly believed it was an act of Providence.

****

Louisa C. H. Va
Apr 10 1862

My dear Harriet,

When I wrote you the enclosed letter at Orange C.H. on the 5th I expected to remain long enough to finish it that evening or the next day. Sunday morning Pete Temple and Lyons asked me to go with them out into the country and get a good dinner. I went and when we returned just before night I found our Regiment preparing for a long march somewhere so I just had time to pack up my few little things and fall in ranks.

Longstreet's whole Division started for Fredericksburg just as the sun set and marched sixteen miles that night but very suddenly turned about the next morning and marched back towards this place. We have been marching all the time and I have had no time to write but I have carried your letter all the time and if we had got into a fight I should have destroyed it.

Just before we started on Sunday evening I got your letter of the 4th April and you had not got my reply to some of your letters. I have recd all except one and that one is 14th March. I hope by this time you have my reply to them all. In your last you informed me of the death of Sarah's baby and this is another misfortune but remember dear Harriet that those who have must lose and we must not complain at these visitations of Providence.

You complained of your failing health. Now my sweet wife don't let your health give way under any circumstances. If you allow yourself to give way to trouble and grieve, then your health will fail but if you will just keep up against misfortune you will certainly be healthy.

Go up to my mother's and stay as long as you please but I think you would hardly be satisfied at Womack's place by yourself in a large cold house. Just take your clothes and shut up all your furniture in one room of the house and give Sarah orders to take care of it. Don't mind expense and sell anything you please for where my wife is concerned I don't care about money.

If you are not satisfied at my mother's you can go to your father's or anywhere you please and I will hereafter pay any bill you make anywhere. Do as you think proper and I will be satisfied.

In the last five days we have marched fifty or sixty miles and when we once get settled for a few days I shall write you a long account of our trip. We had snow and rain and hail nearly all the time and hundreds of men gave out and strayed off to the country. The mud was knee deep in some places and we waded rivers in our journey. This Division is about 8,000 strong and we expect to go to Yorktown. From here we go by R.R. to Hanover Junction near Richmond. Write your letters addressed as I back the envelope inside until you hear again from me. All our company is up in Camp today except one and we are looking for him.

My love to all. I am doing well tho' very tired. Keep in good spirits.

Your devoted husband,
Henry

****

Henry mentions the men he is with in camp do not observe the Sabbath. Maybe for many who participated in the war saw such violence and carnage that their beliefs waned.

****

Camp near Yorktown
April 20th 1862

My dear Wife,
     I have written you once since arriving in the Peninsula and first chance in that time was four days. Our marches have been so constant and fatiguing that I could not write before today.
     It appears a hard case that we are down here and remain in ignorance of affairs at home but such is the case. I have not heard from you since we left Orange C H 13th April and yr letter was dated the 4th Apr. It seems several weeks since I heard from home and I am very anxious to get a letter from you. One of my letters was initiated in Richmond but we passed through so hastily I could not visit the Office. We do not get any mail and all the Boys are anxious to hear from friends.
     This is a perfect wilderness place and since I got here have not seen much cleared land. All woods so thick and tangled that a man can hardly move through them. The land is as level as can be and covered with frog ponds. We are camped far off in the gloomy pine forest and the rain is pattering down upon our oil cloth shelters.
     It is Sunday but the soldiers seem unaware of the fact. Very little respect is paid to the Sabbath in the army. The great guns of the enemy are thundering at us from a distance and their bombs fall a little short of us. They have not been able to reach us here but we have had several men killed at the breastworks and some little fighting is going on below us about a mile off.
     I have just recd your letter of the 9th and while it tells me of you at a later date than the previous one of the 4th it is yet so old I am anxious to get another from you. I know several are on the Road and shall continue to hope for them to reach me after awhile. I am sorry you complained of the headache to Smith and fear you think too much and trouble yourself too much. Just let things have their course and not grieve at anything.
     Some of the Boys have the mumps and some are sick various ways. Ten or a dozen have been sent off to the hospital.
     You can do as you please in respect to Ada and I will be satisfied. Whatever you do will please me.
     I have no news to write and will have to close my letter.
     I have seen Billy Mottley and Meridith Watson and P. Fowlkes and Dick Dyson since coming down here. They all look well and their troop is on a pocket near lands end some ten miles

from us. If it had not rained today I reckon several of them perhaps would have visited us.

Write often dear Wife.

I am very truly yrs,
Henry

****

It is evident in the following letter that Henry did not dwell on his situation and did not want Harriet to get melancholy. The letter tells us that Henry truly believed Providence was his protector.

****

Camp near Yorktown
April 24th 1862

My dear Harriet,

Your kind letter of 22nd has just come to hand and is good opportunity offered for me to send a reply. I avail myself of the chance to write you a few hasty lines tho' nothing occurs here in camp that can possibly interest you.

I was truly glad to hear from you and to learn that little Hattie has gotten well bless her little soul. You must bite her good for me and squeeze her properly like a peach and touch up the others lightly for me.

I send this one by Capt. Graves of the Danville Blues. He goes to get provisions in town.

I am sorry Louis Morton is sick and I fear since he has kept no better care he will not get well. Tom Jones sends his best to his father.

We were doing first rate in the wilderness here and the cutting line but the bombshells were falling and bursting over us all the time. We lost six men and Magruder is a capital general and has made the strongest defense here I ever saw and can whip ten to one easy if they advance on in. It is reported that the Yankees are advancing on Richmond by way of Fredericksburg and I expect we shall be hurried back there in a day or so.

You must not allow yourself to sit down and think too much. If you do you will most certainly get in bad health. You must enliven us and cheer yourself anyway but don't despond. Nothing troubles me so much as to hear that you are miserable and I am miserable until I hear again from you. Let arise what will do and not give way to these trying times. Providence will yet bless us and make us happy. I am satisfied that I shall not be hurt by the

108

Yankees and all that I need to make me satisfied under my severe trials is to know that you are not miserable.

Take care of yourself and regards to all inquiring friends.

Most truly and devotedly Yrs

H. T. Owen

****

Henry even urged his children to pray in the following letter. Part of home schooling the children probably included teaching them about the religious belief system of the parents.

****

Camp before Washington N.C.

April 6, 1863

Wife & Millie Owen:

My dear Daughter

I have expected a letter from you and looked for one in vain until I begin to think you have forgotten your "promise" to write to me very often and I must remind you that you owe me a letter and I shall remind you to be more punctual in payment of your just debts. I am anxious to hear from you and see that you are making constant improvement in your studies. I am far away from home in a cold, dreary country undergoing many hardships in the shape of long toilsome marches through gloomy swamps, sometimes wading through streams of dark rolling waters and sometimes standing watch all through the long, cold nights in some dismal looking place and often suffering the severest pangs of hunger and want of rest, but I still each day and night think of my little children at their distant home and feel that they will learn fast and be good and kind that I shall be repaid for all my toil and suffering. You must not forget to pray   (PAGES MISSING) …forgotten how flour bread tasted. Now Meadows had one biscuit in his haversack that he brought from camp and he called up one of the woman's little boys about the size of Michael and gave him the biscuit. The little fellow did not know what it was as he had never seen one before and after turning it about and looking at it closely for a time he put it down in the middle of the floor and got a chunk of fire and place it on top of the biscuit saying it was a little terrapin and that he wanted to see him crawl. He would not believe that it was anything else until Meadows broke it in two and showed him it was something to eat.

We did not have many snows here while it was snowing so heavy in Va but we have a hard rain in place of the snow. It is a great deal warmer here than where you live and we see strange looking birds here that are never seen in your country and farther we go South then the greater the change and the more you see these animals and birds that are strange and new to us.

Your affectionate father
H. T. Owen
****

While camping in one of the spots he had previously camped in, Henry stated he was tired after a march. Henry rarely complained. He speaks of a vow he made after listening to some sermons preached by Dr. Pryor. Henry seeks Dr. Pryor out to confess his sins and to profess his faith. He even admits he is not particular in wanting to join some type of church.

****

Rappahannock County Va
June 16th 1863

My dear Harriet,

We left camp below Culpeper C. H. yesterday morning and are now camped at one of our old camps on the road to Winchester. The main turnpike is about a mile above us and we do not yet know which end we shall take. The left hand leads towards Front Royal and Winchester and the right leads to Warrenton and Manassas. I am very tired after a long day's march and can't write a long letter.

I made a vow at Boonsboro last Sept. that if God would permit me to have another opportunity for repentance that I would not refuse to accept it and after listening to three able sermons last Sunday the 14th by Dr. Pryor who is preaching in our Division, I resolved, as he preached next day, that I would make a public renunciation of my sins and profess Christ. The next morning early (yesterday) we got orders to start at 12 o'clock and as Dr. Pryor was to preach at 4 o'clock, his meeting was put off and I determined not (to) allow the opportunity to pass so I sought him and told him I had come to acknowledge my resolution to sin no more and that I wished to unite with some church and I had no prejudices. I would make choice of the Presbyterian and have written to Mr. Martin on the subject. I wish you would follow my example. God has been kind to us and we should be willing to serve him. My love to all. I will write more as soon as I can.

Yr affectionate and devoted husband
Henry

****

Henry admonished Harriet in several letters to attend preaching on a more regular basis. In a letter of June 21, 1863 (See Chapter 3), Henry tells Harriet about a dream he has about William Henry. The dream is so real that it troubles Henry.

Near Christmas of 1863, Henry encourages Harriet after a misfortune and reminds her he has been watched over during the war. He mentions another dream. In this dream, there is a shadowy figure, an angel perhaps, protecting Henry. He is overcome with emotion and humbled by this experience. The war has deepened his belief system.

****

24th & Franklin
Richmond Va
21 Dec 63

My dear Wife,

Yr letter of the 19th is received. I am truly sorry you met with the misfortune to lose your trunk and the articles of such value to you but it might have been a great deal worse and instead of grieving over the mishap I hope you will take it easy. God will certainly protect us and care for us under all circumstances if we found worthy his attention and I hope you will not give way to what may be considered of small moment in comparison to what might befall us in one moment if God should neglect or forget us. All the substance of this like is as chaff and we should learn to submit to our trials when they come. You seem to forget how God has shielded us and cared for us in past time, given us life and health and prosperity and what claim had we to expect these blessings? You seem to forget that I have passed through half a dozen desperate battles when death reigned around and men fell by hundreds on every side and still came out unhurt and unscathed tho' my company, my commander, my messmates and bedfellows have been taken time and again. If God did not watch over me and cared for me what could have saved and protected me in these desperate conflicts? Man could not avail anything then for in such times man can not save himself. Who saved me at Gettysburg when 29 out of 31 officers were struck down killed or wounded and all my company except one other man? One night several weeks after Battle of Gettysburg I lay down very much dissatisfied about my condition and situation and after spending several restless hours in thinking over my grievances and how fate, as I imagined it, I fell asleep and dreamed as follows:

We were advancing in line of battle upon the enemy troops on my right and left shot dead away as far as the eye could see all pressing on the fearful conflict. I could hear the fearful reports of five batteries of cannon and the perpetual roar of fifty thousand muskets while a dark cloud of smoke hung over the field mantling everything as the gloom of dusky sunset. Far away to the front I saw the dim outlines of lofty hills, broken rocks and lofty precipices which resembled Gettysburg. As we advanced further I found we were fighting that great battle over again and I saw something before me like a thin shadow which I tried to go by but it kept in front of me and whichever way I turned it still appeared between me and the enemy. Nobody else seemed to see or notice the shadow which looked as thin as smoke and did not present myself to the enemy distinctly thru' it. I felt troubled and oppressed but still the shadow went out before me. I moved forward in the thickest of the fray trying to loose sight of it and went all through the Battle of Gettysburg again with the shadow ever before me and between me and the enemy and when we came out beyond the danger of shot it spoke and said to me " I am the Angel that protected you. I will never leave nor forsake you."

The surprise was so great that I awoke and burst into tears. What had I done that should entitle me to such favours beyond tho' hundreds of brave and reputed good men who had fallen on that day leaving widowed mothers and widowed wives, orphan children and disconsolate families to mourn their fates? I felt that I was blessed beyond my deserts and shall not complain at the little misfortunes of this life.

God sees us always and provides for us as he sees fit. He means this little misfortune as chastisement for some neglect of duty and awakens a sense of dependence upon him. Look to him and be industrious and serving and all things will work well in the end. This war has been a blessing to me and you will honestly say so or thinks so, still it had been the cause of a change in me that all of the eloquence of the best sermons could not have produced. Real suffering and danger has taught me to rely upon God above and it has saved me from sickness and death. You must cheer up and not repine at these little things. I am afraid you are not enough like Job and don't practice patience enough under trials.

If it appears necessary I will sell my Negroes and it may be best for us to do so but unless it is absolutely necessary I think it a sin and prefer retaining them.

I will look around and see what I can do for you. I have very good acquaintances in Richmond but I never have failed where I fixed my will to do anything. If I ought to get out of the War, God will point out the way and unless I am following his will I must remain. He will find a way to inform me what to do.

Be cheerful and don't repine. I am using every effort to get a leave of absence and will come as soon as I can.

Until then I am as ever Devotedly Yrs,
Henry

My love to Ma & Brothers
****

A letter penned to daughter, Mamie, speaks of Providence. Henry professes that life and death are not mere chance, but born of God's wisdom. He cites two examples of this belief.

****

2601 E. Franklin St.
Richmond Va. Jany 29th 1919

Dear Mamie,

The box of candy reached me safely and it is a wonder I kept it two days before I let anybody know I had it, then I felt so proud I wanted the girls to look at the beautiful assortment and invited Hattie and Sallie to take a look.

They made the greatest screams of admiration but Sallie said, "just looking was mighty poor satisfaction" so I had for manners sake to invite them to taste and I watched them tasting. It appeared to me their tasting had been sharpened by fasting. I ought to have fed them on brown sugar two or three days before I let them see the box. I will know better next time if there ever comes a next time.

I was thankful to God that Mr. Styll was providentially saved from the accident at the bridge. Many people look upon these escapes from death as mere chance, but not a sparrow falls to the ground without the will of God.

About twenty-five years ago a poor farmer in Dinwiddie, ten miles from Petersburg, had business in Richmond. He rode to Petersburg where he left his horse and took the cars for Richmond. Late in the evening when he went to the depot to take the train back, there was a man there selling "accident tickets" good for 24 hours for $1,000 for

113

25 cts.   This farmer saw several people buy these tickets and asked them if they were of any value.   He had never seen one before so he bought one, and that night, while riding home, he crossed a bridge where his horse dropped through and a broken plank and the man was thrown over the horse's head and broke his neck where he was found next morning.   His wife and little children would have been left destitute but for the accident ticket.

I have been to hear Billy Sunday six or seven times and he is wonderful.   Some days fifteen or twenty thousand people are turned back from the doors of the auditorium.

We are all well and hope you and Mr. Styll can pay us a visit soon.

Affectionately Yr father

H. T. Owen

****

In July of 1920, Henry writes a long letter to his son "Mich", (Michael), espousing some of his knowledge about the Bible and his thoughts on its scripture. In this letter Henry goes off on a tangent about Queen Victoria. It is puzzling to the authors how he learned of such intricate details.

****

2601 E. Franklin St..

Richmond Va.

July 23, 1920

Dear Mich,

Your letter with copy of the Pathfinder received yesterday and the Editorial on the question, "Shall the Jews rule World?" is very interesting and instructive. I am more concerned about them and their movements than about any other people and watch them very closely as all history has been shaped by them and will be wound up and ended by them.

The Hebrews are the only race on earth that has supplied the world with a list of prophets to foretell coming events, sometimes hundreds or thousands of years before they occurred, but were fulfilled exactly as predicted.   Nebuchanezzar, King of Babylon, had a vision of a great triage with a head of gold that Daniel told him represented his kingdom, to be followed by one of silver, (the Persians), then one of brass, (the Grecians), then one of iron, (the Romans). With the feet and toes mixed with clay as partly weak and partly strong.   This was about 600 years B.C. and the Roman Empire was broken up and divided into ten kingdoms about 475 years after

114

Christ, 1175 years after Daniel's dream. We are now living in the last of the Iron Age and clay mixed. All nations on earth are rapidly changing to Democracies and mixing up into mud and iron.

When I first voted it was on a certain amount of property and ability to read and write. Then the Democrats extended the right to every man 21 years old and now to the women, who will have to bear arms and be, at once, degraded. Democracy is the strongest form of government on earth and at the same time it is the weakest because every question must be submitted to the people before the nation can decide what to do in the matter. But when a question is decided by majority, they accept it until repealed. The Germans had defeated the Belgians, the French, the English, the Italians and Russians before the Americans got there and they found a different kind of enemy, one they could not drive, but would drive them. And this they admit since the war ended.

After Nov. election we shall know whether or not to sign the League of Nations. I am opposed to any mix up with foreign nations as Washington and Monroe were and I was with Senator Lodge in all his arguments against the treaty but will vote for it as a religious duty though the Bible says we shall "cry Peace! Peace! But there shall be no Peace!" until after Armageddon. We are fixing for Armageddon as fast as we can. The League of Nations has decided to drive the Turks out of Europe. This will start a war in which all the peoples opposed to Christianity will combine against it and Armageddon will begin. The prophet stood on the hills of Palestine and saw a vast army coming. They covered the earth as far as the eye could see and were on horseback, with smoke and flames coming out of the mouths and nostrils of the horses. These were not our animals, called horses, but it was the bicycle loaded with poisonous gasses. The reason he said horses, he had never seen men mounted on anything else so like a horse. The Prophet saw a lion with eagle's wings come out of the sea and take control of Palestine. This is England and U. States combined now together planning to take control of all that country. The Governor of Jerusalem now is an Englishman filling the office that Pontius Pilate, the Roman, occupied in the crucifixion of Christ. This Lion is followed by a Leopard, whose spots represent all the nations of the world, to join in the great battle in defense of their faith. It is during the last contest when the Christian army, vastly outnumbered, are being driven back, that Christ with one hundred and forty four thousand Christian Hebrews appears at the head of the army and speaks a

115

word that blasts the whole heathen host in front and it will take seven years to bury the dead. Then he is to reign in profound peace on earth a thousand years. The inspired scribe of Genesis states that the world was made in six days and in particular in telling what was made each day, and saying "the morning and the evening was the first day" and so on, "the morning and the evening was the second day." All geologists agree that the days were long periods of thousands or perhaps millions of years, but they also agree that the Creation shows six different and distinct constructions. Up to the fourth day the waters covered the earth and darkness rested upon the deep. On the fourth day the Sun, Moon and stars were made and the morning of the fifth day the Sun rose for the first time bright and clear to light up a darkened world. Each day is typical of events to come and Christ was born at Bethlehem on the night that closed 4,000 years afterwards. Then there came the fifth and sixth day in which the latter of which man was made and the Lord rested on the seventh which day was typical of the millennium in which Christ reigns on earth. It is stated that each "day is as a thousand years and a thousand years as a day with the Lord" and the usual construction put upon this sentence is that the Lord pays to attention and does not take note of time as in watering a lot of flowers you would not care to notice whether you used a pint, a quart or a gallon of water, but the manner in which the phrase is used shows another meaning the inspired writer meant to impress upon his readers which was each day was typical of a thousand years and on the fourth the light for the intellect of the world be created and appear on the fifth thousand while the seventh represented the Millennium. We count this as the 1920th year since the birth of Christ but do not know exactly what the year is, for time has been changed several times and our year is not the same length as the Jew's year. Bishop Usher, after long study of all the facts he could obtain, decided the birth of Christ was in the year of the world 4004, but since his time it has been determined that it occurred in the year 4000 at the close or end of that year and I think that is correct as it agrees with the typical day of the Creation of light for the terrestrial globe. But in the dark ages extending from the downfall in A.D. 476 to the middle of the 13th century, about 900 years, we are in ignorance about all Europe. If we were certain this is 1920 then the millennium should commence in about 80 years or the year 2000 to agree with the seventh day. But there again, Christ said, "the time would be shortened or no flesh would be saved." And the people are doing their best to bring on the

116

last great war. The false prophet was to treat Jerusalem under foot 1260 years. Mahomet captured it in 635 and a Jew could not stay all night in the city until 1895 when the Sultan gave them liberty to settle there and now there is about 70,000 settled in Palestine and becoming Christians. How strange that the Sultan was induced to let the Jews go back by a letter from the Queen of England delivered to him by a Jew and how strange that Sultan was educated in England and that she was named <u>Victoria</u>.

She reigned 57 years, a longer period than any other king or queen since Ramasees of Egypt, in the time of Moses, 1500 years B.C. She was more widely respected, more generally beloved and universally obeyed than any crowned head that ever graced a throne in the world.

She lived a pure clean life and by her example did more to correct the immorality among women of England and America, in fact to cleanse society and raise the character of all the inhabitants of the civilized nations of the earth than any other person that ever lived. She was evidently a Providential selection for that purpose.

Her uncle, George IV, King, in middle age and robust health bid fair to live many years. In case of his death, one of his younger brothers would succeed him, as he had no children. There were three brothers and when little Victoria was born in 1819 there was no prospect of her ever succeeding to the throne as her father was the youngest of the King's three brothers, but the others died with no children and her father also when she was just 20 months old and she became the only heir to the Kingdom, but the strictest orders were given to the family and to all her attendants not to tell her nor to mention the subject in her presence, and was kept a secret from her. She was reared by an old aunt, as wise as Solomon, who taught her to sew, to knit, to cut out and make her own clothes and do all kinds of housework, in which she became an expert and functioned through life. The best teachers were employed and she learned rapidly acquiring a knowledge of language and figures with ease, and the ablest accountants in England found out when she became queen, they could not fool her with shifty reports. She had a very sensible, discreet maid who took long walks with her, for exercise, in the evening when her lessons were over and one evening when little Victoria was about eight years old, Providence so arranged matters they took a new route and came to a high brick wall which they followed until they came to an iron gate with cross bars, through which they could see beautiful gravel walks, lined by plots

117

of various kinds of colored flowers, and far back in a grove stood a grand old building that looked like a castle. Vick asked the Maid who lived there and she replied that she didn't know, as they hadn't been that way before. Then Vick said "she reckoned some great old genie lived in that castle and if he came out and caught them peeping through his gate he would eat them up, but she wished she could go in and walk over the grounds to look at those pretty flowers." At this an old grey haired man got up from a seat in the inside of the wall where he had heard this talk and opened the gate for them to come in, saying he would show them over all the place. They soon came to some bush in full bloom of white roses that Vick admired very much and pointing out a particular half bloomed bud, she said "it was, she believed, the prettiest she had ever seen," and the old man started to clip it off for her, but she laid her hand on his arm and told him not to touch it. He replied that "the old genie who lived in the castle would let him clip all the flowers he wanted." "But he can't let you clip them for me, leave them where the Lord placed them for the bees and butterflies. If you clip it, in an hour it will wither and be useless, so let it stay where it is." At this he took a long steady look at her and they passed on over all the grounds and he walked with them back to the gate where he gave her a key and told her she could come in at any time and go freely over the whole place. Whether he then knew who she was or not, is not related but he probably did know. However, she became a frequent visitor and she and that old man were soon fast friends. She went to his place oftener than anywhere else and began to consult that old gentleman about all subjects that concerned, or interested her. She found him a man of great learning, profound wisdom, strict integrity and always frank and candid, with an eye to truth and justice, without prejudice or partiality to any person or subject submitted to his opinion for decision. He was a Jew and became her advisor through life. I was invited by the Jews of Richmond to the celebration of his hundredth birthday and he lived two years longer. When Victoria was eleven years old the great lords and ladies of England gave a feast and at its close told her she was heir to the throne and was going to be queen upon the death of the king. She listened and sat in silence for five minutes or more before she said "some children would think this is a great honor and be delighted at the information, but the troubles and trials of a sovereign are often greater than any pleasures or joys of that position. I don't want to be queen, but if I have to be, then I will try to be a good one." As soon as the crowd left she went to see the old Jew, Count Moses Montefiore, and upbraided him for not telling her of this. She said to him "you have known this all the time and kept it from me, I have thought if there was a person on earth that would never hide a secret like that from me it was yourself." He explained to her that the strictest orders had been imposed upon him not to tell and he had to obey the command. She scolded him a long time but finally made it up and became friends as before.

In 1839, when the great lords, earls, and dukes met at ask her to marry some prince of their selection, she listened quietly to all they had to say and then as quietly and respectfully told them, "a husband is a matter I shall settle for myself and not consult nor consider the wishes or opinions of other people, and to settle this matter beyond dispute I am already engaged to a man I have decided to marry." This ended the question and she was married that year and King George died in 1844 when Victoria became Queen. Her husband never interfered nor meddled in her official duties and they lived a long and happy life together.

When official documents of great questions were presented for her signature, she at once sent her carriage for old Count Montifiore and gave him the papers saying, "read these papers and tell me what to do with them." She generally followed his advice, but not always, for she had opinions of her own, which she seldom had to repent or regret. Her whole life was a clear case of Providential selection, control and management all through.

I return your copy of the Pathfinder as I might misplace it and not be able to find it again when we wanted to and it is too valuable to be lost.

I hope you will be able to get a substitute for your place so you can pay us a visit for several weeks. We are looking for Helen about 1st Aug and if you can come at that time you can meet her here. There is now only Sally, Kenneth and myself here with two boarders and their roomers.

All of us are well except myself. I am getting diseased and going down very fast, but next Thursday, if I live till then, will be 89 and may expect the end not far off. I am not alarmed at the prospect of death for I have lived to learn that occurrence is Providential.

Give my best compliments to all your people and a large share for yourself.

Very truly Yrs.
H. T. Owen

CHAPTER 10 – GETTYSBURG

"On swept the column over ground covered with dead and dying men, where the earth seemed on fire, the smoke dense and suffocating, the sun shut out, flames blazing from every side, friend could hardly be distinguished from foe."
Henry T. Owen, **on Pickett's Charge.**

From the diary kept by Henry covering the period from February 10, 1863 to July 10, 1863 and from his letters during that time, we learn that the 18th Regiment, having spent much of the spring of 1863 in the area around Washington , North Carolina, was sent to Suffolk, Virginia in May and remained there until later in the month when it started the long, almost continuous march to Chambersburg, Pennsylvania, arriving there on June 27. Henry later wrote "The men were footsore and wearied, their faces were tanned by winter's storms and summer's heat and covered over with unkempt beard."

****

Notes From a Diary Kept During the War of Rebellion
By Capt. Henry T. Owen

Procured a "leave of absence" at Guinea Station Feb. 10th 1863.

Curtis deserted on night of 11th Feb.

The Division marched south and I joined the Regt at Petersburg 2nd March.

March 9th two Regts boarded the cars in front of Jarratt's Hotel and leaving Petersburg behind passed through Weldon, Halifax and Rocky Mount reached Tarboro on the evening of the 10th during a heavy snow fall and was invited by the citizens to occupy their house as shelter during the inclement night.

Left Tarboro on 12th March and marched twenty miles in direction of Greenville and camped on left side of road two hours before sundown. Hiram O. Fowlkes of Old Va said the Camp was a very still venue and silence reigned supreme because "from the fullness of the heart the mouth speaketh" and their stomachs were empty."

Mar 13th 1863. Continued march S.S.E. leaving Greenville 2 ½ miles to the right and taking the road towards Little Washington. Camped at Great Swamp Church and had inspection of arms, expecting a battle in a day or two. We remained in camp all day waiting for rations. I explored the swamp for several miles finding a dense thicket of bamboo, briars and underbrush too thick to penetrate easily interspersed with Cypress trees and the ground wet and boggy.

Sunday 15th. Continued march on road toward Williamston and Washington through young forests and swamplands over long elevated foot logs, where the water usually two to three feet deep and so clear and still that the white sand at the bottom could be seen distinctly as in a mirror and course of the stream could not be determined as the waters were apparently unmovable. These foot bridges were often a mile or two long and zig zagged through the forest and among the large Cypress trees of the swamp. After a march of about fifteen miles we camped.

On Monday 16th marched twelve miles and went into camp after crossing a creek at the head of tide water.

Tuesday the 17th at 6 o'clock A.M. faced about and marched back and encamped at Siloam Church at 4 o'clock P.M.

March 18th. Continued march towards Plymouth. About 4 o'clock P.M. stampeded a Yankee picket and chased the party into town and shelled the fleeing cavalry who dropped their hats, sabers and carbines along the road in their hasty flight. During the day saw a company of guerillas composed of old men and young boys 12 or 14 years old, the only defense for this country. ("Republics are ungrateful. Aristides was banished from Athens and Miltiades her greatest general was allowed to die in prison of wounds received in defense of their liberties because he refused to pay an unjust fine.")

19th March. Remained in camp all day, rain and snow. Sent out wagons for forage. Went to Mr. Johnson's and heard music on piano and violin, manner's of soldiers before ladies very courteous, refined generally.

20th. Continued to rain all day and the weather very cold the ground wet and miry staid in an old granary at night, the planks torn off the sides, the floor hard, the wind chilly but it was a palace compared with the camp in the forest.

21st. Broke camp and returned toward Greenville, raining very hard, rivers overflowed and we had to wade several swollen streams. Camped at Siloam Church where we had camped on night of 17th. I staid all night with Major Sheppard and after a thorough drying out slept well.

Sunday 22nd. Commenced marching at 12'clock crossed river on a dam, river very high, transported caissons and ammunition across in boats, passed in one mile of Williamston and camped two miles from the village.

Monday 23rd. Guarded wagons and my company had special charge of seven wagons which had frequently to be lifted out of the mud by the soldiers. Crossed a river several hundred yards wide and waist deep.

24th. In command of Battalion of four Companies A, B, C and D. Returned march and after wading a river ¼ mile wide (the Vinedell) and several smaller streams we reached our former camp at Great Swamp Church that we had left on the 15th. Sent "blockade runners" to Still House for corn juice.

27th March. Fasted. On night of 27th a dozen soldiers went serenading to Mr. Moore's and to two other places. At the former got up a dance with the young ladies. Music – two violins, banjo and flute. Old man Moore sat in the corner and smoked. As the dance progressed and the wise edge wore off so that Miss Charlotte came down thick on the haul back and rattled her heels together like rocks in a basket. The old man sung out "mind how you stomp Charlotte, cow skins is dam high now." This brought down the house but the dance went on and warmed up as the time rolled on. On the 26th had serenaded at two or three houses and at one found four young ladies who had never seen a flute or a violin and were frightened nearly to death.

On 29th marched at 12 noon and marched seven miles toward little Washington.

30th. Marched 17 miles on the Washington road via Factotus, rain and cold.

31st. Camped in sight of Washington, were on picket on night of 1st April near the town and were relieved early on the morning of the 2nd by the five left Cos. of the Regt.

2nd of April. Crept near the town and took a view of the defenses of the place.

3rd. Viewed the town from an eminence on the right. (Miller and the owls in which Miller was frightened by the owl's talk and asking him "who cooks for you!

Who cooks for you?" Meadows and the biscuit taken for a terrapin by the small boy at or near Great Swamp Church.)

On picket on alternate days either on the right above or on the left below the town. x x x x x x x x x x x x x x Notes here indistinct during which is related the return to Tarboro, from thence by rail to Franklin Va then at Suffolk. Then at South Quay on 4th May capture of Lieut Watkins who had cramp colic from eating half boiled beans.

Then marched to Petersburg and on to Richmond and at Martin's crossing heard of the death of Stonewall Jackson at Chancellorsville.

Then marched to Hanover Junction down on Rappahannock and returning two of us passed the house of Mr. Sale. Left Hanover on the 8th for Culpeper and crossed at Sommerville Ford on the 10th _ above Raccoon Ford. Went into camp near Culpeper C. Ho. June 11th. Left there on 15th June reached Gaines X roads on 16th and at Paris on 18th. Borum and I got supper during rain storm at house where two beautiful ladies waited on us. Reached Snicker's gap on 19th and crossed and recrossed the Shenandoah seven time. Strawberries on the mountains and cavalry fighting in the distance. At Berryville on 20th two stragglers from Armistead's Brigade put in Div. Guard House. Genl Pickett released them at my request and I took charge of them. Left Berryville on 24th June passed thru Smithtown and camped at Darksville. Orders read out and Reily to be shot for desertion. The soldiers and the settlers grumbled. On 25th passed thru Martinsburg jeered and abused by the women who praised Lee. Crossed the Potomac at Williamsport and shot Reily in presence of Brigade. On 26th passed thru Hagerstown, Middletown and camped near Greencastle. Passed a school where the boys would not be called "Seash." Passed thru Greencastle on 27th, thru Marion and Chambersburg and camped three miles beyond the latter place.

29th. Returned thru Chambersburg and camped 2 miles from the town.

July 2nd. Marched thru Chambersburg and took the turnpike toward Baltimore.
Passed thru Fayetteville, Greenwood and camped in sight of Gettysburg at 3 o'clock.

July 3rd. Engaged in Pickett's Charge on Cemetery Hill.

4th. Guarded prisoners and took the road to Hagerstown.

124

5th. Passed thru Fairfield and camped at Monterey Springs.

6th. Passed thru Waynesboro and on 7th thru Hagerstown and camped near Williamsport.

8th. Crossed to the Va side.

9th. Started with prisoners to Winchester. Camped at Big Spring 3 miles from Martinsburg and reached camp at Hopewell Church 6 miles from Winchester on 10th.

****

JULY 3, 1863, PICKETT'S CHARGE

On July 2nd the Regiment marched most of a sleepless night from Chambersburg toward Gettysburg reaching the crest of a hill in sight of the battlefield about 3 P. M. The Regiment did not go into battle until the next day as a part of Pickett's Charge where it suffered the highest losses of Garnett's Brigade. During the battle the 18th lost its hallowed battle flag and when it was over, barely fifty men were left in the Regiment.

One of the longest and most acrimonious controversies of the War, which still continues to this today, was centered around the reasons for the Confederate defeat at Gettysburg. It began in earnest shortly after General Lee's death in October of 1870, first by General Jubal Early in a speech given at Washington and Lee University in 1872.   He contended that General James Longstreet had been ordered to attack on the second day of battle and was not in readiness until 4 P.M. on the third day. Longstreet then replied in November of 1876 with an article in the *Philadelphia Times* which placed much of the blame on Lee. Early then replied to this article with his own in the 1877 issue of the Southern Historical Papers. In 1878 Longstreet wrote a second article for the *Philadelphia Times* which was followed by a second article by Jubal Early published in the *Southern Historical Papers* also published in 1878.   In 1899 Henry Alexander White wrote an article for the *Richmond Dispatch* which attempted to settle the Longstreet/Early controversy.

Beginning in January, 1878, Henry corresponded with several survivors of the Battle of Gettysburg whose ranks ranged from from Private to Lieutenant General to compare their experiences and observations of the battle before writing his own account of Pickett's Charge. The first article was published in *The South-Side Sentinel* around 1878 and was entitled "Pickett's Division, The Truth of History" and the second article, "Pickett At Gettysburg" was published in *The Philadelphia Times* on March 25,1881. These articles appear later in this chapter.

His first letter was written to Col. Charles Marshall who was a Staff Officer to General Robert E. Lee.

****

Green Bay P Office
Prince Edward County Va.
24th January 1878

Col. Charles Marshall
Baltimore Md.

Dear Sir,
A letter from Genl Longstreet in the Philadelphia Times of 3rd Nov. last, upon the Battle of Gettysburg has provoked quite a sharp discussion upon the events and orders, movements etc. of our army during that eventful campaign.

Your position was such that you were aware of most, if not all, the movements of the different Corps and Divisions and can well determine where the different accounts of the great battle are in error. Col. Freemantle states that after the repulse of Pickett's Division General Lee rode among the broken lines and rallied the men without difficulty "that there was much less noise and confusion than on an ordinary drill or review etc."

Now after Pickett's Division was driven back there was a gap in the line occupied by artillery alone, this upon the left of his line of attack. I did not see Genl Lee during the evening at all. I tried to rally the men first on the slope in front of the artillery below its range
and was assisted by a Captain wearing a miniature palm tree upon his cap. Suppose he was a S. Carolinian. Failing to rally a single man in front we came back to the woods just in rear of our artillery and there I endeavored to rally the men to protect the artillery. That lost the S.C. Captain and I never saw him again. Failing again I fell back to the road and found a good position for a picket, with a bluff on one side and a swamp on the other. Here I succeeded by persuasion and various appeals in rallying some thirty or forty men and kept back the stream of men forming back in the rear. We had stopped some two to three hundred men when Genl Pickett came by (crying) and said "Capt do not stop any of my men. Tell them to come to camp we occupied last night." He passed on and any man

we had detained got up and said he belonged to Pickett's Division and not knowing better I let them pass then closing up my line prevented others from passing. About twenty minutes after Genl Pickett had gone past you came galloping up the road and inquired what that company was doing then. Your words were "What's this?" A soldier replied " a picket." "Who placed it here?' "That officer yonder." "Who is he, call him here." I was on the opposite side of the road from you and came forward when you again asked me what I was doing there and by whose orders. I explained to rally the stragglers and had no orders. You then asked my name and said you would give me orders, that the stragglers were flanking my picket and ordered me to take position along the river a few hundred yards in rear and gave me a written order (in pencil) signed Charles Marshall A.A. Genl. You afterwards came down after the stragglers several times and I suppose carried back   (pages missing)

****

Henry next wrote to Col. H. A. Carrington who was second in command of the 18th Regiment giving him a detailed account of his experiences and observations during the Pickett's Charge. He mentions a flanking movement by the Federal troops that occurred during the charge. "Old Pete" was the nickname given to Lt. Gen. James Longstreet.

****

Green Bay R.&D. R.R. Va.
27th January 1878

Col. H. A. Carrington:
Dear Sir,

Yrs if 21st inst duly recd and I would not trouble you with a second letter upon this subject but for the reason I think you missed "Old Pete's" letter when you say "he was mistaken when he says that the men of Picketts Division did not get more than half way across the field." I have reread his letter today and he says "they (the Div.) went half way up the height." He also quotes Col Freemantle who in company with an Austrian and Prussian Officer found Genl L. sitting on a fence in full view of the charge and riding up Col F. said to Genl Longstreet " I would not miss this for a thousand pounds." Genl L replied "The devil you wouldn't. I would give everything in the world not to see it." Col F. "Why Genl, they have carried the heights." "Yes and won't be able to hold them for five minutes." "I then turned to look again (says Col F.)

and sure enough saw Picketts men slowly falling back down the hill."

Again you say we were driven out of the enemy's entrenchment x x by a body of the enemy I suppose not more than a brigade, which struck us on the right flank after we reached the wall etc. Now in regard to this flanking party, I think I am well posted and you will understand me to have the highest respect for every officer's report, especially as we all know that no two men ever could see all the incidents of a battle alike. When we came into line upon the crest of Cemetary Ridge where the assaulting columns were formed there were troops upon the right and upon the left of our Division. Longstreet does not mention this but Major Daniel in his address before the Survivors of the A. N. Va. states that Wilcox was upon our right and Heath or a part of his command upon our left. The distance from crest to crest of the two heights is said to be 2000 yds. When half way down the slope we were ordered to "oblique" to the left which threw us more to the center of the field. While marching obliquely I looked to the left and saw the troops sent as our support falling back in great disorder. When we again "fronted" and assumed the direct front march I looked to the right and saw only the 8th Va. Regt. and the support had completely vanished. I then knew as well as I do now that Picketts Div was alone. Now about that flanking party. When we were about six hundred yards from the stone wall a Sergt. Dalton of my Co. asked me "what troops are those on our right, are the our men or Yankees?" I looked and made him no answer for a few minutes and then said just loud enough for him to hear me (he is still living) Yankees march straight ahead and say nothing. I measured the distance with my eye as accurately as the best surveyors compass and chain ever constructed could do. There off on our right was the grandest sight I have ever seen – a body of Yankees 800 or 1000 yards away coming at a double quick "right shoulder shift," uniforms looking black in the distance, muskets glittering in the sunlight and battle flags fluttering in the breeze created by their quickened motion. I saw at once they were men let loose by the withdrawal of our support on the right. Their line was perpendicular to our own and they were hastening to strike us before we reached the stone wall. I saw it was to be a race and as Genl Garnett came along saying several times "faster, faster men" I put my men to the double quick and each time was ordered on quick time. I have always thought that Garnett perhaps saw this flanking party but then there is no way now of ever deciding that point. Your position being more to the center of the line you did not feel the shock of this attack on our right which struck us at least 100 yards from the stone wall and I saw their men up in 60 or 70 yards of the right flank of the 8th Va. and deliberately fire into out whole line. In a few minutes all was confusion and companies belonging in the 8th Va. were in a few minutes fighting on my left while I found myself with a part of my company upon the left of Capt Cocke and part of his Co. E and we on the right advanced upon the stone wall 15 or 20 deep. I saw men turn deliberately and coolly commence upon this new enemy while others shot to the front. At one time I saw two men cross their muskets one fired to our right and the other to our left. There was a part of the 8th Va. and part of A, B, C, and E that fought this body upon the right and never reached the stone wall. I think the nearest I got to the wall was about 50 yards. I had 5 or 6 only of my company, the others going to the right and front. Capt Cocke probably as many and with other companies I suppose 100 or perhaps 150 were all we had, these men scattered and fought without any order or command. This body did not advance for twenty minutes I suppose and when we fell back we had to run down the face of their line I thought for a quarter of a mile. I knew from the first that not one soldier in a hundred would see this flanking party while advancing upon an enemy in full view of their front. I tried to estimate their numbers by their flags which seemed to be fifteen or twenty and they were six or eight lines deep. I have always estimated their numbers at 10,000 (double our force). They certainly came from the extreme left of the enemy's line. Major Daniel says in speaking of the charge "that when half way down the slope the line was halted and reformed." Now I do not remember any halt and think he is mistaken. Perhaps our oblique movement to the left to get nearer the center of the field had mislead him or his informant. If you can recollect that we did halt and reorganize the lines please say so and I shall be satisfied of the fact.

Col Freemantle says "after the repulse that Genl Lee rode among the men saying 'This is all my fault and we will talk over all this hereafter. I want all good men to rally now' and that the men readily fell into place. There was less noise and confusion than upon an ordinary review or drill." This is not true. I did not see Genl Lee during the whole evening. On rising the slope in front of our artillery which was <u>still firing</u> – (ammunition all gone they say !!) a Captain with a palmetto tree upon his cap ran up to me and asked me to assist him in rallying the stragglers. I agreed and we made the attempt but not a single man <u>nor officer</u> could we stop. We then agreed to try just in rear of the artillery and in passing through the artillery I lost my Captain and kept on to the road below. Here, where the road made a sharp turn with bluff on one side and swamp on the other, I thought a favorable point and tried again. I made all sorts of appeals but not an officer did I succeed in stopping. I succeeded in rallying about 30 men, all privates from various commands and with these thrown across the road presented a barrier to all straggling that way. Genl Pickett came along (crying) and said "Capt do not stop any of my men. Tell them to come to the camping ground we occupied last night." As soon as he passed every straggler we had in front claimed to belong to Picketts Div. I opened the seine and let them out. Closing up again Capt Linthicum came by, told me you were a prisoner, Col. Hunton wounded, Genls Armistead, Garnett and Kemper killed etc. I began to wish I was somewhere else but saw no good excuse for it and held on for a while longer 'till I caught a few hundred more, then Major Charles Marshall came up from the direction Pickett had gone and arriving at the other end of my picket opposite to where I was, asked "What's this here?" A soldier replied "a picket." "Who put it here?" "That Captain yonder." "Call him here. Who is he?" I came forward and these questions were repeated. I answered that I had rallied the men and put them there as picket to stop stragglers. He asked orders from Lee and the inference is made he had no control of Pickett's "by whose orders." I replied that I had no orders. He said he would give me or orders which he did and sent me back to the creek where we deployed and as we collected the stragglers he marched them back to the battle field. During the evening I saw only two 18th men that I knew to be such. One was from Cumberland shot through the thigh and I had him sent to field hospital. The other was Thackston of Farmville unhurt and I started him on to our camp as Genl Pickett had directed but he deserted and was reported a prisoner.

I have written to Genl Hunton, Genl Kemper and Col Marshall. I wish to show by Col Marshall, if his memory is good, that the men were not rallied so easily as Col F states and I never saw it so on any battle field. I have asked Genls Hunton and

Kemper why Genl Pickett started for Gettysburg on the evening of 1st July and after marching about a mile halted and remained in the road all night. He no doubt had some good reason for doing as he did. But you notice Genl Longstreet says Pickett was at Chambersburg under movements.

On the evening of the 1st July Stuart was at Carlisle and had summoned the town to surrender. The authorities held a counsel and asked 'till the next morning to consider the question of surrender. About night fall a courier from Lee reached him with orders to come at once and in all haste to Gettysburg. Stuart called up his Lieutenants the Lees, Harrington and others and asked their opinion of what he should do. They replied that "they could not take the responsibility of advising him in the face of express orders." He replied "then I will send another summons that the town surrender at midnight." He did so and was asked to wait for daylight. Several messages passed and the townspeople smelt a mice and at daylight refused to surrender. Stuart then shelled the town and left, reaching Gettysburg on the evening of the 2nd, ought to have been there early on that morning.

I have written at some length but my excuse is that Longstreet has stirred up the whole issue afresh (as he has a right) and at his bugle blast we fight our battles o'er again.

I am with high respect

Yr Obt Servt etc etc

H. T. Owen

****

On January 28, 1878, Col. Charles Marshall wrote Henry in answer to a letter written on January 24, 1878. In this letter he describes General Lee's actions and statements after Pickett's Charge, the movements of troops preceding the battles at Gettysburg and the orders directing Gen. Pickett to move his troops from Chambersburg to Gettysburg.

****

Balt.

28th Jany 1878

Cap. H. S. Owen
Green Bay
Dear Sir,

Your letter of the 24th inst reached me today and I avail myself of a spare moment to reply to it very briefly as I cannot, without a full reference to papers and correspondence not immediately accessible to me reply to it fully.

I think Col. Freemantle mistakes the facts a little so far as he speaks of the effect of anything said by Genl Lee to the men.

I remember very well that I was separated from the Genl by some duty at the time he rode up to the field to my right of the woods you mention and did not join him until he had been there some time. Before I was sent off on the duty you referred to, however, I had been riding by the side of the General and was with him when he met Genl Kemper being taken to the rear on a stretcher. I heard him speak to Kemper and it was obvious that I heard the words "it is my fault" or something like that, addressed. I did not hear such words spoken to the men to rally them, though of course, they may have been in my absence. As soon after Kemper passed us Genl Lee rode on and sent me back to assist in getting up the stragglers and preparing to resist an advance of the enemy which he then expected.

I went back for that purpose and first proceeded to a place some distance in rear of the spot where I afterward saw you and where I had seen a considerable number of men as I came forward. After trying to restore order to these men and impressing upon such officers as I could find the importance of rallying them and preparing to resist the enemy, and directing them to advance towards the position where the guns were. I went back to report to the Genl and on my way came upon you as you describe. I have a general recollection of all the circumstances you narrate so far as I was concerned and shortly after leaving you I returned to Gen Lee who was sitting on his horse when one or two members of his Staff, and Col. Freemantle being dismounted, lying down a short distance behind him. Gen Lee, upon receiving my input, spoke again very earnestly of the importance of rallying the men but there were no men near him there that I saw except some artillerists whose guns were a little further back. I think I went back for men who had been stopped by your men then me. While you were where I met you with your guard, Gen Lee was on the other side of the road through which you had come back in the open field beyond. We had gone there before I saw you but did not go the way you first saw me coming towards you but were upon the opposite side of the woods above mentioned not through them.

2nd (June) The only orders Gen Pickett had (so far as I know and I think I know this part of the matter correctly) as to him remaining in Chambersburg, were the following: As the army advanced into Pa. Gen Imboden had crossed above us at or near Hancock and had moved in on the left up to a place called McConnellsville (or McConnellsburg) west of Chambersburg and ------- was moving west from Chambersburg. When we started from Chambersburg to go east what we did was under the belief that the Federal Army was moving west from Frederick. (It must be remembered that having no report from the Cavalry we did not know where the enemy was.) Imboden was ordered to move east from McConnellsburg and occupy Chambersburg so as to protect the trains that Ewell had been ordered to send back towards Chambersburg from Carlisle and Gen Longstreet was ordered to leave Pickett at Chambersburg until Imboden got there and then to order Pickett to follow his Corps. This was on the 30th June the day Genl Lee left Chambersburg. When we got through the mountains the next day and found the enemy at Gettysburg Gen Lee send back to Longstreet to move up with his whole Corps. I suppose Genl Longstreet sent back for Pickett under this order, and am rather surprised to learn as I do now for the first time, that Pickett lost any time coming to us, as Gen Longstreet must have ordered him to move on at once. Pickett was not detached, and received all his orders through Gen Longstreet.

The delay on the 1st of which you speak would indicate that Pickett had not received a sufficiently urgent order or that he did not appreciate the importance of dispatch.

The arrival of Pickett on the morning of the second would have added greatly to the force of the attack we made on our right that day. His inability to take part in it was much regretted but never explained except by the statement that he had a long march that day and did not get up in time to participate. I never knew until now that his failure to get up earlier was due to any cause that could have been averted. If there was any neglect to impress him with the importance of joining us at once or as speedy as possible, it must have been from a failure to appreciate the urgency of the order sent back from Gettysburg by Gen Lee as soon as he found the enemy then in force, directing all the troops behind to be moved up as speedily as possible.

I remember that Gen Lee in answering back to Gen Longstreet to order up Pickett, advised him to order Pickett to notify Imboden the he (Pickett) was to move eastward from Chambersburg and to signal Imboden to hasten on to take his (Pickett's) place. But there was no order that Pickett should wait for the arrival of Imboden at Chambersburg. I have and indistinct recollection that Longstreet was told that if Imboden had not reached Chambersburg, Pickett should have a brigade of some force at Chambersburg to wait for the arrival of Imboden and come on with the rest of his division. I have the means, however, to verify this (and) will do so.

I believe I have answered your letter as fully as I can at this moment and am obliged to you for it as it has brought to my attention a fact that I had not known before which tends to explain a very important part of the history of the battle.

Very truly yours,

C. Marshall

****

On February 1, 1878 Henry received a letter from James L. Kemper, who was a Brigadier General in Longstreet's Division, stating that he was not cognizant of orders passed from Gen. Longstreet to Gen. Pickett regarding the march from Chambersburg to Gettysburg or whether Longstreet sent for Pickett to support Hood.

****

Madison, Madison Co. Va.
1st February 1878

Dear Sir,

My memory is not clear in regard to the subject of the inquiries propounded in your letter of the 28th ultimo, but I think you correctly state the particulars of the movement of Pickett's Division from Chambersburg until its arrival at a point near Gettysburg on the afternoon of the 2nd of July. I was not, however, cognizant of what passed between Longstreet and Pickett after our arrival, and I do not know that Longstreet sent for Pickett to support Hood in an attack on the right that evening nor that Pickett objected on the ground that his men were exhausted and would have to be rested before going into the fight. Such communication between Longstreet and Pickett might have passed, just as you state, but I know nothing of them or, if I did, I have forgotten all about them. I take it for granted your recollection in the premises must be correct and I would cheerfully

134

corroborate it if I could, but I think I was too busy looking after my own command to pay any attention to what was passing between my Corps and Division Commanders.

Very truly and respy yours,

J. L. Kemper

****

On February 23, 1878, Major Charles Pickett, brother of Maj. Gen. George S. Pickett and a Staff Officer wrote that all of the Division records were destroyed during the retreat but that he estimated the size of Pickett's command at Gettysburg to be 4,800 men.

****

C. Pickett

General Insurance Agent

No. 52 Roanoke Avenue

Norfolk Va., Feby 23d 1878

Captain H. T. Owen

Green Bay P. O. Va.

Dear Sir,

Your favor of 18th to hand. All the records of our Division were destroyed in the retreat, hence I have nothing official but my recollection is that we took in to the Battle of Gettysburg about 4,800 men composed of Garnett's, Kemper's and Armistead's Brigades Corse and Jenkins having been detained around Richmond by orders from Secy of War.

With kind regards

Very truly yours

C. Pickett

****

A second letter from former Brigadier General Kemper dated March 4, 1878 stated the composition of Pickett's Division as well as regiments making up his own Brigade at Gettysburg.

****

Madison Va.

4 March 1878

Capt. H. T. Owen

Dear Sir,

In connection with your inquiry of the 28th ultimo I notice that General Longstreet in a communication to the Philadelphia "Times" of the 23rd ultimo says that two brigades of Pickett's

135

Division, to int. Corse's and Jenkins' were left behind when we invaded Pennsylvania.

It is barely possible that by some special order Jenkins' brigade might have been temporarily attached to Pickett's division about the time of that advance but I do not remember to have heard of it, and I don't think it was so. Pickett's division was made up of Armistead's, Garnett's, Corse's and Kemper's brigades. Corse's brigade was left behind. All the five regiments composing my brigade were at Gettysburg. To the best of my knowledge and belief, Armistead and Garnett carried all their regiments into the battle. You err in supposing that the 32nd Regiment belonged to my brigade which was composed of the 1st, 7th, 11th and 24th.

Very truly yrs

J. L. Kemper

****

Z. A. Blanton succeeded Richard A. Booker as Captain in command of Company F, 18th Virginia Infantry. He was wounded and captured at Gettysburg on July 3, 1863. He wrote the following letter in answer to more of Henry's questions on Gettysburg.

****

Farmville Insurance and Banking Company

Farmville Va., March 15, 1878

Capt. H. T. Owen

Dear Sir,

I will reply to your letter to Col. Ligen the best I can. The first question in the Gettysburg Campaign was the 33rd Regt. or 32nd left at Winchester in the advance. I answer "they were not." Corse's brigade did belong to Pickett's Division. Armistead commanded his own brigade and so did Kemper command his on the 3rd day of July 1863. Because Kemper was wounded and Armistead was killed that day after the Battle. I know nothing what troops or how many was left behind in the advance. I do not know. I do not know how many regiments was in the Battle. Your Brigades composed Pickett's Division as well as I recollect. Mr. S. W. Paulett who belonged to my company says this is his recollection but he said a Mager from Lynchburg commanded our brigade after the Battle. I regret I cannot give you any definite information.

Yours truly

Z. A. Blanton

****
The following letter is the first of four written by Lt. Gen. James Longstreet. This letter addressed the movements of Jenkins South Carolina Brigade, the assignment of Gen. Pickett's Division to Gen. Lee and efforts to rally the troops after the repulse of the charge. He also states that Gen. Lee expressed the words "It is all my fault." Longstreet also stated that "Gen. Early's writings are surer criticism upon himself and his friends than upon me and will be so regarded when the historian take them up to thoroughly digest them."

****

Gainesville Ga
March 24th 1878

Capt. Henry T. Owen
Green Bay Va
My Dear Sir,

I have through the kindness of Philadelphia Times office your esteemed favor of the 18th inst. In reply to inquiring of Jenkins brigade being part of Pickett's Division, I have to say Pickett succeeded to the command of my old Division according to my recollection, and Jenkins S.C. brigade was part of my Division. This, Gen. Kemper will surely remember if he will go back to 2nd Manassas. For he and Gen. D. R. Jones were near together on that field and Jones was then the Commander of the brigade to which Jenkins was promoted. Jenkins brigade moved with Pickett from Fredericksburg when we went down on the south side (of the) James, and served with the Division all of the time at and around Suffolk. When recalled from Suffolk by Gen. Lee to join him for Chancellorsville Jenkins was left on south side down in Blackwater. But up to that time, if my memory is not totally at fault, Jenkins Brigade had always served with the division, and as regularly as any other brigade of the Division. In regard to this and other points in my accounts of Gettysburg, I think that I can establish them all by evidence that cannot be doubted. If I had not been satisfied that I can address this evidence I should not have ventured to make these points.

Your remarks under your number "2" are I believe correct, except that I did not send an order to Gen. Pickett from the time I left him at Chambersburg until he reported to me again. Because when he was detached he was taken away from my command and could only receive orders from Gen. Lee, until he again reported to me for orders. You mentioned Gen P. received "a message or orders" from me before he joined me. He may have received a message, but as I have just explained I had no right to order him, as he was only under the orders of Gen. Lee at that time.

I have not had the pleasure to read McCabe's book or Maj. Daniels, so I cannot aid you in regard to their views. I should judge from your letter however that you were more right than they.

Gen. Lee did ride up just after the repulse and made the appeal that you quote, in pretty much the words given. Lee's appreciation of the efforts to rally the men is more correct however than that of others present. For myself I can only say that I considered any effort to rally the men at that moment as useless. That therefore, I sent some of the staff to aid in trying to get the men together somewhere in this war whilest others were sent with orders to prepare the troops on other parts of our line for an advance by the Federals, and I saw to my Artillery as the only support that I could give it at that point, determined that we should hold even to the sacrifice of all the guns in it. For that part of our line pinned, the Army of Northern Virginia would have but little chance of escape.

I am pleased to know that you are inclined to put these points in response to the repulse in their true right. The repulse was as you describe it, and such as an inevitable in a disastrous repulse such as ours was. There is no doubt but my troops did as splendid fighting as ever known in battle, but we were beaten and serious soldiers should admit it.

This is already rather a long letter, but I am not satisfied that I have made myself well understood in my efforts to meet your wishes. If there are other points in which I may be of service to you I hope you will not hesitate to write again. I have felt a desire to close up all questions you seem to have to make impartial and correct conclusion(s) from them.

When you write I hope that you may be able to pursue the same just appreciation of the position of one who writes in vindication of truth and for the benefit of the historians. The details you allude to are particularly interesting, as they are really the most important items in summing up the general and leading features in this conflict of war and yet as a rule they are in the entirety unprinted or put down so carelessly or inaccurately that their value is unavailable.

I don't remember to have seen Gen. Lee on the afternoon of the 3rd except for a moment when he expressed the words "It is all my fault." I was at this time moving on to observe, and hold our Artillery line against an anticipated attack from the Federals, and remained out in anxious watch for the apprehended charge. All of the items that you allude to seem material following of our efforts and you seem to have had better opportunities for observing and knowing this effort of efforts to rally the men than I when connected with the War, but the efforts made by writers to throw undue responsibility upon me were made public. Now I feel anxious that everything should be made public particularly from the day that Gen Lee was assigned to command of the Army of Northern Virginia. Gen. Early's writings are surer criticism upon himself and his friends than upon me and will be so regarded when the historian takes them up to thoroughly digest them.

I am very truly yours

James Longstreet

****

A second letter was written by Capt. Z. A. Blanton recounting the march from Chambersburg to Gettysburg, stating that he did not remember that Gen Pickett refused to send his men into battle until they were refreshed. He also said that he was wounded, was left on the field and captured.

****

Farmville
March 28th 1878

Capt. H. T. Owen
Dear Sir,

Your forms of the 18th inst was received and I have been so busy with tobacco I have not replyed and now I write. I really can't give you any points more than you know and better than I do. I remember marching from Chambersburg to Gettysburg on the 2nd July and arriving about 4 o'clock and Pickett refusing to let his men go into the fight until they were refreshed and the next morning moving to the right of Gettysburg and going into the charge about 3 o'clock on the 3rd July at which time I was wounded after having driven the enemy from this works and could not hold them when Kemper's brigade was driven back on our right and our flank. That was the time I received the wound that knocked me senseless and was left on the field and captured and remained a prisoner one year.

I do not know anything about the retreat. Mr. S. W. Paulett thinks you are mistaken in regard to stacking arms in the road and remaining all night. Thinks when we left camp we went straight through to Gettysburg. I do not remember. I do not know. Capt. Morrissett's address – some where near Bristol Tenn., I think.

Yours truly,
Z. A. Blanton

****

The second letter of Major Charles Pickett, Staff Officer, stated his recollections of the time of the march to Gettysburg and the troop position prior to the July 3rd charge.

****

C. Pickett
General Insurance Agent
Norfolk, Va., March 30th 1878

Capt H. T. Owen
Green Bay P.O. Va.
Dear Sir,

Your favor of Mch 26th duly to hand. I have no recollection of any orders either from Genl Lee or Longstreet reaching us on July 1st. I do remember breaking camp and moving out, but I think it was due to a report coming from Gen Imboden, the Comm., and of some cavalry that a body of the enemy were threatening us, which however, turned out to be a mistake. The order to move to "Gettysburg" or "Cash Town" was received after midnight of the 1st probably about 1 o'clock AM or a little later on July 2nd. As well as I can remember, the whole Division was on the march by daylight of the 2nd. We reached a point near Gettysburg about 3 o'clock PM on the 2nd and the Command was halted and went to work cooking rations. I knew of no order received even then by Genl Pickett but do know that after giving us instructions for the men to halt and cook he immediately rode to the front where McLaws was attacking the enemy accompanied by one of his Aide-de-Camps Capt. E. R. Baird and reported the position of his command whether to Genl Lee or Longstreet I don't know. But at any rate he returned later in the evening to the Division and we lay in bivouac till early on the 3rd when we moved up to our position in front of Cemetery Hill. I am sorry to be unable to give you further information. Would suggest that you propound the same questions to Capt E. R. Baird – Occupacia P.O. Essex Co. Va. and Capt. W. Stuart Symington –

140

Baltimore. These gentlemen were both aides of Genl Pickett and their memory may be better than mine.

Most truly yours,

C. Pickett

****

Lt. Col. George C. Cabell, Field and Staff Officer, 18th Virginia Infantry, wrote that he was not at Gettysburg but that he knew that Pickett had five brigades and that Corse's Brigade was left at Gordonsville. Cabell served in the U. S. Congress after the War.

****

House of Representatives

Washington D. C. April 7, 1878

Capt H. T. Owen

Dear Sir,

Your letter of 28th Febry came to my address whilst I was confined by a violent attack of pleurisy and pneumonia or it would have been answered sooner. I am just getting about again.

I am sorry that I can't give you all the information you seek. I was not at Gettysburg but I knew the fact that Pickett had but five brigades, and one of them Corse's was left behind at Gordonsville. It rejoined the command near the Shenandoah as the army returned from Gettysburg. I rejoined my Regiment at or near Shepherdstown as the army moved back from Gettysburg and assumed command of the brigade being senior field officer and remember at Manassas Gap receiving the 17th Regiment of Corse's brigade which had become involved in a fight with Merritt's Cavalry in the Gap. Joining Garnett's Brigade to the 17th we cleared the Gap.

The other questions that you ask, I am sorry that I cannot from personal knowledge answer.

I am truly yrs

Geo. C. Cabell

****

William J. Morrissett was a 1st Lieutenant in Company F, 18th Virginia Infantry at Gettysburg and was promoted to Captain in 1864. He wrote that his letters of 1863 were destroyed but attempted to describe the march of Pickett's troops to Gettysburg.

****

141

Bristol, Tenn.
April 8, 1878

Capt. H.T. Owen
Dr. Sir,

Your favor of the 5th was duly received. I kept no diary during the war, relying mainly upon my letters which I wrote home being kept and that from them I might refresh my memory if occasion called for it. But, really, there was so much that was unpleasant about the war that I really preferred forgetting much of the past and look only at the future and even thus far it has not been pleasant or prosperous as we would have desired or hoped for.

My war letters of 1863 were destroyed by my wife, who was near Richmond when Richmond fell. This she did as a precautionary measure, but there was really no use for such precautions as she was not interrupted. I will try to answer your questions as nearly as I can from memory prefacing them with this remark. As a soldier, I felt it my duty to obey orders from proper authority without question and hence I seldom knew who sent order to Genl. Pickett nor how answered.

1st I remember the bivouac a short distance South of Chambersburg on the thirtieth of June. I am not as certain of the distant cannonading heard on the 1st and have some recollection of orders to march on the evening of the 1st and marching through Chambersburg on the morning of the 2nd early and reaching the vicinity of Gettysburg after a forced march about 3:or 4 o'clock P.M. and bivouacking for the night and as it began to grow dark, distant cannonade could be heard and the bursting of shells could be seen over Gettysburg. I do not remember the order to Pickett "to bring his division on the right at once." From my own knowledge of Genl. Pickett I am inclined to believe that he received no such order from Lee or Longstreet else it would have been obeyed and if not obeyed he would have been relieved from command at once. The troops were tired, it is true, but the same march has been made many a time by troops and then go immediately into action.

I am sorry I cannot give you more satisfactory answers. I am glad to hear from you and will be glad again.

I did not hear from Genl. McCulloch during the war and of course cannot give you his address. Perhaps Genl. F.H. Smith of the VA Mil Inst might as I think he was from Rockbridge Co.

Hoping you success in your undertaking, I remain,

142

Yours very truly,
W.J. Morrisett
****

John S. Hayes was a dispatch bearer and orderly for General Robert E. Lee. In his first letter he stated that he would attempt to answer further questions on what transpired between Gen. Lee and Longstreet and was with Gen. Lee all of the time from during the Gettysburg Campaign until Lee returned to Virginia.
****

Afton, Va. - April 8th, 1878

Capt. H.T. Owen
Green Bay, Va.
Dr Sir,

Yours of the 3rd just came duly to hand. I have been sick in bed for a week. Now just able to sit up. As you know I have lost one eye by congestion of the nerve and my other eye is affected. I write more by grasp than sight. Now as to your information desired about the battle of Gettysburg, if you will write and (I see you are a good writer) the matter in questions, that you wish information on, I will cheerfully answer to the best of my recollections and to what transpired between Genls R.E. Lee and Longstreet. I would prefer to give first to Genl Longstreet if he makes a request. I will merely inform you that I was with Genl R.E. Lee all the time from the morning we left Chambersburg day and night until we returned to Va. I heard and delivered his orders etc. (I was his special dispatch bearer and orderly).

As to the hour of Genl Pickett's arrival, I do not know, but this I do know that on the morning of the 3rd days fighting, a little after sunrise, Genl Pickett's Division left its camp on or near the pike leading from Chambersburg to Gettysburg about 1 1/2 or 2 miles this side of Gettysburg, took a bee line across the fields in double quick for our extreme right etc.

Capt. as I am sick in bed and can't use my eye much, I close and if you think I can give you any information you desire, write it out in questions and I will answer. Where is Genl James Longstreet -his residence Post Office, etc.?

Yours very Respt.
J.S. Hayes

James A. Holland was a Lieutenant in Company A, 18th Va. Infantry. He was wounded and captured at Gettysburg. He wrote that Pickett's Division served extra duties as teamsters and cattle drivers while in Chambersburg, the arrival time at Gettysburg on July 2nd and estimates of the losses on July 3rd.

Glade Hill
Franklin County
April 14, 1878

Capt. H. T. Owen
Dear Sir,

Your favor of the 8th instant is just to hand and I hasten to reply. Capt. Robt McCulloch's address is St. Louis Mo. and can doubtless give you as much or more information than almost anyone for you know he recollects well.

I think we went into camp about 4 o'clock on 2nd July. I do not recollect to have heard that Gen Pickett was sent for to support Hood on the 2nd. There is one fact that may have escaped notice and it is this that while we were at Chambersburg you know the detail made on the Division as teamsters and cattle drives etc. were very heavy and reduced our strength very much. While in prison I saw an article in Blackwoods English Magazine written by one Lt. Col. Freemantle (on.til) of the British Army who accompanied our army at the time and was the guest of Gen Longstreet. He said in his description of Pickett's Charge that the loss was about 3,500 out of 4,300 carried into action. This report was freely shared by the officers of our Division Adj. Dick Ferguson Bearklys etc. and seemed to be received as a correct statement at that time. Now if you would count Artillery Corps, sick, etc. it would probably not make it up to Maj. Charles Pickett's reports.

I would like to see your report when it is published. Can you send me a draft.

I am very respectfully
Your friend etc.
James A. Holland

The second letter of John S. Hayes, dispatch bearer for Gen. Lee, gives detailed accounts of conversations between General Lee and General Longstreet during the first day of the Battle of Gettysburg and stating that the two Generals were together nearly all of the time during the fight.

Afton, Va.
April 15, 1878

H.T. Owen, Esq.
Green Bay P.O. Va.
Dr. Sir,

Yours of the 9th inst to hand. Contents noted, in reply will state on the first days fight of Gettysburg Genl R.E. Lee, staff and about 150 assts and couriers; with Genl. James Longstreet and staff at the head of the First Corps (his) two divisions Hoods and McLaws arrived from Chambersburg about 3 o'clock P.M. on the flat or level, about a mile or mile and a half from Gettysburg and halted, just as the firing ceased, when some scouts reported that the 1st & 3rd Corps had driven the enemy back through and beyond Gettysburg viz. Genl Lee at once sent, first one and then another of his staff and a number of couriers in search for the commanding officers of the 2nd and 3rd Corps, as he wanted to see or hear from them before proceeding. In the meantime we (Genls Lee, Longstreet and myself) concluded to reconnoitre along the ridge or hill South and East of Gettysburg-on our right. After fully taking in the situation as far as we knew and could see, the following conversation took place between Genls R.E. Lee and James Longstreet.

Longstreet addressing Lee "Well General what do you think best to be done?"

Lee: "The best thing that could be done, would be to drive those people off of that ridge, and if I could only see or hear from the commanders of the 2nd and 3rd Corps, we would press those people (by which term Genl Lee always addressed the enemy), back at once."

Longstreet - "I can take my First Division, which is up and has had over one hours rest, thrust them in here (pointing to the place which was to the right of Gettysburg Heights) and drive the

145

Yankees back and take back possession of those heights long before dark, if you say so."

Lee - "Let's wait a little while longer to hear from the commanding officers of the 2nd and 3rd Corps." (about this time some of the staff officers and couriers returned and reported that they had not been able to find the commanding officers of the 2nd and 3rd Corps. Genl Lee told them that he must see or hear from them, so they went off again.)

After 1/2 an hour or more spent in reconnoiting viz, Longstreet said "General we are losing precious time."

Lee - "Well let's see if we can get a good position for a battery of artillery on that Hill, and if we can, you may try what can be done in driving those people away from that position, before they are reinforced by fresh troops; oh! I would know what to do if I could see Ewell or Hill."

Longstreet-"Yes, but if we don't drive the Yankees this evening out of that position, we will loose this battle; for before day-light tomorrow that Hill will be nothing but breast-works and masked batteries which then will be impossible to take."

Lee - "That's so."

The Hill for the artillery spoken of above by Genl Lee was examined by artillery officer and after some time spent reported that is was accessible viz. About this time I left my horse with Genl Lee and Longstreet and went down to a log-cabin in the hollow near the Yankee lines, and had a conference with the man of the house which I reported to Genl Lee in the presence of Genl Longstreet. From the conversation between Genls Lee and Longstreet, their actions and movements, I think it was Genl Lee's desire and wish to have the Yankees moved from the Heights, on the evening of the first days fight, but he did not seem or desire to move in the matter until he heard from Ewell and Hill: and Genl Longstreet was quite anxious to pitch in right then and there, in other words at once, and take possession of the Heights, capture, kill or disperse the Yankees.

The artillery ordered to get into position on the Hill selected, was delayed by balking horses viz viz until it was too late to make the attack. (dark.) Then Genl Lee and Longstreet went back a short distance and struck tents for the night. About 9 o'clock Genls Ewell and Hill reported, there upon a conference was held between Genl Lee and his three Corps commanders; when it was thought best to attack the enemy at day-light the next morning - if the Yankees made no change during the night. Long before day-light reports came in that the Yankees were building breast-works viz and had been re-inforced by another corps coming up viz, then the day-light attack was abandoned.

To be brief, Genls Lee and Longstreet were together nearly all the time during the fight at Gettysburg and I can add from the time we left Chambersburg until we recrossed the Potomac River on our return to Virginia, I do not think there was anything done unless both were cognizant of it. There was unison between them.

I think the above covers your questions and owing to my illness and loss of sight viz I conclude.

Yours very Respectfully
John S. Hayes

My office is in Richmond Va. - the Guide & News - living up here on acct of my health by order of my physician Dr. McGuire will be glad to see anything in regard to operations of the Army of Northern Va. and especially the battle of Gettysburg by yourself, Genl Longstreet or anyone else. I will cheerfully assist you viz. J.S.H.

****

In Lt. Gen. James Longstreet's second letter he addressed Henry as "Major" and stated that his memory agreed with Gen. Lee's report regarding the time of arrival of Pickett's Division at Gettysburg. He also stated that when Pickett was left at Chambersburg he was under the orders of Gen. Lee until he was placed back under his command on the morning of July 3rd. In his postscript, he wrote that he did not expect to write more for publication and that he did not object sharing any details to "friends who are within."

****

Gainesville Ga
April 21st 1878

Maj. H. T. Owen, Va
My Dear Sir

I have your esteemed favor of the 9th inst. with enclosures. In regard to the arrival of General Pickett at Gettysburg my memory agrees with General Lee's statement in his official report. I have used the diary of my Chief of Staff for details of this character, but have not that nor the diary of Col W. M. Owens of New Orleans to refer to now.

When Gen Pickett was left at Chambersburg he was actually taken from my command, and was only under the orders of Gen Lee until the morning of the 3d when General Lee ordered him to report to me for service, and he did report on that morning. I don't think he received any message or order from me whilst he was on detached service except a message from Gen Lee to march from Chambersburg as soon as relieved by Gen Imboden's Cavalry, but a message or order was sent him from Gen Lee, and it is possible that General Lee gave the order to one of my Staff who wrote and sent it by one of my couriers. I don't think Gen Pickett sent the message attributed to him to anyone and was too true a soldier to hesitate about a positive order. He may have made some such remarks in reply to someones conjectures in regard to orders which afterwards took the shape of orders. I do not believe that Gen Lee knew that Pickett reached the vicinity of Gettysburg on the afternoon of the 2nd at all. Nor do I think that I was advised of Gen Pickett's approach until so advised by Gen Lee.

It seems a little irregular if Gen Lee knew of the arrival of Pickett at 3 o'clock, that he allowed me to engage and fight from 3 until 7 with only two divisions against the entire Army of the Potomac, more strongly posted than it was at Malvern Hill.

Unless your correspondents have notes taken and recorded on this field showing that General Pickett actually reached the vicinity of Gettysburg at a specified hour on the afternoon of the 2nd I shall not be able to accept the theory that he was on the ground when the battle of the 2nd begun.

I have no recollection of sending order or message to Gen. Pickett from the time we left him at Chambersburg till he again reported to me nor do I think it possible that I could have done so for he not in my command until again ordered to me by Gen Lee. I have an idea that Gen Lee's order for him to march was sent by one of my staff and this if a written order may appear as mine but it was in reality Gen Lee's. This was nearly always the case and it was not uncommon for him to use my staff for communicating his wishes to myself or any part of my command when it was convenient so to do.

The only rumor that I heard in regard to the division was that General Pickett felt hurt at being left at Chambersburg whilst the balance of the Army was expecting to enter a battle. This and the rumor that he was ordered or asked for the battle of the 2nd and failed to be in time do not agree. I cannot visit the contention that

148

Gen Lee did not know that Gen Pickett was up or nearly up on the afternoon of the 2nd. I could only know of it through Gen Lee or by his orders.

I have not seen Maj. Daniel's address. Should like to see if you find one. It appears to be getting quite common with the Virginia politicians to increase their capital by reflections against me. I have heard nothing as yet of his argues.

I think I have finished my own account of Gettysburg. If I have failed to make it clear it is because I am not able to do so. It is all clear to my mind and I thought I had made it so to all.

Yours Truly
Longstreet

P.S. In my remark "I have finished my own accounts of Gettysburg" was meant that I do not expect to write more for publication. I do not object to share any details that I have to friends who are within.

****

In the third letter from Gen. Longstreet he admits that he and Gen. Lee were both mistaken regarding the time of arrival of Gen. Pickett on the field of Gettysburg.

****

Gainesville Ga
May 5th 1878

Dear Sir,

I have your very interesting letter of the 23rd Apr and am pleased to admit that both General Lee and I were mistaken as to the time of arrival of General Pickett upon the field of Gettysburg. As he was left at Chambersburg under General Lee's orders I knew nothing of his movements until he reported to me on the morning of the 3rd except through General Lee.

I remain very truly yours,
James Longstreet

****

Captain Edmund R. Cocke was the Commander of Company E, 18th Va. Infantry at Gettysburg. He was captured at the Battle of Sailor's Creek in April, 1865.

****

149

Oakland Va.
July 9, 1878

Capt. H. T. Owen
Green Bay Va
Dear Sir,

I owe you many apologies for not answering sooner your interesting letter. It was received on the eve of my leaving home and since my return I have been much occupied.

In reply to your inquiry as to the time of our reaching our bivouac near Gettysburg - I would say certainly no later than half after four P.M.

As to the report in regard to Hood making an attack and wishing Pickett for a support - my recollection at this time is too indistinct to make any assertion. I am sorry I cannot throw more light upon this interesting discussion. Reciprocating cordially your wish that we might meet again.

I am most
Truly yrs
Edmund R. Cocke

****

Capt. Edward R. Baird was an Aide-de-Camp to Major General George Pickett. In the first of two letters he stated that on July 2nd, Gen. Pickett had personally reported the arrival of his troops to Gen. Longstreet and that Gen. Longstreet then ordered him "to put his men into camp where they were until they were wanted." He also stated that on the morning of July 3rd, the Division was ordered to the front reaching the battle field about sunrise where it rested until the order to attack was given 5 or 6 hours later.

****

Occupacia
Essex Co. Va.
August 18, 1878

Capt. H. T. Owen
Dear Sir,

Yr two letters were duly recd and I must say in explanation of my not answering the first that about the time of it's reception I was confined to my bed and did not know when I got out whether the information you asked for would be in time for yr purpose. I got yr last letter day before yesterday and reply at once.

150

In reaction to the dispatch received through a courier on the evening of the 14 of Aug. while the Division was at Chambersburg it is impossible for one to say from whom it came, Gen. Lee or Gen. Longstreet. After this lapse of time my memory may not be reliable but my impression is that I never saw it but always supposed that it came from Gen. Longstreet as I have no recollection that we were at that time considered ourselves as being taken from under his command excepting in so far as the command moved into duty of guarding the rear of the Army keeping open the communication with Va in which of courier Gen Pickett necessarily exercised his own judgment as both Gen. Lee and Gen. Longstreet were too far from the scene of action to know much about it. Still we always considered ourselves a part of the 1st Corp – liable to be excused of that duty and ordered to join the rest of it at any moment. I promise, therefore, that the order referred to came from Gen.Longstreet. I was never AAG of the Division but ADC to Gen Pickett and therefore a dispatch of the kind referred to could not necessarily have come into my hands but into those of Pickett's AAG.

The Division arrived near the battle field of Gettysburg as nearly as I can remember about 3 P.M. on the 2nd after one of the best infantry marches I ever knew having come from Chambersburg (said to be 25 miles off) since about day break. When we reached there I have some indistinct impression of a currier that we were wanted at the front, and that we all thought the condition of the men after the march was such as to render it inadvisable to put them into a heavy fight if it could be avoided. About this, however, I am by no means certain.

As to what actually did occur I can only think it possible that my memory can deceive me. It was as follows – Gen. Pickett and myself rode a little ahead of the troops to the front and he reported to Gen. Longstreet personally. Of course I cannot say exactly what passed between them but at the end of the conversation Gen. L. told Gen P. "to put his men into camp where they were until they were wanted." This was done with no apparent reluctance and I have no reason then or afterwards to suppose that Gen. Longstreet either intended or decided to have put our Div. into action that evening. This conversation took place just as Hood and McLaws were going into action and Gen. P. and myself waited on the field some little time to observe the fight then rode back out (to) the Div. and put it into camp as ordered.

During the interview I have mentioned as near as my memory serves me, there was no one present but Gen. Longstreet, Gen. Pickett, and myself but I am very confident that Gen. Pickett could corroborate my account if he was living. The next morning the Div. was ordered to the front and reached the battle field about sunrise on the 3rd where it rested until the order for the charge was passed down 5 or 6 hours afterward. Had it been intended by Gen. Longstreet to attack at sunrise I know of no reason why our Div. should not have taken part. Whatever inducement there may have been to postpone the attack it certainly cannot (be) due to so far as I can see to any delay in Gen. Pickett's movements. Of course when Gen. P. reported to Gen. Longstreet the evening of the 2nd the troops were some little distance behind him but I see no reason why they ought not have been brought up in a short time if it had been thing to massing to put them into action in their then fallen comrades. I have always been desirous in re the war to avoid any controversy on the subject. I now join this statement only as an act of justice to the "Va. Div." and it's gallant Commander. The impression of persons engaged in a battle are so often different when both parties are equally honest, that unless when it is absolutely necessary to clear the memory of those from blame who are no longer able to speak for themselves. I am unwilling to be drawn into any discussion of the past for I now wish to be understood as casting any blame upon Gen. Longstreet or expressing any opinion as to the propensity of his actions. I simply state the facts – that the Div. arrived near Gettysburg about 3 P.M. on the 2nd – that it's location was reported to Gen. Longstreet personally and by his direction it was camped where it was. Further than this I have nothing to say about questions in respect to which my inferior rank necessarily constitutes me a very poor judge.

I shall be pleased if you choose to give me yr "Chapters on Gettysburg" as they are published. I never see the paper and am always interested in the project.

Hoping that you may be able to elucidate the truth out of the mass of conflicting evidence which always surrounds such discussion I cheerfully contribute what little information is in my power.

The truth the truth the whole truth and nothing but the truth is all that the best friends of Gen. Pickett and his Division could possibly desire.

Very respectfully yrs
Edw. R. Baird
Late ADC to Maj. Gen. Pickett
****

In Gen. Longstreet's fourth and final letter he discusses conversations between himself and Gen. Lee that took place concerning the time to make an attack.
****

Gainesville Ga
Sept 6th 1878

Maj. H. T. Owen
Green Bay Va
My Dear Sir,

I have your favor of the 4th with its inclosures.

There have been many other incidental occurrences of the campaign that have escaped my mind and the arrival of Gen Pickett at Gettysburg or its vicinity at 3 or 4 P.M. of the 2nd may be one of the as my orders were to make my battle with Hood's and McLaw's Divisions. The arrival of Gen Pickett on the field at the moment of battle was not likely to make an impression upon my mind, as he could not be of service to me for the incursion. I asked for the Division on the 1st and I was told that it would not be available for the occasion. No further thought of using it was entertained. So with the suggestion spoken of by Mr. Hayes I clearly remember the first thought upon seeing the positions that the Federals were in the act of organizing when I joined Gen Lee which was that it left the left and rear of the Federal Army open and presented a favorable opportunity for us to make the move we so much desired viz secure a position which might force the Federals to the attack, and this was my first remark or something to the same effect upon Gen Lee's pointing out this position. It is possible that upon finding Gen Lee inclined to abandon his preconceived plans, that I may have said it would be better to attack, if his mind was fixed, on that afternoon instead of postponing for the next day. I have Gen Sorrel's diary of occurrences and conversations with Gen Lee. He was my Adjutant General and has noted all other points of conversations except that mentioned by Mr. Hayes. I am inclined to think therefore that the mention made by Hayes on the 1st if really made was done for the purpose of diverting Gen Lee's mind from his proposed attack on the following day other than with the idea that we could and should

153

attack on the afternoon of the 1st. Thanking you for your kind interest and impressions.

I remain very Truly Yours,
James Longstreet
****

The following undated article was published in the *South Side Sentinel*. It is believed that it was published in late 1878 after receiving the above letters from the Gettysburg survivors.

****

PICKETT'S DIVISION THE TRUTH OF HISTORY

Audi Alteram partem arrectus qurilus

In the invasion of Pennsylvania Pickett's Division was detached, by order of General Lee, to guard the rear of the army and on the night of the 30th of June 1863, bivouacked in a body of woods about two miles below Chambersburg. In April a part of the division was around Greenville and Washington (North Carolina) then at Suffolk, and now went into camp from an almost continuous march of more than five hundred miles.

The men were foot-sore and wearied, their faces were tanned by winter's storms and summer's heat and covered over with unkempt beard. Boys, who enlisted in their teens were changed by the weather and by the hardships of war into men of middle life. The bright uniforms and braided caps of earlier days were gone and had given place to the slouched hat, the faded threadbare jacket and patched pantaloons. Their tents were burned early in the war and their baggage had been reduced from time to time, until the men marched for weeks and months together without a change of raiment, climbed mountains, waded rivers, slept upon the bleak, snow clad hills under a single blanket and the cold bare heavens for a covering, shivering in the chilly blasts upon the outpost or tramped barefoot the stony turnpikes and tangled swamps, often the van in battle the rear in retreat, they breasted alike the storms of the weather and of war and though thinly clad and poorly fed fought long and well for the "Just Cause".

The missiles of war had ploughed their ranks and fallen comrades had been left upon every field, whose bleaching bones marked the tract of the division and must tell as a monument where the contest raged fiercest. Disease too, that fell destroyer of armies

154

had followed in the wake of the sword and the angel of death had flapped his broad sable wing over the camp and the hospitals as well as the field and erected new burial grounds for each campsite.

Various recent details made upon march in addition to heavy detachments left behind, had reduced the division to less than one half its former strength, but though its numbers were reduced, its prestige was still unbroken, the insatiable vampire disease had been outstripped upon the long rapid march, the weak and the feeble had fallen by the way and were left behind, while those now answering to the roll call were the strong on the march and the strong-in-battle to whom scenes of peril and carnage had grown familiar.

The three brigades present, in camp near Chambersburg, were composed entirely of Virginians and nearly every family of honorable mention, in the brief but brilliant annuals of the commonwealth, had its representatives here, either among the officers or among the privates marching in the ranks of this celebrated body of soldiers.

There marched in the line presidents, professors and students from universities of learning, graduates of law and of medicine, editors and divines, men of learning, of reputation, of wealth, and refinements, and these men actuated by personal or family pride often displayed upon the field of battle the loftiest heroism in the charge against superior numbers, were held firmly in front of the hotly worked batteries, decimating their ranks or fell back slowly and sullenly disputing every inch of ground, for with them the fear of ridicule and disgrace was stronger than the fear of death and nerved them to look on the surrounding dangers with an indifference akin to contempt.

There was another class of volunteers present that followed in the wake and influence of these proud cavaliers, no less deserving of mention. The yeomanry of the Old Dominion, the plowman, the mechanic, the laboring men from the town and country, whose stout hearts and brawny arms had sprung from a warlike ancestry, whose individual names and acts in war are unrecorded upon the scroll of fame, but mustered as a mass, worthy scions and worthy sires, as Briton, Dane, Saxon, Norman, English and Virginian, can point to deeds in arms by sea and land, in every clime that have made the race famous on the historic page for more than a thousand years.

Strict military discipline, the regular daily drill and proper handling of this material in the first two or three battles, where victories were gained, soon converted the raw recruits into efficient soldiers, and as that flush of successive victories followed, these soldiers in time became almost invincible.

A reputation once required by a corps or division is easily retained and hard to break as each single soldier, if not himself a hero, believes every other man upon his right and his left is one and he is soon converted by association and conviction into a reliable veteran.

Major General George E. Pickett was a graduate of West Point, had passed through the war with Mexico and was bronzed by his long service in the old army upon the distant frontier, from the Rio Grande to the mouth of the Columbia.

Generals Armistead, Garnett and Kemper had also seen service in Mexico and among the officers of lesser grade there were many graduates of military schools, while all from the highest to the lowest in rank had seen very much arduous service and possessed a vast and varied experience of all the perils and hardships of war long before they reached the memorable "Heights of Gettysburg."

There were men here who fought under Sam Houston at "San Jacinto," others with the celebrated British Legion in the Don Carlos war, others with Walker in Nicaragua, others again with Wheat and Garibaldi upon the classic plains of Italy. There were men here who found under Taylor from "Palo Alto to Monterey," and with Scott from Vera Cruz to the castles of Chapultepic and Cherabusco, while their later experience might be summed up as with Longstreet at Bull Run, and with Beauregard at Manassas, with Johnson at Williamsburg and Fair Oaks and Lee for "Seven Days around Richmond." At "Second Manassas, Chantilly, Slaughters Gap, Sharpsburg, Fredericksburg and Chancellorsville." Whenever and wherever the division had marched or charged victory had marked its pathway or defeat had been made glorious by its stubborn fight and sullen retreat.

The morning of July 1st, 1863, was hot and sultry --scarce a zephyr breathed to stir the loosened leaf and the birds, awed by the unusual sight and sounds amid their quiet bowers had sought the deeper shade and ceased to sing.

Through camp, scattered over hill and dale, the jest, the laugh and patches of Southern song kept up a busy hum that ever and anow rose and fell, while many hundreds were busied in mending their tattered garments or engaged in writing long letters back home to distant friends and loved ones, many of which were their last kind messages and would be received and read after the hands that penned those endearing lines were cold in death.

The morning wore slowly away and about noon stragglers returning into camp reported that out upon the hills beyond the bustle and hum of the camp there could be heard heavy, distant cannon firing. So distant this heavy rolling sound seemed to ripple upon the bosom of the sultry summer's air and fell upon the ears like a trembling echo. So far off, with the mountains intervening, that the direction of the firing was difficult to determine, but was thought to be east, northeast, yet the continual dull heavy sound showed that a great battle had begun. A bird's eye view would then have seen every rod in Southern and Central Pennsylvania filled with clouds of dust and long dark columns of cavalry, infantry and artillery rushing on with hasty forced marches to the bloody conflict going on around the sequestered village of Gettysburg. The distant cannon's roar was as a summons to the feast of carnage and death.

About 4 o'clock P.M. a courier, bearing down on a mad gallop, in front of a cloud of dust, burst into camp and dashing through without slack of rein called as he swept on, "Where will I find Gen. Pickett?" The men pointed, for there was scarce time to reply and the half turned head of the fierce rider seemed to see the sign, for onward like an arrow he flew towards division headquarters. His orders were soon delivered, whatever their import, and back again through camp he swept, looking neither to the right nor left, and disappeared like a fleeting shadow upon the course he came- the color of his steed had changed to a darker hue, while flecks of froth from the champing bit, had fallen like snow flakes here and there upon his neck and smoking flanks and hung there like locks of cotton.

But he had come and gone in a cloud of dust and within half an hour Pickett's Division was upon the march. Taking the road towards Chambersburg the division was marched about a mile and halted.

A rumor went along the line that the enemy's Calvary was threatening the rear of Lee's army and a message from General Imboden, giving the information, had caused this movement of Pickett's Division to prevent the threatened attack. The rumor turned out to be a false alarm. Storm clouds collecting among the mountains soon united in one dark mass and came drifting over

Chambersburg and down upon Pickett's Battalions drawn up in line of battle awaiting the enemy. The air grew dark, the lightening played in orbit flashes, the thunder roared and the wind blew. Strong out the rain came down a heavy drenching shower. An hour's tempest is soon over, the men are wet to the skin, the clouds have broken above, the thunder is dying away, all is bright again, the birds now dared to sing and soar aloft. Rain drops sparkled on every twig and blade of grass, but hour after hour rolled by and the sun sank behind the trees, still the division moved nowhere in march.

Night came down and rolled along, over the long dreamless hours till the dawn of day and found the division watching under arms in the road. During the night a second courier had come clattering along the road in search of Pickett bearing a more potent message and at day break the column was put in motion and about sunrise of this 2nd day of July passed through Chambersburg and took the road to Gettysburg. The day was extremely hot, the distance twenty-five miles and the march a rapid one.

Upon the road couriers were met coming in hot haste down the dusty lanes and like "Mother Cary's Chickens," or the Petrel upon the billowy deep they were recognized as precursors of a booming tempest.

About 3 o'clock in the afternoon the head of the column reached the crest of the hill that overlooks Gettysburg. In the distance, and in sight of the battle field beyond. Here Gen. Pickett halted the division and rode forward with Aide-de-camp Capt. E.R. Baird and reported his arrival to Longstreet.

A rumor floated through camp that General Longstreet apprised of Pickett's arrival sent him this message:

"Bring your division around on the right at once. Hood is about to attack the enemy and I want you to support him."

To which Pickett replied, "Tell General Longstreet my men are exhausted and must have rest before they go any farther."

The division was therefore halted in the woods and proceeded to cook rations, while many of the officers and men came out upon the summit to view the distant battle field and listen to the uproar of that fierce onset of Hood and McLaws, whose combined divisions of 13,000 men contended for near four hours for the disputed field against 65,000 of the enemy, drove them back over entrenchments and in their head-long charge overthrew the Third corps, the Second corps, the Fifth, the Eleventh and part of the

Twelfth, and was only prevented by the darkness of night and the arrival of Sedgewick with the Sixth corps from gaining the most brilliant victory of the whole war. Hood and McLaws having penetrated the Federal center until they were outflanked by greatly superior numbers and having no reinforcements to protect them upon right and left were ordered to retire which they did in good order, leaving upon the field 4,529 of their men - more than one-third of their total numbers engaged.

Picketts Division was a silent spectator in hearing and sight of this sanguinary conflict and the golden opportunity to change the course of history was lost.

History is filled with instances of long forced marches, fierce conflicts and great victories gained by wearied troops until the truth is well established that while some armies might fight well when rested, all armies fight better when carried into battle from a long rapid tiresome march. Dessaix made a long march from early morning till 4 o'clock in the evening and going straight into battle with his wearied division of six thousand soldiers drove back a powerful victorious Austrian army and changed Napoleon's defeat into the splendid triumph of Marengo.

Buio and Blucher came upon the field of Waterloo at 6 o'clock P.M. from a long harassing march and saved the allied armies of Europe from complete overthrow.

The forced march of Claudius Nero with seven thousand men against Asirubal led to the great battle and victory on the Metaurus and saved Rome. The most successful leader in the late war was Stonewall Jackson, who accomplished all he did by forced marches, sudden surprise and derce onset. He marched forty miles a day and saved Beauregard at Mansassas.

And thus it has ever been in the history of war since Daniel's prophetic vision saw Alexander's fleet army moving across Asia Minor with such celerity as to seem not to touch the earth in its ever victorious career to the present time. But no better instance is needed of the timely arrival of troops upon any field than that of Sedgewick at Gettysburg on the 2nd day of July at 6 o'clock from a forced march of thirty-five miles, made night and day, to reach the field just in time to check the victorious career of Longstreet, and save the Union army from a disastrous defeat.

****

After the *South-Side Sentinel* article was published, Henry continued to pursue the truth about the Battle of Gettysburg and received letters from survivors as late as 1908.

W. F. Clark of Company I, 56th Va. Infantry, wrote the following letter giving the composition of his regiment and some of the casualty figures at Gettysburg.

****

Keysville Va.
May 24th 1880

Capt. Owen:

Mr. Jeffries handed me your letter which was received yesterday morning.

Corse's Brigade only had 4 Regiments.

I think you mistaken about Jenkins being in Pickett's Div. Jenkins belonged to Longstreet's Div. but after the reorganization at Winchester in the fall and winter of 1862 Corse's Brigade was given to Pickett at Culpeper Court House just before he went to Fredericksburg Va. and Jenkins was transferred to McClaws, Anderson's or Hood's Div. I am not certain which when Hood and McClaws reinforced Bragg's Army in Oct. 1863 Jenkins you will find was with them. The 56th Regiment had two Companies from Charlotte, I and G, two from Mecklinburg, A and B, one from Hanover, K, two from Louisa, H and C, one from Buckingham, D, one from Albemarle, H, one from Brunswick, E. This writer was not in the Battle but was on duty not far from the battle ground. My cousin, Capt. Charles I Clark of Aspenwall Charlotte County Virginia commanded the company I belonged to (I) in the Battle of G (Gettysburg). The Co. (I) numbered 47 muskets as it stood in line to advance. Capt. Clark and 1st Lt. S. D. commanded the company. Officer Clark was severely wounded in breast and escaped capture. Lt. Aronino severely wounded and taken prisoner. 56 Regiment went in with 350 muskets and came out with 42. Lieut. Matt Brown commanded Co. D in the Battle and was wounded in the knee.

Lieut Frank Nelson	Co. A	
Capt J. W. Jones	Co. B	he lives in Brunswick
Capt Tim Smith	Co. C	Louisa C. H.
Lieut Thomas	Co. F	Louisa C. H.
Capt Nat Flournoy	Co. E	
Lieut Barns	Co. G	
Capt Wyant	Co. H	

Capt Timothy Co. K   Timothy was from Clarkesville Va.

Col W. D. Stuart Commanded the 56th Regt and was mortally wounded and died at his home in the Valley of Va.

I am unable to give you the numbers of killed, wounded and missing of each company but you may be able to get some information from some members of each company by writing to their county. Any question I can answer I will do so with pleasure and give you all the information I can.

A young man by name of Wharton of Richmond City was Adjutant of the 56th Va Regiment. If he is living he could give you a great deal of information.

Yours truly,
W. F. Clark

Corse's Brigade was left at Hanover Junction to guard the North and South Anna Bridges and had a little brush with the enemy during Pickett's absence in Pennsylvania.

****

Edmund R. Cocke, Captain and commander of Company E, 18th Va. Infantry, wrote the following, stating that all in his company were killed, wounded or captured and recalling his own escape from the battlefield.

****

Oakland Va.
Sept 17, 1880

Capt H. T. Owen
Richmond
Dear Sir,

Yours of 14th inst has just reached me. I fill out the blanks in the space for Co. E and return it herewith. I have no roll of my Company and cannot give the names of the men in the Battle of Gettysburg but I distinctly remember that a total of 23 officers and men went into that engagement, of this number 9 men were left dead on the field and the remaining 14 were either captured or wounded. Not a single one escaped.

I will with pleasure furnish you any additional information in my power and would be glad if you could suggest the points to me. I shall ever remember our almost miraculous escape together from that field of death and carnage.

Respectfully truly yrs
Edmund R. Cocke

****

The following article is the second that Henry wrote on Pickett's Charge at Gettysburg. In the opinion of the authors, this is one of his best writings. As previously stated, he continued to pursue the details of the battle after this article was published and corresponded with survivors as late as 1908.

****

PUBLISHED BY *PHILADELPHIA TIMES* – MARCH 26, 1881
ANNALS OF WAR – CHAPTERS OF UNWRITTEN HISTORY
PICKETT AT GETTYSBURG, HIS DIVISION AND ITS PART
IN THE PENNSYLVANIA CAMPAIGN

ON THROUGH THE CLOVERFIELD
A PARTICIPANT'S DESCRIPTION OF THE DESPERATE CHARGE ON JULY 3.
HOW THE 18TH VIRGINIA MELTED AWAY
Only thirty seven officers and men left out of three hundred and nine.
By H. T. Owen, Late Captain in the Eighteenth Virginia Regiment

In February 1863, while the ground was yet covered with snow, the rivers locked in ice and chill wintry blasts swept over the hills and howled through the forests of Northern Virginia, Pickett's Division was ordered from Fredericksburg on a foraging expedition.

It marched down through Richmond and Petersburg into the South Side counties, while a part of the command was sent as far south as Tarboro, the snow still falling at intervals for several weeks. The command reconnoitered around Greenville, Plymouth, and Washington, North Carolina, and skirmished occasionally with the enemy until the month of May, when it returned to Suffolk in time to start upon the memorable Pennsylvania campaign. Selected by General Lee as rear guard of his invading army, Pickett's Division was detached from Longstreet's Corps to perform the arduous duty of keeping open the communication with Virginia and to guard all of the roads, mountain passes and fords to the rear. The division was ever on the alert while others slept (or on the march while others rested), to meet some real or rumored advance of the enemy and the men often retraced their steps for many miles, and then countermarching passed over much of the same ground three times or more. Thus climbing over the Blue Ridge through Snicker's Gap and wading the Shenandoah River breast-deep at Castleman's Ferry, the division moved on down the valley but was recalled and detained several days to be in supporting distance of Stuart's cavalry that was skirmishing along the eastern side of the mountain. A part of Pickett's command crossed and re-crossed the Shenandoah River no less than six times before the enemy disappeared and then had to hurry forward by long forced marches to overtake Lee's army, now far in advance toward Pennsylvania. On the night of the 30th of June 1863, Pickett's Division bivouacked in the woods about two miles south of Chambersburg. The men were footsore and weary and went into camp from an almost continuous march of almost a thousand miles.

TRUE VETERANS

The bright uniforms and braided caps of earlier days were now gone and had given place to the slouch hats, the faded threadbare jackets and patched pantaloons. The veteran's faces were tanned by summers' heat and winters' storms and covered with unkempt beard. Boys who enlisted in their teens appeared with long tangled locks, changed and weather beaten, now apparently, into men of middle life. The tents had been destroyed early in the war and their baggage had been reduced from time to time until the men often marched now for weeks together without a change of raiment. They waded rivers, climbed mountains, shivered beneath a single ragged blanket as they slept or watched upon the frost-clad hills or tramped barefoot stony turnpikes and tangled swamps. The missiles of war had plowed their ranks, and fallen comrades, left thickly strewn on many fields, pointed as landmarks the track of the division and the course of battle. Heavy losses in many battles and still greater losses by disease, besides various recent details, in addition to the two largest brigades being left behind in Virginia, had reduced the division now to about one-third of its former strength. But though its numbers were lessened its prestige was still unbroken; each bloody conflict that thinned its ranks had spread a wider fame and forced confidence in the terror of their name. Upon the long rapid march the weak, the feeble and the sick had fallen by the way and then left behind, and those now answering to roll-call were the strong on the march and the stout in battle, who paused at no obstacle, quailed at no danger, and to whom scenes of carnage had grown familiar. Strict military discipline, regular drill and the proper handling of these troops in the first two or three engagements, when victories were gained, soon converted the raw recruits into efficient soldiers, and as the flush of successive victories followed, these soldiers had become in time almost invincible. A reputation once acquired by a corps or division is easily retained and hard to break as each single soldier, if not himself a hero, thinks every other man upon his right and left is one, and he is soon converted by association into a reliable veteran.

LIST OF VICTORIES.

Major General George E. Pickett was a graduate of West Point, had passed through the war with Mexico and was bronzed by long service in the old army upon the distant frontier from the Rio Grande to the mouth of the Columbia, and among the officers of lesser grade were many graduates of military schools, while all from the highest to the lowest rank, had seen very arduous service and possessed a vast and varied experience in all the perils and hardships of war long before they reached the memorable "Heights of Gettysburg." Scattered through the different regiments was a sprinkling of restless, roving adventurers, seekers after excitement, whose passion, past time and pleasure had been war and revolution for the last quarter of a century--some who had fought under Sam Houston at San Jacinto, others with the celebrated British Legion through the Don Carlos war, others with Walker in Nicaragua, and others with Wheat and Garibaldi in Italy. There were men who fought under Zack Taylor from Palo Alto to Monterey and with Scott from Vera Cruz to the City of Mexico, while their later experience may be summed up with Longstreet at Bull Run and with Beau regard at Manassas; some with Buckner at Fort Donelson and some with Johnson at Williamsburg and Seven Pines, and with Lee around Richmond, at Second Manassas, at Chantilly, South Mountain, Sharpsburg, Fredericksburg and Chancellorshville. Each regiment had now inscribed on its torn and tattered banner all the noted fields over which it had been borne to victory.

ON TO GETTYSBURG

Wednesday morning, July 1, was hot and sultry; scarcely a zephyr breathed to stir the loosened leaf and the birds, awed by the unusual sight and strange sounds amid their quiet bowers, had sought the deeper shade and ceased to sing. Through camp, scattered over wooded hill and dale, the jest, the laugh and snatches of Southern song kept up a busy hum, while the ragged rebel mended his tattered garment or wrote a message to distant friends and loved ones at home--the last, perchance, he ever sent--to be received and read after the hand that penned the lines was cold. The morning wore slowly on to noon, when stragglers returning into camp reported that out upon the hills beyond the noise of camp there could be heard heavy, distant cannon firing. The ball had opened, the play had begun and a bird's-eye view would then have disclosed every road in Southern and Central Pennsylvania filled with clouds of dust and long dark clouds of infantry, cavalry and artillery rushing along to unite in the bloody conflict going on in and around the village of Gettysburg. About 4 o'clock General Pickett received a message from General Imboden that a column of the enemy was moving in the direction of Chambersburg, and Pickett moved his division out upon the road above Greencastle and drew up in lines of battle to await the threatened attack upon the rear of Lee's army. during the evening a storm of wind and rain and loud peals of thunder passed over the battalions and the men were drenched in the shower, but the tempest was over in an hour and the sun went down bright and clear. The night came and rolled along over the long hours until dawn to find the division still drawn up in lines of battle, watching under arms for the approach of the enemy. The rumor turned out to have been a false alarm, but one o'clock at night a courier came clattering along in search of Pickett, and at daylight on Thursday morning, the 2nd of July, the columns of wet, worn and sleepless men were put in motion on the road to Gettysburg. The sun rose bright and clear, rain drops sparkled on every twig and blade of grass, a cool refreshing breeze, laden with sweet perfumes of summer flowers, lifted the tangled lock upon the heated brow and fanned the care-worn cheek, until along the long lines of rough and ragged veterans, trampling rapidly forward, could be heard here and there some humorous jest or joyous laugh, but before noon the day was hot and sultry.

"ONE BOOT OFF."

At 3 o'clock the division reached a crest of a hill that overlooked Gettysburg and in sight of the distant battlefield beyond, having come since daylight twenty-seven miles. Here the division was halted and a rumor circulated along the lines that General Longstreet, apprised of Pickett's approach, sent him this message; "Bring your division around on the right at once. Hood is about to attack and I want you to support him." To which General Pickett replied; "My men are exhausted and must have rest before going any farther." General Lee replied to Major Walter Harrison, who reported to him the approach of Pickett's Division; "Tell General Pickett I shall not want him this evening; tell him to let his men rest and I will send him word when I want them." And soon afterward meeting General Pickett, General Lee said: "I am glad you have come; I shall have work for you tomorrow." General Hood relates a conversation that occurred early in the morning, in which he said to General Longstreet; "General Lee seems a littler nervous this morning." To which Longstreet replied: "He wishes me to attack. I do not wish to do so without Pickett. I never like to go into battle with one boot off." When the division came in sight of the battlefield at 3 o'clock it was halted by Pickett, and he, accompanied by his aide, Captain S.R. Baird, rode forward and reported in person the arrival of his division to Longstreet who, upon learning the jaded condition of the men, ordered them into camp where they had been halted. Many of the officers and men of the division came out upon the hill to view the distant battlefield and to listen to the uproar of that fierce onset of Hood and McLaws, which began at precisely 3 1/2 o'clock and lasted until 7 1/2.

THE LOST OPPORTUNITY.

General Longstreet says these two divisions combined, numbered scarcely 13,000 men, and that for four hours they contended for the disputed field against more than 50,000 of the enemy, and their grand and headlong charge overthrew the Third Corps, the Second Corps, the Fifth Corps, the Eleventh Corps, a part of the Twelfth Corps, and were only prevented by the darkness of night and the arrival of Sedgwick with the Sixth Corps of 15,000 fresh troops, from gaining the most brilliant victory of the whole war. Hood and McLaws fell back at dark, leaving upon the field 4,529 men, being a loss of more than one-third of their numbers carried into action. General Lee says; "It being now about dark General Longstreet retired and determined to await the arrival of Pickett." Pickett's Division was silent, within sight and hearing of this sanguinary conflict, and, perhaps, the opportunity to change the course of history was lost. For had Pickett's Division, upon its arrival on the field at 3 o'clock, been led straight into battle, or had it supported the assault of Hood and McLaws at any time after an hour's rest, it is possible the Battle of Gettysburg would have ended there without a third day's bloody sequel, for history is filled with instances of long forced marches, fierce conflicts and great victory gained by the wearied troops, until the truth is established that while some armies have fought well when rested all armies have fought better when taken into battle from a long, rapid, tiresome march. Dessaix made a long forced march from early morning till 4 o'clock in the afternoon and going straight into battle without pausing, with his six thousand wearied soldiers drove back a powerful victorious Austrian army of more than twenty thousand men and changed Napoleon's defeat into the splendid victory of Marengo. Blucher came upon the field of Waterloo at 6 o'clock from a long, fatiguing march and changed the tide of battle in time to save the allied armies of Europe from complete overthrow. The forced march of Claudius Nero with seven thousand troops, marching night and day, led to the great battle and victory over fifty thousand Carthaginians on the banks of the Metaurus, the death of Asbrubal, and eventually saved Rome. The most successful General of the late war was Stonewall Jackson, whose victories were due to his rapid forced marches, sudden surprise and fierce onset. His infantry will live in history as "the foot cavalry of the valley." But no better instance is wanted of the timely arrival of troops upon any field than that of Sedgwick at Gettysburg on the 2nd day of July, from a forced march of thirty two miles, made night and day, to reach the field just in time to check the victorious career of Longstreet and save the Union Army from defeat.

SIGNAL GUNS.

On Friday morning, July 3, Pickett's Division left its bivouac at dawn of day and moving around to the right reached the position assigned it in the ravine behind Cemetery Ridge soon after 6 o'clock. Long dark lines of infantry were massed along the bottoms, concealed from the enemy's view, and orders were given "to lie down and keep still to avoid attracting the attention of the enemy." About 8 o'clock Generals Lee, Longstreet and Pickett, in company, rode slowly along up and down in front of the long lines of prostrate infantry, viewing them closely and critically as they rode along. They were not greeted with the usual cheers, as orders had preceded them forbidding this, but the men voluntarily rose up and stood in line with uncovered heads and hats held aloft while their chieftains rode by. This review over, strong detachments were thrown forward to support the artillery stationed along the crest of Oak Ridge and Cemetery Ridge, composed of about one hundred and twenty cannon, and stretching along the brow of these ridges for a mile. The supporting detachments were placed about a hundred yards in the rear of this line of batteries and lay day in the tall grass with a cloudless sky and a bright July sun pouring its scorching rays almost vertically upon them for five long, weary hours, while they listened and watched in painful suspense for some sound or some movement to break that profound stillness which rested over the vast battlefield and depressed the spirits like a dreadful nightmare. At 1 o'clock this awful stillness was suddenly broken and the men startled by the discharge of a couple of signal guns fired in quick succession, followed by a silence of half a minute, and then, while their echo was yet rolling along the distant defiles and mountain gorges, an uproar began as wonderful as had been the previous silence. Lee's one hundred and twenty guns opened at once with a crash and thunder sound that shook the hills for miles around from crest to base, and were instantly replied to by almost eighty guns ranged by General Meade along the front of Cemetery Ridge, about one mile in front.

No sound of roaring waters, nor wind, nor thunder, nor of these combined, equaled the tremendous uproar and no command, no order, no sound of voice, could be heard at all above the ceaseless din of thousands of shrieking shot and shell falling thick and fast on every side and bursting with terrific explosions, while others by thousands came bounding, skipping, racing and chasing each other over the hills and down the slope, hissing, scoffing, spitting and moaning like relentless demons as they dashed through the detachments and went on with a crash among the reserves far back in the rear. The bursting shell in mid-heaven are upon the earth scattered death wherever its fragments flew, and the shrill shot overhead or bounding madly across the field would both alike dip through a line of prostrate men and tear away with a wail to the rear, leaving a wide track of blood behind. The air was filled with clouds of dust and volume of sulphurous, suffocating smoke rolled up white and bluish-gray like frightful storm clouds, and hung like a pall over the field, through the rifts and rents of which the sun with dim light looked down upon the ghastly scene.

After two hours the firing suddenly ceased and silence again rested for half an hour over the battlefield, during which time the Confederates were rapidly forming an attacking column just below the brow of Seminary Ridge. Long double lines of infantry came pouring out of the woods and bottoms, across ravines and little valleys, hurrying on to the positions assigned them in the columns. Two separate lines of double ranks were formed a hundred yards apart, and in the center of the column was placed the Division of Pickett, said to be "the flower of Lee's army"--4,481 privates, 244 company officers, 32 field officers and four general officers, making 4,761 all total. In the front line was placed Kemper and Garnett's Brigades side by side, covered by Armistead's Brigade in the second line.

THE MEMORABLE CHARGE

The column of attack, composed of Wilcox's Brigade, Pickett's and Heath's Divisions and several other commands, detached for this duty, has been variously estimated, but probably numbered about 13,000 troops, the command of the whole line given to General Pickett, a brave and fearless officer and a fit leader of this forlorn hope, thrown forward to retrieve disaster or turn by fierce conflict the waning fortunes of a dying cause. Riding out in front, Pickett made a brief, animated address to the troops, and closed by saying to his own division; "Charge the enemy and remember old Virginia." then came the command in a strong, clear voice: "Forward! Guide center! March! " and the column, with a front with more than half a mile, moved grandly up the slope. Meade's guns opened upon the column as it appeared above the crest of the ridge, but it neither paused nor faltered. Round shot, bounding along the plain, tore through their ranks and ricocheted around them; shells exploded incessantly in blinding, dazzling flashes before them, behind them, overhead and among them. Frightful gaps were made from center to flank, yet on swept the column and as it advanced the men steadily closed up the wide rents made along the line in a hundred places at every discharge of the murderous batteries in front. A long line of skirmishers, prostrate in the tall grass, firing at the column since it came within view, rose up within fifty yards, fired a volley into its front, and then trotted on before it, turning and firing back as fast as they could reload. The column moved on at a quick step with shouldered arms, and the fire of the skirmish line was not returned. Half way over the field an order ran down the line, "left oblique," which was promptly obeyed, and the direction is changed forty five degrees from the front to the left. Men looking away, far off toward the left flank, saw that the supporting column there were crumbling and melting rapidly away.

General Pickett sent his brother, Major Charles Pickett, gathering swiftly to rally, if possible, the wavering lines, saying to him; "Unless they support us on the left, my division will be cut to pieces." Major Pickett and other officers rode along the breaking battalions and vainly attempted to restore order, but hundreds and thousands of fugitives from the front could be seen fleeing from the field and went rushing pell-mell towards the rear like dry leaves before a gale. Order was not restored upon the left and Pickett's support there was gone, excepting some brave Tennesseeans and North Carolinaians, who never wavered in the storm, but closed up by the side of Pickett's Virginians went as far, fought as long, bled as freely and fell as thick as Pickett's men.

"FASTER, MEN!"

The command now came along the line, "Front, forward!" and the column resumed its direction straight down upon the center of the enemy's position. Some men now looking to the right saw that the troops there had entirely disappeared, but how or when they left was not known. The enemy in front, occupying an elevated position and watching closely every movement of the advancing columns, say "the right gave way first, then the left broke up and fled the field, but the massive center, composed of Pickett's veterans of iron nerve, wounded in scores of battles, were coming sternly on." Guns hitherto employed in firing at the troops on the right and left sent a shower of shells after the fleeing fugitives, and then trained upon the center, where the storm burst in ten-fold fury, as converging batteries sent a concentrated fire of shot and shell in, through and around the heroic column. The destruction of life in the ranks of that advancing hosts was fearful beyond precedent, officers going down by dozens and the men by scores and fifty. Kemper has gone down terribly mangled, but Garnett still towered unhurt, and rode up and down the front line, saying in a strong, calm voice; "Faster, men! Faster! Close up and step out faster, but don't double quick!" The column was approaching the Emmetsburg Road, where a line of infantry, stationed behind a stone fence, was pouring in a heavy fire of musketry. A scattering fire was opened along the front of the division upon this line, when Garnett galloped along the line and called out; "Cease firing," and his command was promptly obeyed, showing the wonderful discipline of the men, who reloaded their guns, shouldered arms and kept on without slackening their pace, which was still a "quick step."

The stone fence was carried without a struggle, the infantry and the skirmish line swept away before the division like trash before the broom. Two thirds of the distance was behind and the one hundred cannon in the rear were dumb and did not reply to the hotly worked guns in our front. We were now four hundred yards from the foot of Cemetery Hill, when away off to the right, nearly half a mile, there appeared in the open field a line of men at right angles with our own, a long, dark mass, dressed in blue, and coming down at a "double quick" upon the unprotected right flank of Pickett's men, with their muskets "upon the right shoulder shift," their battle flag dancing and fluttering in the breeze created by their own rapid motion, and their burnished bayonets glistening about their heads like forest twigs covered with sheets of sparkling ice when shaken by a blast.

Garnett galloped along the line saying; "Faster, men! Faster!" and the front line broke forward into a double quick and Garnett called out; "Steady, men! Steady! Don't double quick. Save your wind and your ammunition for the final charge!" and then went down among the dead and his clarion voice was no more heard above the roar of battle. The enemy were now seen strengthening their lines, where the blow as expected to strike, by hurrying up reserves from the right and left, the columns from opposite directions passing each other double along our front like the fingers of a man's two hands locking together.

The distance had again shortened and officers in the enemy's line could be distinguished by their uniforms from the privates. Then was heard behind that heavy thud of a muffled tread of armed men that roar and rush of trampling feet as Armistead's column from the rear closed up behind the front line and he (the last brigadier) took command, stepped out in front with his hat uplifted on the point of his sword and led the division, now four ranks deep, rapidly and grandly across that valley of death, covered with clover as soft as a Turkish carpet.

NO CHEERS FROM PICKETT'S MEN.

There it was again! And again! A sound filling the air above, below, around us, like the blast through the top of giant cedar or the whirring sound made the sudden flight of a flock of quail. It was grape and canister, and the column broke forward into a double quick and rushed toward the stone wall where forty cannon were belching forth grape and canister twice and thrice a minute. A

171

hundred yards from the stone wall the flanking party on the right, coming down on a heavy run, halted suddenly within fifty yards and poured a deadly storm of musket balls into Pickett's men, double quicking across their front and, under this terrible cross fire the men reeled and staggered between fallen comrades and the right came pressing down upon the center, crowding the company into confusion. But all know the purpose to carry the heights in front, and the mingled mass from fifteen to thirty deep, rushed toward the stone wall while a few hundred men, without orders, faced to the right and fought the flanking party there, although, fifty to one and for a time held them at bay. Muskets were seen crossed as some men fired to the right and others to the front and the fighting was terrible--far beyond all other experience even of Pickett's men who for once raised no cheer, while the welkin ran around them with the "Union triple huzza." The old veterans saw the fearful odds against them and other hosts gathering darker and deeper still.

The time was too precious, too serious for a cheer; they buckled down to the heavy task in silence, and fought with a feeling like despair. The enemy was falling back in front while officers were seen among their breaking lines striving to maintain their ground. Pickett's men were within a few feet of the stone wall when the artillery delivered their last fire from guns sheltered, to the muzzle--a blaze fifty feet long went through the charging, surging host with a gapping rent to the rear--the survivors mounted the wall then over and downward, rushed up the hill close after the survivors who waved their rammers in the face of Pickett's men and sent up cheer after cheer as they felt admiration for the gallant charge. On swept the column over ground covered with dead and dying men, for the earth seemed to be on fire, the smoke dense and suffocating, the sun shut out, flames blazing on every side, friend could hardly be distinguished from foe, but the division in the shape of an inverted V, with the point flattened, pushed forward, fighting, falling and melting away, till half way up the hill they were met by a powerful body of fresh troops charging down upon them, and this remnant of about a thousand men were hurled back out into the clover field. Brave Armistead was down among the enemy guns, mortally wounded, but was last seen leaning upon one elbow slashing at the gunners to prevent them from firing at his retreating men. Out in front of the breastwork the men showed a disposition to reform for another charge, and an officer looking at the frowning heights, with blood trickling down the side of his face, inquired of another; "What shall we do?" The answer was; "If we get reinforcements soon we can take that hill yet." But no reinforcements came, none were in sight, and about a thousand men fled to the rear over dead and wounded, mangled, groaning, dying men, scattered thick, far and wide, while shot and shell tore up the earth and mini balls flew around them for more than a thousand yards.

A STAMPEDE.

Colonel Freemantle says; "General Lee rode among Pickett's men after the repulse and with a few kindly words rallied the broken troops, and that he saw many men with an empty sleeve seize a musket and turn ready into line; that there was less noise and confusion than on an ordinary review." Here are the facts of this rally of Pickett's Division. An attempt was made on the brow of Seminary Hill, in front of the Confederate batteries, by a couple of officers who rallied the fugitives but the effort (under a heavy cross fire from both sides now) failed, and then commenced a rout that soon increased to a stampede and almost caused demoralization of all the survivors of this noted charge without distinction of regiments or command.

A few hundred yards behind the Confederate batteries there is a ravine along which runs a country road that makes at one place an abrupt angle by turning or bending to the left. At this point there is a bluff on one side and a slight swamp on the other, creating a narrow path, through which the fugitives without distinction of rank, officers and privates side by side, pushed, poured and rushed into a continuous stream, throwing guns, blankets and haversacks as they hurried on in confusion towards the rear. Here another effort was made to rally the broken troops and all sorts of appeals and threats made to officers and men who turned a deaf ear and hurried on, some of the officers even jerking loose with an oath from the hand laid on their shoulders to attract attention. At last a few privates harkening to the appeals, halted and formed a nucleus around which about thirty others soon rallied and with these a picket was formed across the road as a barrier to further retreat and the stream of stragglers dammed up several hundred strong.

PICKETT'S GRIEF

General Pickett came down from the direction of the battlefield weeping bitterly and said to the officer commanding the picket; "Don't stop any of my men. Tell them to come to the camp we occupied last night;" and passed on himself towards the rear. Other officers passed by, but the picket was retained at this point until Colonel Charles Marshall came galloping up from the rear and inquired "what this guard was for and who placed it here?" Finding the officer without orders, he moved the picket back a few hundred yards and extended the line along the stream or little creek found there. Here the guard did his duty until sundown, arresting all stragglers from the battlefield, and Colonel Marshall took them back to General Lee. The fugitives were formed into squads and Colonel Marshall took them forward himself, with no other help, to where General Lee was on the field, and it was to these men that Colonel Freemantle heard General Lee address his kindly words, but none of them had empty sleeves, as all the wounded were allowed to pass to the rear. When Colonel Marshall first came up to the picket across the road he had come from a point still farther in rear, where he had been sent by General Lee to rally the stragglers, if possible, and failing to do so was returning to report to General Lee. Colonel Marshall came down several times before sundown after the stragglers collected by the picket and carried up to the field, probably a total of four or five hundred men during the evening.

The Comte de Paris makes a mistake in estimating the strength of Pickett's Division at Gettysburg at 5,500 as he includes Corse's Brigade, which had been left behind in Virginia, and was not with Pickett in this campaign. The total loss in the battle is given by Colonel Harrison, A.and I. General of the Division as 3,393. General Armistead and Garnett were killed and Kemper wounded and captured. Colonel Hodges, Edmonds, Magruder, Williams, Patton, Allen, Owens and Stuart were killed and Colonel Hunton, Mayo, Terry, Gantt, and Aylett were wounded. Three lieutenant colonels were killed -- Calcott, Wade, and Ellis. Seven lieutenant colonels were wounded--Swindler, Otey, Berkley N., Cannyton, White, Whittle and Martin. Of nine majors, one was killed, seven wounded and one escaped unhurt, being the only field officer left out of thirty two that went into battle. The Eighth Virginia Regiment went into battle with 173 privates and lost 157 leaving one captain and sixteen privates. The Eighteenth Regiment carried 281 privates and 28 commissioned officers and lost 246 privates and 26 commissioned officers.

****

Robert O. Bright, Staff Officer to Gen. Pickett wrote the following letter listing the members of Pickett's staff who rode with him into the July 3rd charge at Gettysburg and his role as a courier for Gen. Pickett.

****

Williamsburg
July 20, 1887

Capt H. T. Owen
Dear Sir,

Your letter of July 18th is to hand. I am unable to answer the letter which you mention as having appeared in Richmond Dispatch of last Sunday not having seen it, but it will give me pleasure to answer any question about the war asked by so gallant an officer as you always proved yourself to be.

Those of Genl Pickett's Staff who rode into the Gettysburg Charge with him on the 3rd of July were Maj Charles Pickett, Capt Baird, Capt Symington and myself. We took no couriers with us. Col Lewis Williams 1st Va was mounted, he having asked me when I gave the order to Genl Kemper to go in on foot, to allow him to ride because he was not well and said to me "remember Williamsburg," which was my native place and he had been shot in the shoulder there. He rode a sorrel mare from which he was killed and Lieut Marshall of Stribling's Battery, having had his own horse killed, caught Col Williams mare and rode her off the field. The four members of the Staff mentioned were not with Genl Pickett all the time during the charge. We were sent about the field, with messages and orders. I carried a message just before we reached the Emmetsburg Road to Genl Longstreet and brought back his reply to Genl Pickett. I afterwards carried an order to Dearing's Battalion of artillery and another to Genl Wilcox, who had been placed under Genl Pickett's orders by Genl Longstreet, a message sent Genl Pickett by me to him but now about another piece which you know but was in Richmond Whig. It says the Div was reported to Genl Longstreet by members of Genl Pickett's Staff who reported the men much fatigued by their long march. Genl Longstreet asked me as to the fighting condition of the men and I said when the men reach this point will be able to go into anything only requiring an hour or two of effort but are not in a condition for a fight of six or seven hours having marched when they reached this point some 28 miles.   I was the Staff Officer who reported the Div to Genl Longstreet and he told me where to encamp it and said tell Pickett I will have work for him tomorrow.

Please excuse the paper.   I am out of my usual kind and nearly out of this kind also and now hoping to see soon

I remain yours sincerely

Ro. A. Bright

****

Capt. Edward R. Baird wrote the final letter on Gettysburg concerning a meeting held in 1894 of former staff officers to vindicate the conduct of Gen. Pickett at Gettysburg.

****

Edw. R. Baird

Superintendent of Schools

Essex County, Va.

Occupacia Va. Sep 22 1908

My dear Sir,

Yr letter of 19th put to hand and I reply at once.   I have gotten a letter from Maj. Perkins few days ago, but as his covered a longer period it required more examination of our positions is not yet answered.   The meeting referred to by Col Lock was <u>not</u> held in vindication of Pickett's Staff as he states, but of <u>Pickett himself</u> and in answer to some charges made I believe by Maj. Otey of 11th Va. it was held at Murphy in Decr 1894.   Maj. Pickett, Capt. Symington, Lt. Col. Martin 53rd Va., Thos Frank, Thomas Harrison and myself were present.   A statement of the facts connected with Gen. Pickett's presence and conduct on the battlefield at Gettysburg <u>was drawn up and signed </u>by <u>all</u> of these gentlemen and was published in the <u>Times</u> of I think, the 19th Decr or there about.   It set at rest by the testimony of AGC witnesses the question which seems incredible that anyone could ever have raised.

This publication was made before the Times and Dispatch were merged but I have no doubt it can be found at the present office of the paper.

The charge referred to as coming from Gen. Rosser and Col Venable and Mosby were not before that meeting at all and I never heard them until a few days ago thru Maj Perkins.   I have reply to his letter in a day or so and I think I shall be able to satisfactorily.   If you get the paper please have a copy of the card made and also of Mr. Wm Royal's editorial comments on it.

If I can serve you further please call on me.

Res.

Edw. R. Baird

Late ADC Pickett's Div

Cap R. A. Bright was also present at the meeting referred to.

****

Henry apparently could never accept the premise that Gettysburg was lost due to General Lee's hesitation. Lee apparently wanted to wait until he had the full strength of his army before making a concerted charge against the Union forces. Henry apparently believed the battle could have been won if the 18th and the rest of Pickett's Brigade had been put into battle on the day they arrived at Gettysburg.

Major General George Edward Pickett

(Photo Courtesy of Mr. Randy Chadwick)

George Edward Pickett was born January 25, 1825 in Richmond Virginia. He attended West Point and after graduating in 1846 served in the Mexican War. He remained in the U.S. Army until 1861 when he resigned his commission to enter the Confederate Army as a colonel. In January of 1862 he was promoted to Brigadier General and commanded the 3rd Brigade of Longstreet's Division in the Seven Days and Gaines battles. He was promoted to Major General in October 1862 and commanded Pickett's Division of Longstreet's Corp at Fredericksburg, Suffolk and Gettysburg where the ill fated charge was made against the Federal center on July 3 with the brigades of Brigadier Generals James L. Kemper, Richard B. Garnett and Lewis A. Armistead. He later fought in the battles at New Berne, Petersburg, Five Forks and Sayler's Creek.

Following the war he was an insurance salesman in Richmond. He died in Norfolk Virginia July 30, 1875 and is buried on Gettysburg Hill, Hollywood Cemetery, Richmond, Virginia..

Pickett Monument, Gettysburg Hill, Hollywood Cemetery, Richmond, Virginia

(Photo by Erik Lander)

Major General George Edward Pickett died July 30, 1875. The monument was erected by the members of Pickett's Division Association consisting of the survivors of his Division at a cost of $2,500 and unveiled at a ceremony on July 3, 1888. The monument committee was made up of members from each brigade. Henry was appointed to represent Garnett's Brigade. Mrs. Pickett was at the unveiling ceremony. She died March 22, 1931 and was buried in Arlington National Cemetery. In 1998 she was re-interred at the foot of the monument. Her gravestone is at the bottom of the photo.

179

Major Charles F. Pickett

(Photo courtesy of The Pickett Society)

Major Charles F. Pickett, younger brother of Major General George E. Pickett was born June 1, 1840. He served as Assistant Adjutant General in "Pickett's Division." After the war he owned an insurance agency in Norfolk, Virginia. He died March 25, 1899 and was buried in Elmwood Cemetery, Norfolk, Virginia.

The obverse side of his marker reads as follows:

"I would also bring to your notice the name of Capt Charles Pickett, Asst Adjt Genl, who acted with the most conspicuous gallantry, carrying a flag by my side at the head of the brigade on foot (having lost his horse), and urging forward, all the time forward, until shot down seriously wounded, and then begging those who went to bear him off the field to leave him and go to the front; if they could not bear him off conveniently, but leave him his flag, which he still held, and let him die under its folds."

Report of Col J. B. Strange HQ 3rd Bde 2nd Div CSA
Fraziers Farm, July 15, 1862

CHAPTER 11 – SOUTHERN HOSPITALITY SHOWN TO A FEDERAL

"He said I fulfilled the Scripture in that when I found mine enemy hungered, I fed him."
Henry T. Owen - July 18, 1863

After Lt. Col. Carrington was wounded at Gettysburg Henry was put in command of the 18th Regiment which was down to about 50 men. The brigade was assigned the duty of guarding several hundred Federal prisoners on the march back to Virginia. General Lee expressed concern if they were up to the task.

Henry T. Owen continues to involve the reader in the many facets of his personality. In the following letters, the reader observes Henry is a kind, gregarious human being. He does not like the men in his command "taking advantage of the poor prisoners." (Archived letter in collection at the Virginia State Library)

The reader also meets a Union soldier named Captain Frank R. Josselyn who was commander of Company F, 11th Massachusetts and was captured at the Battle of Gettysburg.

In the letter from Bunker Hill, Berkley County, Virginia, the reader sees common humanity at its best. Again, the reader sees how Henry not only had a strong belief in Providence, he lived what he believed. Josselyn tells Henry he has acted as a Christian by feeding a hungry enemy. Henry tried to find Frank Josselyn after the war.

****

Bunker Hill Berkley Co Va
July 18th, 1863

My dear Harriet,

After the great battle of Gettysburg our Division had charge of a large lot of prisoners – some two hundred officers and thirty three hundred privates. We guarded them from Gettysburg to Winchester and had charge of them eight days. Our provisions were scarce and the Yankees have no utensils to cook with and had to work up the little flour that was issued to them in their tin cups and cook their small rations of beef on the coals. The officers were fine looking men in neat uniforms and more intelligent than are lot of prisoners I have seen before at all. They parted with their canteens, knives, gold pencils, combs and many little trinkets to our soldiers for bread or meat and I was sorry to see a disposition with our men to take all the advantage possible of the poor prisoners.

One day while at Williamsport on this side of the Potomac I went along the line of sentinels to see if all was safe and as I went strolling by a crowd I found a young, fine looking officer trying to trade off a neat little pocket flask, silver mounted for a half cake of bread and our soldiers were trying to see how small a piece he would agree to take. I told the officer that he would soon have beef and flour issued to him and advised him to wait awhile but he said had had never worked any and did not know how to fix up his flour and beef right. Said he was very hungry and wanted a piece of bread. Some officers standing by were trying to dispute with him about the War but he told them that he was a prisoner and it was unfair to argue the matter since if he spoke his sentiments freely they would be offended and that any arguments they might have would not affect the War at all nor end the strife a day sooner. They persisted but he kept his eye and mind fixed upon the bread and I tried to get him off from the party. I had not gotten my rations that day and it was 9 o'clock. I told him however that as soon as they came I would divide with him. Soon afterwards one of my men told me that he knew a house not far off where I could get breakfast and I went and got the Yankee officer and told him if he would promise not to try to escape I would take him out to breakfast. He readily promised and away we went over hill and dale together without even a pistol, chatting gaily as we journeyed together. We reached the house and got a splendid breakfast. The old lady and three daughters saw my old grey uniform and the Yankee's blue cloth and they stirred about like the house was afire. We were both hungry and ate heartily of the old lady's light bread, fried ham, coffee (genuine) and honey. When we got through the old lady did not want to take my Confederate money and the Yankee pulled out a full purse of his, purchased three dozen biscuits and we jogged along back to camp. He was very thankful for my kindness and wanted me to accept his flask as a present but I told him I did not charge for favors and that I had only done my duty to my fellow man in distress. He said I had fulfilled the scripture in that when I found mine enemy a hungered I fed him. I told him that was my religion. His flask was the neatest one I ever saw – silver mounted and covered with bamboo and whalebone with a nice cover. It cost him $5.00 and he said he had often been offered $10 for it. It was all he had to carry water in and I did not think it right to accept it. I told him all I wanted of his people was to be let alone and unless they stopped the War we would fight them for a thousand years. His name was Capt. F. R. Josselyn of the 11 Mass. Reg. Co "F" from Boston. Before we parted several for whom had done little previous came round and bade me good bye and promised that if any of our Reg or my Company ever fell into their hands they should be kindly attended to. When they left for Richmond they all regretted to part with our Brigade and one or two came forward and for the others thanked the Brigade for their kindness and courtesy while with them and said they had found the bravest soldiers were the kindest to prisoners. They said they wished we could go on with them to Richmond and regretted to part with us. Capt Josselyn and myself had met in battle twice before without knowing it, once at Williamsburg and once at seven Pines. He was one of the handsomeness men I ever saw and smart as a steel trap. I took his name and gave him mine when we parted.

I have written an obituary notice of Lieut Watkins and sent it to the Whig. The editor will send you and Mrs. Robertson a paper with the notice as soon as he publishes it. I wrote to him to do so. I have also written and article signed "Cyrus Cassunder" which I expect he will publish in the same paper and an advertisement of a lot of deserters from the 18th Reg among them George Anderson, Jos Leath and Hiram Fowlkes. I expect this will set the Leath family all in a blaze of wrath with me again. These boys were not hurt and while we were fighting just straggled off and are trying to make their way home.

I am the only Capt left in our Reg and find a good deal of trouble in managing the refractory men. I almost feel like deserting myself and if I was to do so don't you think you would kiss me and say it was all right.

I am writing with a miserable pen and expect you will hardly be able to read my scribbling.

I don't think we shall be called on soon to fight as we have been so cut up. My trust is in God for safety.

Yrs faithfully as ever
Henry
****

Stephen Stanley pens Henry a letter from the Office of Stanley Brothers in response to an inquiry by Henry about Josselyn. It seems Josselyn had died sometime after his meeting with Henry.

****

Office of Stanley Bros.
Atteboro Falls, Mass., Oct. 17th 1884

H. T. Owen
Dear Sir,

Yours of the 9th inst recd. I have delayed answering, thinking that I might hear of something to write you concerning B. F. Joselyn. This A.M. I recd a letter from the National Tribune Washington D.C. They say "that the Roster of the 11th Mass. Vol (officers) show that Capt Frank R. Josslyn missing since the Battle of Gettysburg. The record does not show any officer by the name of B. F. Joselyn." This is all that I have recd in regard to Joselyn up to the present time. I feel confident that I shall hear more. The names do not seem to be the same. But now both say "captured at Gettysburg" so I think that I am on track of the right person. You know as well as I, that he might have died while a prisoner and was never heard from afterwards. It looks that way from the records of the Regt. I cannot think but what if he died while a prisoner that the fact would have sooner or later reached his Regt or his home. But it is a fact, that you as well as I very well know, that thousands of poor fellows were lost and it was impossible to ever get any trace of them afterwards and possibly Capt Joselyn may have been one of them. If I cannot get any further information from those I have written to I will try and find out from what towns and cities the 11th Regt came from, and it cannot be possible but what I can find someone that knew him and knows whether he ever came back from captivity. You can rest assured that I will do all that lays in my power to find this man or find out what became of him if it is possible. We know that he was alive after the Battle of Gettysburg and a prisoner. I presume it would be an utter impossibility to get at the Confederate Prison Records, even if they are in existence. Yes we might trace him. At present, however, I should think it would be best to let the matter rest until I find out whether he came back from captivity or not. Trusting that I may be able to write you the desired information soon I remain

Respectfully
Stephen Stanley

184

****

Stephen Stanley persists in trying to assist Henry in finding Captain Josselyn. It seems Stanley has a great response to his inquiries about Josselyn which indicates that he was well known and well revered.

****

STANLEY BROS.,
MANUFACTURERS OF
GOLD STOCK PLATED CHAIN
New York Office, 200 Broadway
Atteboro Falls Mass., Jan 2nd 1885

H. T. Owen
Dear Sir,

Enclosed you will find a letter which I rec this A.M. in regard to Capt Joselyn which I thought might be of interest to you. This letter I rec in answer one that was sent to me offering information about Capt J.

I wrote them that I had recd the desired information and had sent the same to you, then came this letter, which I send to you. Since I wrote you last I have recd letters from all over God's creation nearly but as they all told the same story, I did not write you. But I should judge from them that this Capt Joselyn was a man that was thought much of by all that knew him.

We are having a very dull time here at present, most of the shops are closed, no trade at all. But I think that we both have seen harder times than the present so I will wish you a Happy New Year.

Stephen Stanley

****

Finally, Henry hears from George T. Bosson of Boston. Bosson reveals that his wife was the youngest sister of Captain Josselyn. Mr. Bosson and his wife plan to visit Henry in Richmond.

****

Boston - May 6, 1886

H. T. Owen Esq.
Dear Sir,

About two years ago a request appeared in the public papers of this city for the address of Capt Josselyn, 11th Mass Regt.

I answered it, among others, and rec'd from Mr. Stanley of Atteboro Falls Mass a note relating to the circumstance of meeting with you and your desire to know what had become of Capt J.

My wife is the youngest sister of Capt Josselyn and ever since hearing from Mr. Stanley has had a strong desire to hear from the lips of one who was with her brother the story of the march from Gettysburg to Richmond, one as captive and the other as captor.

Capt Robert Josselyn, an uncle of Capt F. R. Josselyn 11th Mass, was in the early years of the war private secretary to Jefferson Davis and appointed by him Sec'y of State of the Territory of Arizona. So we have a desire to see the famous City of the Confederacy and if possible to meet one who became so intimate under such peculiar circumstances with our brother.

We hope to arrive in Richmond by Old Dominion Steamer from N.Y. leaving Tuesday afternoon and due in Richmond Thursday noon. We shall stop at Ford's Hotel until Friday and shall try and find Capt Owen as soon as convenient.

I trust you will not consider us in any way intruding on you and shall hope that the nearest relative (an aged father and his widow excepted) of Capt Josselyn will be sufficient warranty to claim your friendship.

Hoping to see you and make your acquaintance.

I am

Very Truly Yours,

George T. Bosson

****

Not long after the above letter, Henry receives a letter from L. Jeannette Bosson (Mrs. George T. Bosson) from Russia Wharf, Boston, Massachusetts. The letter was written after the Bosson's visit to Henry in Richmond, Virginia.

****

Allston

May 25th '86

Dear Capt Owen,

We arrived home Sunday morning, somewhat tired, but delighted with our journey from beginning to end. We enjoyed our visit at Richmond so much and I am so glad that I have seen you and talked with you for it has been on my mind ever since we heard of you and I feel towards you as you said you did towards me as if we were related in some way to each other.

Whenever I have related the story of your kindness to my dear brother Frank, I have wished oh so much that you had met after the war. He was so generous and with pleasure he would have sent for you, but alas, he is gone and it remains for me to thank you from the bottom of my heart for your kindness to him. I can never forget it and I do so much want you to come here and visit us. You do not seem strong and a trip North would do you so much good. Can't you plan some way to come?

I was much pleased with Richmond and wished I could have stayed longer. I reckon I'll come again sometime. My boy Charlie was delighted with his cane (which I carried in my hand all through my journey) and longs to see you and hear you talk about the Civil War. We found Washington a beautiful city and we visited Mt. Vernon and Arlington. The latter is by far the lovelier place. Saw and shook hands with the President and came home more a Democrat than ever.

By the way, <u>can</u> you remember just where you were on the march when you and Frank took breakfast together? Have been asked but could not remember that you told me.

Wish I could have seen your Wife and family. Please tell her that I must write to you once in awhile and that I am so small it isn't worth while to be jealous of me.

Write me soon and tell me how your cold is and remember that I shall always love you for your kindness to my idolized brother. My husband unites with me in sending you a cordial invitation to visit us and I <u>guess</u> you will come. Am so glad you saw me before I wrote you as I am a very poor letter writer and can never express my thoughts on paper. Give my regards to Mrs. Owen and believe me

Yours aff.

L. Jeannette Bosson

My address: Mrs. George T. Bosson, Russia Wharf, Boston, Mass.

****

Mrs. Bosson contacts a friend of hers, B. W. Currier. He writes a letter to Henry about "his old chum Frank.

****

Office of
Chamberlin & Currier
Boston, June 3rd 1886

Capt H. T. Owen
My dear Sir,

You must be surprised no doubt at receiving a letter from me. By way of explanation I will say that Mrs. Bosson, and old friend of mine, told me the other day that she had just returned from Richmond Va where she had met a gentleman who had befriended her brother Frank while he was a prisoner south during the war. I was extremely interested to hear her story about you and your kindness to my old chum Frank.. I felt that I wanted to know you and told her I would write you at once.

You will, I hope, pardon the liberty I take but Frank Josselyn was one of the dearest friends I ever had throughout our school boys days and in after life so long as he lived. He was one of natures noblemen, truly a splendid fellow. During his imprisonment on "Libby" I had the pleasure of sending him cases of condensed food and possibly by your kindness he received them and his life was saved.

I should be glad to see you should you ever come to our city and I will be pleased to extend the hospitality of my home. I am intending a short trip to Europe leaving here the 17th of the month and returning by Sept 1st. In the meantime shall be glad to hear from you by letter. With kindest regard and hoping to be better acquainted at some future time.

I am very truly Yrs,
B. W. Currier
****

Mrs. Bosson refers to B. W. Currier as her "brother's most intimate friend." She inquires if Henry has come across anyone who knows her uncle, Robert Josselyn.

****

Allston, June 27th '86

Dear Capt. Owen,

Your very interesting letter was received on Decoration Day ("The Blue and the Gray") and I have been thinking I might hear from you again after you had visited your home (as you know you owe me a Confederate dollar). Aren't you glad it's not a real dollar? Ha ha.

Its rather and undertaking for me to write you. Your letters are so bright and chatty and I, like most women, can talk but am a poor correspondent. Enjoyed very much your description of your tramp to Gettysburg, particularly your opinion on Parsons. We had quite a laugh over it.

188

I spoke to my brother's most intimate friend, Mr. Currier, about you and he said he meant to write you. Did he do so? If you could only make it convenient to visit us, think it would be very pleasant for you to see how cordially some of the old soldiers would welcome you.

Am very sorry you are not feeling well. Perhaps you need a change. Mr. Bosson says you can tell me all you want to now I am so far away, thinks I am in no danger of wanting to go there this year anyway.

My little folks are well and now that school is over until fall expect to have fine times playing about.

Did you read the Satire? What did you think of it? Have you ever come across anyone who knew Uncle Robert Josselyn?

Yes, I hope some day to visit Richmond again. It is indeed a beautiful city. Have so often thought of the pleasant ride we had around it. Charlie was so astonished at the color of the soil.

Have you been home yet? Hope you found Mrs. Owen and the family well.

This is possibly not so interesting a letter but it isn't me. Whenever we meet again I will talk.

Mr. Bosson unites with me in sending regards. Hoping to hear from you soon and with the sincere wish that you are restored to health I remain

your sincere friend
Mrs. Geo. T. Bosson
****

Mrs. Bosson wrote to Henry on July 30, 1886. She sent him photos of her children and spoke of a visit.

****

Allston, July 30th '86

Dear Captain Owen,

Your favor of the 9th inst. duly received. Have delayed answering it because I wished to send the children's pictures so you might know how they look and know when I speak of them "which is which."

You will see Charlie and Jeanette (our baby) have my complexion and favor our family, while little Ruth, my oldest girl, looks like Papa. Charlie is 12, Ruth 6 and Jeanette just three.

Thank you very much for the $50 Confederate and only wish I could I could send you $50 in our money so you could realize its full value <u>now</u> as you were beginning to do then. Charlie who is all ears for Capt Owen's letters, immediately ran for his child's "History of the Civil War" and said "I know just what is on the back of it" and sure enough, there it was. Charlie wanted to know if you wrote it with your blood. Thank you very much for it. Charlie or <u>Carl</u> as I call him will prize it very highly.

Had the pleasure while in Washington of seeing Mahone and was rather amazed at his insignificance so could appreciate your joke about Mrs. Owen and haven't a doubt she could master him. Mr. Bosson says (and I suppose his experience would warrant his saying it) little people use their feet as well as their hands when cornered in a tussle, so that is the reason we are always victorious.

How I wish I could see your scrap book. It must be so interesting. Frank kept a diary all through the war and letters were published in Taltren paper (The Lynn Bay State) but the files and diary were all burned. We were so sorry. They were so interesting. Send you two scraps for your book. On Wednesday last we (Mr. Bosson, Carl and I) went to Plymouth, saw the wonderful stone, for it isn't much larger now, that our forefathers landed on and relics (pewter platter etc.) in Pilgrim Hall, visited the old cemetery etc. etc., had a pleasant trip but we are having such a heated term, its uncomfortable stirring about much.

We are still looking forward to a visit from you. Mr. Currier is in Europe with his third bride but will soon return. Be sure and write to him. He was my brother's best friend. I will send address if you have lost it.

Mr. Bosson is away, children are in bed so I take this time to write you. Remember me kindly to Mrs. Owen. Hope to meet her some day. Tell her she and I together could lick Mahone all to nothing.

Write soon. Mr. Bosson sends regards,
Yours aff.
Mrs. G. T. Bosson
Russia Wharf
Boston Mass.

****

190

Henry corresponds with Mrs. Bosson in the next letter of this grouping. Apparently, Mrs. Bosson had been to visit Henry and Harriet in Richmond. He comments on politics of the North.

****

State Building
Richmond Va.
August 5th 1886

Dear Mrs. Bosson,

Y'r very kind letter with inclosed articles for my scrap book was recv'd on the 2nd ins't, and the next mail brought me the pictures of the three little dears. I can see a resemblance to their Uncle Frank in each face, but more especially is the case with Charlie, who is exactly like Capt. Josselyn as I remember him, and I had to give the picture a long, searching examination while memory was busy with incidents and accidents occurring more than twenty years ago. I appreciate this present highly and hope you will present my kindest regards to the children and kiss the little girls for me. I am too old and gray and care worn now to send my picture to them in return, but I believe Mrs. Owen has my picture, taken during the war, and I will have a copy for them as they can see how a "ragged rebel" looked when he had charge of Capt. Frank. But you must tell them that I never had the good fortune to kill anybody. All I saw were entire strangers and as I had nothing against them personally I left the matter altogether with my Company.

I received the paper with Genl Longstreet's article on Gettysburg and value it highly. This letter is a reproduction of his letter in the Phil. Times of 3rd Nov. 1877, a copy of which I had at the time, but some good friend borrowed and forgot to return it. I have a number of letters from Gen. Longstreet and a dozen other officers written soon after his letter appeared in the Times. In the main his article is accurate but, as he depended on memory which can't be trusted, he has forgotten, overlooked and neglected some important facts, but upon the whole, he has given us an interesting and very valuable chapter of war history.

I saw, soon after your visit here, a reference to the lecture of Mr. Roper at the Lowell Institute on the Wilderness Campaign and became so anxious to have it complete that I wrote and obtained a copy of his address from himself. He has accomplished a wonderful feat. A civilian, speaking without pride or prejudice, or sectional hate, of a great civil war, and doing so accurately, fairly and impartially is a wonderful surprise. I showed and read his lecture to several prominent citizens here and some thought it a hoax or that some Brigadier General had got loose and broke into Boston.

But we must listen and keep silent, for if we have any friends speaking for us in New England viz telling a plain invarnished story or dares to narrate facts, we are afraid to say "Thank You!" or some society of isms will crucify them.

We have great hopes of New England yet, and think they can be made useful if they ever catch up. Did you know that but for New England Grant would have been nominated for a Third Term? He came within a few votes of securing the nomination and was backed up by all the gamblers, whiskey rings, monopolies, and noisy roughs and then New England, sober, calm, quiet, firm, and determined, stood up between us and a Military Despotism. The country has been drifting for twenty-five years into a consolidated, centralized power at Washington that threatens our liberties.

There is where all the corruption, frauds, bribery, rings and monopolies begin and unless New England decides at once to stop this, and there is no time to waste, we shall drift beyond help of peaceable means and be driven into a revolution the result of which no man can foretell. The South is powerless in this matter for if we speak the cry is raised "Secesh! Secesh!" "States Rights, States Rights!" and we are choked off.

I voted for Grant against Greeley for his second term, had no vote when he was elected for the 1st term, and I was an "Old Time Whig" but had no idea then that such strides would be made in the direction of Centralized Government as would startle me in so short a time. If there is war with Mexico (we hope not) the U. States Government can raise all the troops wanted to conquer if necessary or thrash into good manners Mexico or any other man by just recruiting in the South. Texas, Louisiana, Mississippi and Arkansas can fan them out before frost if it is desired to be done at once.

I wish you would send us some New England farmers down here to settle up our waste places. We have cheap lands and a healthy climate, beautiful landscapes and clear skies and are civilized people.

I was home last week and found my people well. Will write Mr. Currier care of you at any early day.

Very Respectfully
H. T. Owen

In this letter, Henry receives a letter from Maggie J. Baker of Berkeley County, Virginia (Now is in WV). Ms. Baker is the daughter of the couple who fed Henry and Josselyn. She mentions her father's name, Nicholas, but does not mention her mother's name.

****

Berkeley County Va
April 1st 1887

Mr. Owen
Dear Sir

I have just come into possession of a copy of a letter written by you to the postmaster at Williamsport and asking information of the whereabouts of a family living on the Virginia side of the line at the time of Gen. Lee's retreat from Gettysburg. The main object in writing to you is to know if the postmaster ever answered your letter as from the fact there has been no further correspondence and he is very careless of his duty although he told me he had done so. The way it came to be copied was that Mr. Lenon, who lived in the house connected with the ferry at the pike or public road, and who lives there yet, whose son lives in Williamsport, took a copy of it and sent it to his father thinking it had reference to him but the description and surroundings did not agree with his place but all agree that it was a good description of our place and we think it correct except as to distance from the Pike and the latitude of the house. You describe it as fronting the south when it is fronting east directly facing the river and where you entered was the rear or western. You speak of coming through a large yard filled with flowers and evergreens and entering a hall with the dining room on the left, which is all perfectly correct and as to distance you thought about a mile from the road. We think it is something less than a half mile but your recollection of the route by which you came is correct. You came across a field tolerably level until you came in sight of the house when you began to descend a long tolerably steep hill. When you came to the foot you came to a small flat at the bottom after crossing which you came to a good sized branch. After you cross that you ascend quite an abrupt hill for a short distance

193

then a gentle rise until you reach the house which is about fifty or sixty yards from the ravine which stands on a gentle eminence, the ground dropping in each direction from the house and about the same distance from the river.

You wish to know the name of those living here at the time and if they are living and where my Pa is living. Yet here the same place but is quite feeble being in his seventy fifth year having been paralyzed some time ago and otherwise afflicted but he remembers very distinctly all about the circumstances of which you inquire. You speak of coming with a Federal captain. You may have come alone with him but one recollection of it is that there were quite a number took breakfast here but they may have come after you left. I remember one time there was one among some prisoners at one time ate breakfast whose name was Charlie Potter but do not know if it was at that time.

Pa's name is Nicolas F. Baker. Ma died last October a year ago. There were four of us girls at home then, one being small at the time all being away from home but myself now.

You spoke of it being your impression that we were of strong Union sentiment in which you were wrong as our sympathies were with the south and do not wonder that you came to that conclusion as I remember that Ma turned a number of Confederates away that morning telling them that she could not accommodate them. These men were prisoners and not at liberty to seek for their food while they were free to seek further and if she were living now she would be gratified to hear of her service being appreciated as nothing seemed to give her more pleasure than to minister to anyone in distress.

I will enclose an envelope addressed to Pa as I would like very much to have an answer and have all doubts settled. There are sometimes very pleasant incidents crop out of the war. Please answer and you will confer a great favor.

Yours with respect

Maggie J. Baker

****

In the final letter of this chapter, Henry has acquired a letter from George Bosson written to Stephen Stanley.

****

Stephen Stanley   (undated)
Dear Sir,

Yours of Dec 29th rec'd and I was very glad to hear from the request for information relating to Capt Josselyn.

My wife is Capt Josselyn's only living sister and very naturally desired to hear any thing relating to her brother.

His aged father is still living over 75 years old and probably no persons in this wide world (not even excepting his wife) mourn the death of Capt Josselyn more than his father and sister. The father and son were always together and the great sorrow of the old man's life is his son's long lingering sickness, suffering and death.

My wife cannot to this day think of him hardly a moment without being overcome.

Capt J's father had a brother in Richmond during the war and acted in a secretary's capacity to Davis but was not able to help Capt J. much while in prison. Capt Josselyn was for a number of years in N.Y. in business.

A noble hearted fellow he was, none more generous, and if any man could make friends with an enemy it was him.

Be pleased to accept the hearty thanks of Capt Josselyn's sister and father who never weary in hearing good things of their dearest son and brother and if ever an opportunity offers to visit Richmond we shall surely find Capt Owen.

Thanking you for your kind letter
I remain
Yours truly
Geo. T. Bosson
****

As strangers who meet briefly and find some common bond, Henry's kindness to Captain Josselyn endeared him to the good Captain's family.

CHAPTER 12 – TRAVELS AND SUMMARY OF BATTLES

The movement of an infantry unit usually depends on the feet of men and the 18th Virginia Infantry was no exception. During the course of the War the regiment marched over 1,900 miles under all weather conditions, many times with no change of clothing, no shelter, barefoot and little or nothing to eat. On rare occasions, the regiment was moved by train. Following is a chronological account of the 18th's movements and battles.

April 23, 1861 - The Regiment was activated at Burkeville, Virginia . and boarded a train for Richmond. (56 miles)

May 25, 1861 - After a month's training at Camp Lee, near Petersburg, the Regiment traveled 100 miles by train to Manassas to guard the junction of the Manassas Gap and Orange & Alexandria railroads.

Early July, 1861 - Marched to Centreville and camped. (5 miles)

July 17, 1861 - Picket duty at Fairfax Court House. (7 miles) The Regiment fell back to Manassas after an overwhelming attack from the lead troops of Gen. Irving McDowell's army of 35,000 that had marched from Washington D.C. toward the rail junction at Manassas.. (12 miles)

July 21, 1861 - Battle of First Manassas - This was the first major land battle of the War with an estimated 60,680 troops engaged: 28,450 Federal and 32,230 Confederate. In order for the Union army to reach its goal of making an assault on Richmond it first had to capture the rail junction at Manassas. After the skirmishes at Fairfax Court House the armies of Union General McDowell and Confederate Generals Joseph E. Johnston and P.G.T. Beauregard met in battle that started in the morning and raged until dusk. McDowell's forces had crossed Bull Run at Sudley Ford and attacked the Confederate left flank on Matthews Hill driving the Confederate forces back to Henry Hill. In late afternoon Confederate reinforcements arrived and broke the Union right flank. At 2 P.M. the 18th was ordered to the area of Henry House Hill. The 18th, along with Col. Wade Hampton's South Carolina Legion, attacked the Union lines causing them to flee in disorder. The battle was a Confederate victory with the Federal troops retreating back to

Washington, however, the Confederate forces were too disorganized to pursue. Estimated casualties were 2,950 Federal and 1,750 Confederate. The 18th losses were 6 killed and 13 wounded.

Early August, 1861 - After camping near the battlefield at Manassas for several days, an epidemic of typhoid fever broke out due to contaminated water. As a result the Regiment marched to Centreville and camped. (10 miles)

August 28, 1861 - Marched to Fairfax Court House and back to Centreville. (20 miles)

October 9, 1861 - Camped at Fairfax Court house. (10 miles)

November 6. 1861 - Camped at Centreville. (10 miles)

March 12, 1862 - Camp Wise, Richmond, trip probably by rail (120 miles).

March 18, 1862 - Camped at Gordonsville after rail trip of 76 miles.

April 5, 1862 - Marched to Orange Court House (9 miles).

April 6, 1862 - Marched 16 miles towards Fredericksburg.

April 7, 1862 - Marched to Louisa Court House (16 miles).

April 11, 1862 - Henry wrote his wife Harriet about the anticipated march to Richmond on the following day due to the shortage of trains. (See letter of April 11, 1862 in Chapter 8) .

April 12, 1862 - Started march to Richmond through snow, rain, and hail on muddy roads with little to eat (65 miles).

April 20, 1862 - Camped near Yorktown (70 miles)

May 4, 1862 - Marched to Williamsburg (15 miles)

May 5, 1862 - Battle of Williamsburg: This was the first large battle of the Peninsula Campaign and involved nearly 41,000 Federals and 32,000 Confederates. Hooker's division encountered the Confederate rear guard near Williamsburg during the Confederate retreat from Yorktown. Hooker attacked the earthen fortifications at Fort Magruder on the Williamsburg Road but was driven back. General Longstreet's troops threatened the Union left flank until Kearney's Division arrived to help hold the Federal position. Hancock's Brigade then moved to threaten the Confederate left flank. The Confederates then counterattacked unsuccessfully. Hancock did not exploit his success and the Confederate army withdrew during the night Total estimated losses were 2,283 Federals and 1,560 Confederates. The 18th Regiment suffered the highest losses of the Brigade with 14 killed, 21 wounded and 9 captured.

May 5, 6, 1862 - Marched all night to Chickahominy Swamp.(20 miles)

May 11, 1862 - Camped on banks of Chickahominy River (9 miles)

May 21, 1862 - Camped at Laurel Hill Church (35 miles.)

May 31, 1862 - Marched to Seven Pines (10 miles).

May 31 - June 1, 1862 - Battle of Seven Pines. Total estimated casualties were 5,739 Federal, 7,997 Confederate. The battle started on May 31 when Gen. Joseph E. Johnston attacked two Federal Corps south of the Chickahominy River. The Confederate assaults drove back the IV Corp of Maj. Gen. George B. McClellan inflicting heavy casualties. McClellan was reinforced by Sedgewick's III Corp and Sumner's II Corp, which finally stabilized the Federal position. Gen. Johnston was seriously wounded. On June 1, the 18th Virginia Infantry and others were brought up but made little headway. Confederate Brigadier General Robert H. Hatton was killed. The 18th had 18 killed, 28 wounded and 5 missing. Company C had 3 killed, 8 wounded and 2 missing.

June 16, 1862 - Camped below Richmond, on Williamsburg Road (10 miles)

June 25, 1862 - Marched to Gaines Mill. (20 miles)

June 27, 1862 - Battle of Gaines Mill: Total estimated casualties 15,500 with 6,800 Federal and 8,700 Confederate. This was the third day of the Seven Days' Battles when Gen. Robert E. Lee renewed his attacks against Brig. Gen. Fitz John Porter's V Corp which had established a defensive line behind Boatswain's Swamp on the north side of the Chickahominy River. Three brigades headed by Brig. Generals Roger A. Pryor, James L. Kemper and George E. Pickett, were ordered to assault the ridge. The 18th, as part of Pickett's Brigade went forward at double quick. The Confederates had to descend a steep ravine tangled with brush and then climb out. They were met with a hail of musket fire. Col. Withers, bleeding after being grazed on the skull. He later received another shot through the chest. He was struck in the back by another bullet as two men were carrying him to the rear. During the charge, 9 color bearers were killed or wounded as they walked beside his horse. Near sundown the Confederate lines were reinforced and overran the three entrenched Federal lines. This was another Confederate victory as the Federals retreated during the night. The 18th had 14 killed, 99 wounded and 5 captured.

June 30, 1862 - This was the fifth day of the Seven Days' Battles. Huger's, Longstreet's and A. P. Hill's divisions converged on the retreating Union army near Frayser's Farm late in the afternoon The 18th as a part of Pickett's Division was again in the middle of a vicious fight which slowly drove the Union forces back. The total estimated casualties on both sides were 6,500 with the 18th suffering losses of 17 killed, and 57 wounded. After the Battle of Malvern Hill, which ended the Seven Days' Battles, the ten companies of the 18th numbered only 250 men.

July 16, 1862 - Camped below Richmond, Darby Town Road (17 miles)

Late August, 1862 - Marched to Manassas (115 miles)

August 28 - 30, 1862 - Battle of Second Manassas. Total estimated casualties were 22,180 with 13,830 Federal and 8,350 Confederate. On August 28, Gen. Jackson ordered an attack on Major Gen. John Pope's army, which was passing along the Warrenton Turnpike. The initial battle lasted for several hours and resulted in a stalemate. On August 29, Pope thought he had trapped Jackson and ordered a series of attacks against him but was repulsed with heavy casualties on both sides. At noon, Gen. Longstreet's Division arrived from Thoroughfare Gap and took a position on Jackson's right flank. On August 30, Pope again attacked. Longstreet's Division of 28,000 men then counterattacked in the largest mass assault of the war and drove the Union army back to Bull Run. Pope then used a rear guard to retreat to Centreville and was pursued by Lee's army the next day. The 18th was only involved in the August 30 attack as a part of Longstreet's Division and had 3 killed and 33 wounded. This was the most decisive battle of the Northern Virginia Campaign.

Early September, 1862 - Marched northward crossing the Potomac into Maryland near Leesburg Virginia and camped in the vicinity of Hagerstown, Maryland on September 13. During the march Gen. George Pickett was advanced to division level and Brig. General Richard B. Garnett took over the brigade. (95 miles.)

September 14, 1862 - Battle of South Mountain, Maryland: About 11:00 o'clock on this Sunday morning Garnett's Brigade was ordered to South Mountain near Boonsboro, a march of approximately 16 miles, to halt the advance of the advance of Major General George B. McClellan's Federal troops. The 18th Regiment was now down to only 120 men lead by seven officers with three companies lead by sergeants. Reaching the mountain top late in the

200

afternoon, after an ascent of some 14 miles, Captain Owen reported that a count of the five regiments totaled 407 men with an average of just 81 per regiment and only 8 to each company, many having fallen out due to the heat and exhaustion. The little brigade encountered heavy fire from the enemy immediately after reaching the top. The greatly outnumbered Confederates fought very hard until sunset when they were driven back suffering severe casualties. The 18th had losses of 7 killed, 27 wounded and 7 missing.

September 16, 1862 - Marched to Antietam Creek, MD (12 miles)

September 16 - 19, 1862 - Battle of Antietam Creek, (Sharpsburg) Maryland. Total estimated casualties: 23,100. After the Battle of South Mountain, where the 18th had lost over one-third of its troops, on September 17 it was engaged in the bloodiest single day of the war.. On September 16, Hooker's corps had confronted Lee's Army of Northern Virginia at Sharpsburg.

At sunrise on the 17th, Hooker launched an attack on Lee's left flank. Attacks and counterattacks swept across Miller's cornfield and Dunker's Church. The Union assaults against the Sunken Road eventually pierced the center of the Confederate line but this advantage was not followed up. Garnett's brigade, which included the 18th Regiment was on the Confederate right in support of several artillery batteries during the morning. In mid-afternoon the Union lines shifted to Lee's right and massive attacks were launched from the woods adjacent to Antietam Creek buckling the Confederate line and causing the brigade to fall back. Late in the day Burnside's corps went into action and crossed the stone bridge over Antietam Creek. A. P Hill's division then arrived from Harper's Ferry and drove Burnside's forces back. Gen. Lee was outnumbered more than two-to-one but sent in his entire force, while McClellan sent in less than three-fourths of his army, enabling Lee to fight the Union forces to a standstill. Darkness brought an end to the fighting.

The 18th Regiment was directly engaged for just three hours but had 4 killed and 27 wounded leaving just 44 men. During the night, both sides reorganized their lines.

Throughout September 18th, Lee continued to skirmish with McClellan while removing the wounded south of the Potomac. After nightfall, Lee ordered his battered army to withdraw across the Potomac.

September, 1862 - Marched to Winchester and camped. (45 miles) The regiment was down to 25 men.

November 7, 1862 - Camped at Culpeper Court House (75 miles)

December 14,1862- Camped near Fredericksburg. (45 miles)

January, February, 1863 - Camped four miles south of Guinea Station (15 miles)

February 10, 1863 - Capt. Owen took leave of absence at Guinea Station.

Late in February 1863 - The Division marched south to Petersburg. (75 miles)

March 2, 1863 - Capt. Owen joined the Regiment at Petersburg.

March 9, 1863 - Took train to Tarboro, North Carolina. (115 miles)

March 12, 1863 - March toward Greenville, North Carolina and camped. (20 miles)

March 13, 1863 - Marched toward Washington, North Carolina and camped at Great Swamp Church. (15 miles)

March 15, 1863 - Marched toward Williamston and camped (15 miles)

March 16, 1863 - Marched toward Williamston and camped at Siloam Church. (12 miles)

March 17, 1863 - Marched back to Siloam Church and camped. (12 miles)

March 18, 1863 - Marched toward Plymouth and camped. (10 miles)

March 21, 1863 - Marched back to Siloam Church and camped. (10 miles)

March 22, 1863 - Marched to Williamston and camped two miles from town. (15 miles)

March 23, 24, 1863 - Marched through swamps crossing the Tar River and camped at Great Swamp Church. (20 miles)

March 29, 1863 - Marched toward Washington, N. C. (7 miles).

March 30, 1863 - Marched toward Washington N.C. via Pactolus. (17 miles.)

March 31, 1863 - Marched and camped in sight of Washington N.C.. (5 miles)

Late April, 1863 - Marched to Tarboro N.C. (52 miles)

April, 1863 - Boarded train for Suffolk, Virginia, passed through Franklin. (100 miles)

May 5, 1863 - Started March to Richmond via Petersburg. (85 miles)

Early June - Marched to Hanover Junction Va. (22 miles)

June 8, 1863 - Started March to Culpeper Court House reaching there on June 12. (100 miles)

June 15, 1863 - Started March to Warrenton arriving on June 16. (30 miles)

June 17, 1863 - Started March to Paris, Va. reaching there on June 18. (31 miles)

June 20, 1863 - Marched to Berryville, Va. (15 miles)

June 24, 1863 - Marched from Berryville passing through Martinsburg WV on the 25th. (38 miles)

June 26, 1863 - Marched through Hagerstown, MD, and camped near Greencastle PA. (37 miles)

June 27, 1863 - Marched through Greencastle and Chambersburg and camp 2 miles from town. 17 miles)

June 29, 1863 - Marched back through Chambersburg and camped 2 miles from town. (4 miles)

July 2, 1863 - Marched through Chambersburg to Gettysburg. and camped. (27 miles).

July 3, 1863 - The Third Day of the Battle of Gettysburg, about 3 P.M., the 18th Regiment, as a part of Garnett's Brigade and Pickett's Division, were ordered to attack the center of the Federal gun positions on Cemetery Ridge. The Federal artillery was followed by a hail of musket fire, which cut the Confederate lines to pieces as they advanced across the wheat field. The Union line was momentarily breached and was driven back but the Confederates were overwhelmed and fell back with severe casualties. Of the 1,427 men of the brigade, 941 were killed, wounded or captured. Losses in the 18th were again, the highest in the brigade with 50 dead, 77 wounded and 104 missing. Lt. Col Carrington was wounded and captured. The Regimental Adjutant was missing.

During the three days of battle, in which over 83,000 Union and 75,000 Confederate troops were engaged, the estimated casualties were 23,000 Union and 28,000 Confederate.

July 4, 1863 - The regiment, which now numbered just 50 men, started the long march back to Virginia. The brigade was assigned to guarding the prisoners taken at Gettysburg. Due to the small number of men left in the brigade, General Lee expressed concern about its capability to perform the guard duty. Henry Owen was the only Captain left and was in command of the regiment after Lt. Col. Carrington was wounded and captured at Gettysburg. After the regiment's adjutant was missing at Gettysburg, Capt. Owen found his horse near the battlefield and rode it on the march back to Virginia. On July 18, 1863, Henry wrote his wife Harriet that the regiment had guarded two hundred officers and three hundred privates for eight days during the march from Gettysburg.

July 7, 1863 - Passed through Hagerstown and camped near Williamsport. (58 miles)

July 9, 1863 - Marched to Martinsburg (WV) and camped 3 miles from town (21 miles)

July 18, 1863 - Marched to Bunker Hill WV and camped. (14 miles)

July 19, 1863 - Marched to Winchester VA. (14 miles)

July 22, 1863 - Marched to Front Royal and camped (25 miles)

July 24, 1863 - Marched to Culpeper Court House and camped. (51 miles)

September 7, 1863 - Encamped in Orange County. (25 miles)

September 27, 1863 - Encamped near Petersburg. (100 miles)

September 28, 1863 – Ordered to City Point. (75 miles)

December 21, 1863 – Barracks in Richmond. (95 miles)

June 16, 1864 - Marched south from Richmond and battled with Federals at Chester Station driving them back to Bermuda Hundred. Regimental losses were 9 killed and 8 wounded..
(16 miles) The 18th spent most of the remainder of 1864 south of Richmond.

December 22, 1864 - Marched to Richmond (16 miles) and boarded train for Gordonsville to reinforce rail junction. (70 miles.)

December 26, 1864 - Boarded train for Richmond, (70 miles) and marched back to trenches north of Petersburg. (16 miles)

March 10, 1865 - Marched to Richmond (18 miles) and boarded train for Farmville (65 miles).

March 29, 1865 - Boarded train for Richmond (65 miles) and marched to Petersburg. (24 miles.)

March 31, 1865 - Attacked a full Federal Division near Petersburg and drove them back 10 killed, 6 wounded and 36 captured. All of regimental staff killed or wounded.

April 1, 1865 - Marched westward to reinforce other three brigades of the division, which had been attacked on March 31 at Five Forks by Sheridan's cavalry and Warren's corps where the Confederate forces were outnumbered five to one.

April 3, 1865 - Acting as rear guard as Lee's army made its westward retreat from Petersburg, the regiment had several skirmishes with Union cavalry over the next three days during a constant march without food or sleep. On April 6, Lee's army reached Sayler's Creek, near Farmville, after a march of approximately 90 miles.

April 6, 1865 - Battle of Sayler's Creek: Total estimated casualties, 9,980. After Hunton's Brigade and the remainder of Pickett's Division had crossed the creek and were moving up a steep hill they came under attack from Union cavalry and were forced to halt about a mile from the creek. The Union cavalry was reinforced but the Confederate line held. A second Union Charge bent but did not penetrate the line. A third Union charge was made and the lines on Hunton's flanks were breached. Around 5 P.M. the reinforced Federals overwhelmed the Confederate lines by their sheer numbers, inflicting heavy casualties and capturing the Regimental Flag. Eight Confederate Generals surrendered that day: Ewell, Barton, Kershaw, Custis Lee, Dubose, Hunton and Corse. At General Robert E. Lee's surrender at Appomattox three days later, only 43 members of the 18th Regiment were present.

CHAPTER 13 – CONCERNS FOR THE HOME FRONT AND POST WAR CONCERNS

"---(Let me Know) Also how the cow skins came out of the bank. If I stay here long I will see if I can have you and the children some shoes made from the skins"
Henry T. Owen - February 8, 1864

The South was a very different place after the war. All the men who served on both sides, and lived to talk about it, had been changed by the war experience. While still fighting the war, Henry told Harriet to send him her Confederate money and he would get it exchanged for Federal money. Henry advised Harriet to save everything she could. Henry knew, as did all Southerners, that life after the war was going to be difficult.

In one letter to Harriet, Henry mentions the price of cotton increasing after the war.

****

Barracks 7th & King
Richmond Va
Feb 8, 1864

My dear Harriet,

Nothing has occurred since my return to interest you and I spend a lonesome time here with nothing to occupy my time.

Mr. Irving appeared pleased with his trip and promised to return in a short time.

I got a letter from Pat yesterday. He was in Lynchburg and quite well. His Regt has just gone back to the field and his Co begged him to go with them but he wisely declined. I saw Sam Wilson Scott in Richmond last week and he took me to Mr. Brown's. His bro-in-law's C----- has not altered a particle that I can see and she chatted away just as she always did. They have no children and Brown has made a fortune since the War.

Pryor has gotten out and has a chance to go back to the Reserve Inf Corps but says he does not wish to go and wants to remain with me. I shall let him do as he pleases in this matter as I am willing for him to have his choice.

Let me know how C ----- has gotten and if she is quite well. Also how the cow skins came out of the bank. If I stay here long I will see if I can have you and the children some shoes made from the skins.

Let me know whether Cousin Bettie has agreed to take the school or not.

I wrote to Tom Campbell about the cotton but have not heard from him and think if Mr. C----- wants any cotton he had better buy it in Richmond. I could get it last week for $2 but as is going up every day and while he is fooling with Campbell cotton will go up two pnds. I could not find any oats in market at all but will continue to look out for them.

My love to all

Yrs truly etc.

Henry

****

Part of Harriet's life after the war was her appointment as the Postmaster of Green Bay, Virginia.

****

(No. 1835)

AEA

POST OFFICE DEPARTMENT

Office of the 1st Ass't Postmaster General

Washington, D.C. Dec. 7, 1885

Sir:

The Postmaster General has ordered the appointment of Mrs. Harriet A. Owen as Postmaster at Green Bay in the County of Prince Edward and State of Va., in the place of T.J. Price - Removed.

Very respectfully,

K.T. Thomson

First Assistant Postmaster General

Hon. Geo. C.. Cabell
House of Reps,
City

****

The authors are impressed that after the war much correspondence went back and forth between messmates either attempting to locate someone or recall events of the war.

****

Oaks Warehouse Company
Petersburg VA.
March 28th 1897

STITH BOLLING
WM. B. BEASLEY
Capt. H. T. Owen
Richmond Va.
My Dear Sir,

Yours of this date rec'd. I will in a few days send you a list of members of the old company who will likely subscribe to the History of the 9th Va. Cav. and I am sure every one who is able to pay for it will take at least one copy. I should be very glad to see the roll of Co. G before it is published and if it is a copy of a roll I saw published in one of the Richmond papers some time ago it is by no means correct.

I am very truly yours,
Stith Bolling
****

In the following letter from P. W. McKinney to Henry, another facet of Henry is observed – that of financial advisor.

****

Law office of
P. W. McKINNEY
Farmville Va., Jany 7th 1898

Henry T. Owen, Esq.
2nd Auditor's Office Richmond, Va.
Dear Henry,

Will you not be kind enough to look after a little matter for me and give me your judgment with respect to it?

Of course, the information will be entirely confidential. I have five or six shares of stock in the Mutual Guarantee Building and Loan Association of Richmond. I have been paying all of its requirements for nearly three years and the men who compose the company since the death of C. V. Tanner are strangers to me. I have some five or six shares of stock in it and will be glad if you ill inquire whether it is a safe and proper place to invest my money, and to keep the monthly expenses on some five or six shares.

So far it has moved along beautifully, but how it will get along when it has lost its lead I do not know and I wish you would advise me with reference to it. Whether it will be a safe place to continue to invest a few shares.

I send you a list of its officers.

I hope the New Year finds you and your family well.

With all the compliments of the season

I am very truly yrs

P. W. McKinney

I enclose list of officers of the Company.
****

Henry, the author, obviously did a great deal of writing. In the following two letters Roger Pryor rejects two of his manuscripts.
****

74 –76 Wall St. N. Y.

May 16, 1876

Dear Sir,

In compliance with your request I have this day mailed the manuscript. It is a valuable, and to me a very interesting paper; but there is no call here for literature of that character. I tried in vain to dispose of it. Its length precluded its publication. I regret I could not serve you more effectually.

Very truly,

Roger A. Pryor
****

76 Wall St. N.Y. City

15th April 1878

My dear Colonel,

The parcel was duly received and I will endeavor to dispose of them all for your advantage.

I fear, however, that it is impossible to sell it. Indeed, if we can secure its publication I shall be surprised.

The interest in the war is absolutely extinct here and our journals are monopolized by the occurrences of the day.

I am happy to hear of your affairs and to be appraised of your message.

The wealth of my experts shall be communicated.

Very sincerely

Roger A. Pryor

****
Not discouraged, Henry submitted manuscripts to several newspapers in Virginia and several to the Philadelphia Times. Several of these manuscripts were printed. (See also Chapter 15.)
****
This article was written by H.T. Owen and published in a newspaper. Date and Newspaper are unknown.

(Communicated)

A Lecture Upon The State Debt by a Tramp

It was Thursday evening about 4 o'clock, as cold as Christmas, the wind, from due North blowing like the mischief and snowing out doors like all wrath, while five or six of us fellows congregated in front of a roaring hot fire in the counting-room of Ned Dixon's store at the Cross Roads, and were having a hilarious time telling long yarns, when an old tramp came shuffling and shivering up to the door and asked "if he might warm a bit by our fire." Ned replied, "Of course you can"- and the tramp giving his old hat a slap or two against the door facing and kicking the clotted snow from his old shoes came in.

He appeared to be about sixty or sixty-five years of age, a tall, gaunt figure, with long, tangled white beard, and matted gray locks, both wet and dripping with the melted snow; his ragged pants and faded, threadbare coat were patched, with divers colors, in many places, and each needed many more to cover the gaping seams and widened rents through which the freezing blast of winter found easy passage; his well worn slouch hat had holes in the top, and his old shoes, snow worn, had holes in their bottoms.

He carried a dirty bundle, hugged close under his left arm, and as he kept turning and warming before the fire, with his wet garments smoking like a tar kiln, he appeared unmoved by the boisterous glee which suddenly checked by the old tramp's entrance, had soon began again with renewed strength in loud roars of laughter following each good jest.

As the boys showed no impertinent curiosity to inquire his name or business, whence he came nor where going, there were few words from him, but these few were polite, to the point and satisfactory. His sad melancholy face told of campaigns of adversity and suffering, and a restless eye casting occasional, uneasy glances around the room, and then peering anxiously through the half open door out upon the raging storm and gathering gloom of rapidly approaching night, betokened some apprehension or restlessness.

After warming half an hour he said; "He wondered if there was such a thing as an out-house close at hand, where he could sleep in the shucks, for it is a fearful bad night to stop out upon the moor." To this Ned Dixon replied; "Old gent, if you will permit me to display my unlimited love of hospitality and will condescend to accept my invitation to partake of my bachelor fare, you can set at my board and enjoy the soothing influence of toasting your feet before this fire. -My daddy before me was always afflicted with a mania for taking in the wayfarer and used to bet he might some time or other entertain an angel. I am, by inheritance, of like temper, following in the wake of my sire with better chances of success if the number of traveling angels are in proportion to the number of strangers that vex us."

To this the old man replied, "I am no angel," and Ned said; "Well, to be candid, you do not exactly come up to my idea of an angel, but then you may be disguised, and I should say pretty well disguised too; and I would not expect you to admit it, as that would seriously impair the romance of my dream and rob me of all credit. Your gravel grinders do not resemble the pictures I have seen of the sandals worn by the ancients, for theirs had bottoms and no tops - yours have tops and bad bottoms, but I suppose something is due to change of time, season and climate, and especially to snow in place of sand. In the morning I shall try to sell you a new pair or swap you an old pair, so I hope you will allay all excitement about the weather and try to rejoice in the prospects before you."

The old tramp gazed at Ned for a few moments in wonder and then settled down in the corner, evidently at more ease if not decidedly happy, and when Ned's supper was soon after brought in he partook heartily of ham and eggs, coffee, bread, butter etc., and then moving back into the corner proceeded to unwrap his bundle and dry its contents, consisting of a few old ragged garments, a lot of newspapers, pamphlets, and two or three books, at sight at which someone remarked he must be a traveling magazine of information and was evidently possessed of a literary turn of mind, and his stock at once rose to fifty-seven per cent. Observing among other things drying before the fire the "annual report of the auditor of Public Accounts, " Ned asked him to tell us what he thought of the Virginia State Debt, and the tramp said:

"I can make nothing by talking about a matter that does not concern me, and must hesitate to express opinions upon a subject so serious that the truth, which alone should be spoken, will probably subject me to your displeasure."

Being assured by Ned that we could stand quite a lot of serious facts without getting sick; in fact were already complaining for the want of truth, he picked up the Auditor's Report and proceeded thus:

"An oath is a solemn declaration with an appeal to God for its truth," and any form of certificate appended to effect a purpose, assumes the dignity of an oath, and is so recognized in law.

The real estate of Virginia is assessed by persons chosen by the County Judges for that especial purpose, freeholders and residents only being selected with a view to procure the services of Commissioners honest, honorable, well fitted and capable of discharging the duties of their offices faithfully and fairly to the people and for the Commonwealth.

"The law clearly intended that these Commissioners should visit and view each tract or parcel of land within their jurisdiction and assess its value, together with the improvements thereon, before making a report to which was appended the form of an oath which they signed certifying that the duties required had been performed according to law. Yet, in many instances these land Commissioners passed along the public highways and assessed farms and buildings by whole neighborhoods and districts five or ten miles square upon their right and left and never saw any houses or lots except those situated upon the line of their hasty journeys.

In many cases these assessments were complained of as too high, but no instance occurs where a land owner has come to the front and complained that his property was assessed too low.

A farm with all of its improvements of dwelling, barn, stable, orchards etc, is valued at $800, while the owner has his dwelling alone insured for $2,500.

This is a case in point, and your judges, jurors and legislators are all aware that suits are constantly decided in the State Court against Insurance companies for the destruction of property by fire insured at five, ten, or twenty times the sworn value of the same property upon your land books."

213

By some strange course of argument you have convinced yourselves that it is right and proper to swear twice to two entirely different and contradictory reports setting forth the actual value of your property and have simply committed perjury in placing your estimate of insurance too high, and again in placing your assessment for taxation too low.

In some counties your horses are all colts, your cows all calves, your sheep all lambs, your hogs all pigs, and your watches all galvanized brass.

One cow in Clarke is worth more than two in Craig, more than six in Grayson, or three in Nansemond.

There are fifty watches more in Fauquier than in Fairfax, but these fifty (or something else) make a difference between the watches of more than seven thousand dollars. There are only eighteen watches more in Rockbridge than in Shenandoah, and yet there is a difference between the watches of the two counties amounting to nearly eleven thousand dollars. A watch in Roanoke is worth ten watches in Wythe.

The clocks in Sussex are worth ten dollars, in Warwick two dollars, in Highland one dollar. In Alexandria the goats are worth three dollars, in Amherst one dollar, in Gloucester sixty cents, in New Kent four dollars, in North Daville fifty cents.

The hogs in Blaud are valued at eighty-six cents, in Fairfax at three dollars, in Loudon at three dollars, in Carroll and Grayson at about ninety cents.

The same discrepancies exist in regard to the estimate placed by different counties upon pleasure carriages, sewing machines, books, farming implements and all species of property.

The election law of Virginia requires the prepayment of the State capitation tax of one dollar to secure the right to vote. There is a county of 3,000 voters with a delinquent list of 1,200, as appears from the County Treasurer's return, on 1st July or soon thereafter. This law was in force at the November election 1877 and the Auditor's Report for the fiscal year commencing on the 30th September, 1877, should contain some statement of the amount of capitation tax paid into County Clerks on and before the November election - which it does not. If there are 1,200 delinquent tax payers in August, and 800 vote at the November election there are really only 400 delinquents in the final report which should appear upon the Auditor's books.

214

It should be the duty of the Supervisors of election returns to compare the names upon the poll book with the Auditor's delinquent list to see that those who vote are not counted as delinquent.

The Commissioners of the Revenue will inform you that in taking lists of property they find some men willing to swear their sheep are worth only fifty cents per head, hogs fifty cents, cows five dollars, and mules and horses twenty-five dollars, while other men upon neighboring farms will estimate their sheep at two dollars, their hogs at three or five dollars, their cows at twenty or thirty, and their horses and mules at one hundred dollars apiece.

Any increase of ten or twenty cents upon the hundred dollars worth of property will bear hard upon the latter as they value their oath, while the former will beat you swearing and by placing their property at half price escape the increase taxation. No appeal by women, by preachers, and by politicians can reach the man who estimates his property at half price for taxation, and swears to the assessment, and the next day insures it at twice its real value and swears to that estimate also; the man who looks upon the Legislature as a set of gamblers searching out new schemes for appropriation of the State funds, in which they take shares; the man who during the war played lame, played blind, played deaf, and now to encourage immigration is anxious to organize colonization societies with Virginia money to ship men from among the North British and Scotch Irish, and work houses, orphan asylums and chain gangs of New England, while the Virginians whose fathers fell in defense of the soil, emigrate South and West more rapidly than the navies of the world could bring foreigners to fill their places."

Here Ned coughed and said it was bed time, and the tramp retired to his pallet and was soon fast asleep.

****

Owen Family Papers

Apparently the article drew a good bit of comment in political circles. The article was mentioned in later letters to Henry.

****

215

CHAPTER 14 – THE WAR WITH POLITICS AND THE LEGISLATURE

"There will be a lot of green young clerks for me to teach and all their mistakes will fall on me and for many months I should have the whole office to run."
Henry T. Owen - December 17, 1881

Henry T. Owen was outspoken. He actively wrote and said exactly what he thought. There was much discussion about what really happened in Gettysburg. This information is covered in Chapter 10. It seems around 1879, politics drove its way into the Auditor's Office of Virginia where Henry worked. Then around 1881, Henry expresses his views on political corruption.

Henry worked as 3rd Clerk in the state Auditor's Office under Harry Dyson. The 1st Clerk was Shackleford, whom Henry referred to as "Shack." The 2nd Clerk was F. G. Morrison. The political intrusion began when a delegation from the 4th Congressional District tried to change the make up of the Auditor's Office. The squabble became so intense that it made the newspaper and involved Henry in a fist fight with an opponent.

In this first letter of the grouping, William Mahone writes Harry Dyson or perhaps the recipient is unknown and he copies the letter to Dyson. Mahone warns against straying from the protocol for appointment to the office of Clerk in the 2nd Auditor's Office. He mentions irregularities in the bookkeeping. He ends by suggesting a complete inventory be done.

****

Petersburg
Dec. 30, 1879

My dear Sir,

I take the liberty and I feel I may do so with you to suggest that in making appointments to desks in your office that you adhere fully and rigidly to the programme which has been laid down by the care and from which you received your nomination; that is to say, that you shall make no appointment which has not the sanction and approval of the Committee on Nominations. I assume that as yet you have not made assignments to the desks in your Bureau, but be that as it may, I would advise you to let them be made with absolute regard to the programme. It would not be wise in my opinion, to enter upon the duties of your office with an entirely new force, with none acquainted with the duties of the same, in its entirety or in detail. Such a course would involve you and your assistants in a world of unnecessary trouble, if not your office, in incredible confusion. The easier, and therefore the better plan, would be to make your removals by degrees. First establishing your right hand man, who, being bright and quick, would soon familiarize himself with the duties, not only his own, but of the subordinate desks and thus when the work of expurgation shall have been completed, as I take it for granted that your purpose will be to purge your bureau of every clerk, you will find an open course for comfortable sailing. My conviction is that the clerks in this office are by far the most objectionable in the capitol, and the reasons which concluded the caucus readjusters to substitute you for General Rogers obtains an even greater force in respect to his assistants, and my judgment is that their removal, in the manner indicated, is due as well to yourself as to the party which has placed you in position. I seems to be an impression, I cannot say with what foundation in fact, that there can be found great irregularities in the Second Auditor's Office, to reach and remedy which will take time, patience and skill. Irregularities, doubtless, to be traced to the number of different administrations of the office and possibly reaching back to the organization of this Bureau. I have no reason to suspect, nor do I believe that any wrong in act or intent, attaches personally to your immediate predecessor or his staff nor any of his predecessors or their employees, still this impression has been prevalent. Therefore, I would, as a prudential caution, were I in your place, demand an inventory specified in detail of assets and property especially of the books, before I entered in the duties, or gave receipt to the outgoing officer. This on mere business principles is the proper thing but in respect to the retiring and incoming Auditor. Further immediately on the reassembling of the legislature I would demand and insist on a rigid and perfect investigation of the office, at least from the inception lf the public debt to the date of your installation so that you man enter upon an unimpeded and perfectly open tract, and the people may learn at last, what heretofore they have never been able to obtain a certain, undisputed and undisputable statement of the financial condition of the State.

I am very sure that you will appreciate the motives of this letter to be of personal regard for yourself as well as to the people and their party, now dominant, in equal degree.

Confidentially your friend
Wm Mahone

Mr. Treasurer Dyson

****

In a letter penned to his wife, Henry laments that his job keeps him from home and mentions the political mess his office is embroiled in.

****

Richmond Va
17th Dec 1881

Dear Wife,

I have had a busy day and now set down tired and weary to write instead of the intended happy intention of sending myself up to see you. I had hoped all the week to get off to my wife's house Saturday night if not before but work has increased instead of diminishing and I will not now be able to come up before the 30th of Dec. That will be next Friday week. There are a half million dollars of coupons to list and I can do the work as rapidly - so it is said - as any man ever in the office, but there will not be a moment to lose if I can get through with them in two weeks.

I begin work at 7 ½ and work till after 3 o'clock without ever raising my head or speaking a word unless I am called off to attend to other pressing business.

I have been very lonesome since the little boys left for home. I put them on the cars and when it rolled away over the river I felt sad and lonely in the midst of a great crowd. They were company for me and I wish I could keep them with me all the time provided you could be along too.

If I remain here next year I shall make some arrangement for you to come down and stay with me but there is a great quarrel going on here over the different Offices and a big fight is made my Mr. Massie's enemies to remove him and his friends from Office. I may not succeed in getting a place after all. I do not know when the election of the Capitol Officers will take place and it may be after Christmas. Mr. Dyson wants me for First Clerk in place of Mr. Shackleford who will be turned out but I am not willing to assume the great responsibility of First Clerk in this Office. I would much

219

prefer my present position to any more responsible place. I understand my present duties thoroughly and can do as much at this desk as any man in the State but to take a new desk with new work and without the assistance of Morrisson and Shack is more than I am willing to undertake.

There will be a lot of green young clerks for me to teach and all their mistakes will fall on me and for many months I should have the whole office to run.

Write to me and let me know how the little boys liked their trip.

Yrs very truly
H. T. Owen
****

Henry speaks out in a newspaper article he writes to the Editor of a paper on February 10, 1892. He is incensed all three clerks were selected by a caucus and Harry Dyson was not consulted. Henry has been removed from his job and an inexperienced boy installed in his place. The same caucus demands that Henry be appointed 1st Clerk. The 2nd Clerk is a stranger to Dyson. Again, this article mentions bookkeeping irregularities that a legislative committee has brought to the attention of the office and the public. Letter to the Editor - written by H.T. Owen - February 10, 1882. Newspaper unknown.

****

Communicated

We have been requested by the gentleman to whom the following letter was addressed to give it to our readers;

Dear Sir,

The resolution adopted by the Readjuster caucus, as explained by members of both houses (whose names will be given if required) and as it was understood by a majority, no doubt, meant to allow the heads of the different bureaus the right to appoint their first clerk from any section with the privilege of selecting their other clerks also, provided they confined their choice to certain congressional districts. Now look how the resolution was made to work in the Second Auditor's Office after Dyson submitted to the caucus rule.

In the distribution of patronage the Fourth district was entitled to two clerkships in the Second Auditor's Office. Yet, Capt.

Owen, who is from the Fourth district, a Republican and a Readjuster, with two years' experience in the office, was removed by the district caucus and a Negro boy from the Fourth district, whom Dyson never knew before he appeared in the office, was installed at Owen's desk. It now appears that the district caucus met again last week and wrote a joint letter to Dyson asking him to appoint Owen his first clerk, and demanded his resignation in case he refused to do so is second clerk comes from the Fifth or Seventh district and has already been selected by the members from that district. He is an entire stranger to Dyson, whose character and fitness for the duties required he knows nothing. Now, then, what rights has Dyson under the license assumed or practiced under this abominable caucus resolution? All three of his clerks have been selected for him and thrust upon him without his opinion being asked or his feelings or interest in the matter consulted, and in the face of the fact that a legislative committee, at a cost to the State of about $7,000, has just unearthed a startling robbery of more than $90,000 in coupons stolen from the Second Auditor's Office, and in face of the fact that Dyson and his securities are bound to the State to keep records safe, correct, and secure; and, lastly, what allegiance, what obligation, do these three clerks, who obtained their places from other men and were imposed on Dyson against his will and in violation of the letter and spirit of even the caucus resolution itself, as well as contrary to the rules of law and the principles of good government, owe Dyson? Do the Readjuster members, or rather do all of them, know these things and quietly submit to the outrage? Will the people sanction it or indorse their actions?

Yours, very respectfully, &c.,
A Readjuster upon principle
February 10, 1882

Owen Family Papers

****

Henry writes to explain what is going on in the 2nd Auditor's Office. He says the trouble is caused by a delegation from the 4th Congressional District. They have demanded the removal of the 1st Clerk, Henry's friend, Shackleford. They have recommended Henry fill that slot. Henry declines to do that and he tells the reader why. They have removed Henry as 3rd Clerk and put in his place a boy with no experience. Henry expresses his loyalty to Harry Dyson

****

Richmond Va. 21st Feb. 1882

Mssrs. C. H. Bliss
    N. H. Champlin
    A.W. Harris and Others

Gentlemen

Two weeks ago the entire Delegation (15 members) from the 4th Congressional District signed a joint letter, directed to Mr. Dyson, demanding of him the removal of Mr. Shackelford as First Clerk in the Second Auditor's Office and recommending one to fill that position, and I now understand the Caucus intends tonight to insist upon this change being made by Mr. Dyson at once. Allow me Gentlemen to say I have never sought the position of First Clerk in Mr. Dyson's Office, that I have not desired the place and that I now positively decline to accept it under any circumstances. There are several reasons either one of which would itself be sufficient to induce me to refuse to accept the promotion you seek unasked to impose on me.

1st. When the head of the different state offices agreed by letter to submit to the terms of your Caucus Resolution it was stipulated that they should have the privilege of choosing their First Clerks. You now deny them this right when you attempt to select any man and thrust him upon them without their consent. 'Tis true the Caucus has disapproved Mr. Dyson's choice of First Clerk as they request the right to do, but the objections raised to Mr. S. cannot be applied to the experienced clerks in the Treasury and the Land Office who are true and tried readjusters and furthermore if for any reason you find fault with the selections made by the Heads of Bureaus the Resolution by no means confers upon you the right of appointment and I cannot allow you to make me a party to this infraction of your own compact.

2nd. When the Legislature convened you found me Third Clerk in Mr. Dyson's Office with two years experience at a desk where I had given entire satisfaction and wished to remain, yet you removed me and placed in my stead a boy who has no knowledge of book keeping, no idea of the clerical duties of the desk he occupies except as he is then taught by others and whose sole and only recommendation over other men is that he is black.

You also propose to put some other new untrained man at the 2nd Clerk's Desk and then, contrary to my wishes or Mr. Dyson's plans, place me at the head of this raw set, to teach them, do my own laborious work, and shoulder the responsibility of the Second Auditor's Office in Mr. Dyson's absence.

Lastly, I owed my appointment in the Sec Aud Office entirely to the friendship of Mr. Dyson and had no one to recommend me for the place I occupied then. I taught him his alphabet and his first four years at school was under my instruction.

I was ten years afterwards his Captain in the War and more than thirty years we have allowed no one or more persons to interfere either to impair our friendship or to settle our quarrels. Regretting the necessity of this letter I am gentlemen

Yrs respectfully
H. T. Owen

****

FROM THE SCRAP BOOK OF HENRY T. OWEN

Page 195, Newspaper clipping (No date)

"New Clerk in the Second Auditor's Office"

Yesterday morning Captain H.E. Owens, third assistant clerk in the Second Auditor's office, was displaced and a colored man, named R.B. Baptist, of Mecklenburg County, put in his place.

Captain Owen was twice elected to the command of a company in the Eighteenth Virginia regiment of infantry during the war and was a gallant and faithful soldier.

He has been a well known Readjuster, but had to walk the plank in order to gratify the colored senator from Mecklenburg, through whose influence Baptist secured the position.

is in the prime of life, and has had excellent educational advantages, and will no doubt obey caucus rule and party orders with perfect willingness and The new clerk went to work yesterday and it was observed he wrote rapidly and a good hand, and was apt and correct at mathematical calculations. He thereby becomes a proper office-holder.

Owen Family Papers

****

2nd Newspaper clipping (No date)

"VIRTUE IS IT'S OWN REWARD"

How pleasant it is for the heroic survivors of many hard-fought battles who were unfortunate enough to live after their brave comrades had fallen, to look around them and enjoy the fruits of their patriotic sacrifices on the altar of their country's honor.

Fat, greasy, bomb-proof, cowardly cravins that ran into their holes when red battle stamped our old Commonwealth with blood are now the pets of a prostituted government, while the maimed and war-scared soldier is ignored or despised. What a hideous example the corrupt, cowardly and ungrateful human jackals and jackasses of this generation are placing before the next! Heroism and patriotism is punished, while cowardly treason is rewarded. All the soft places of State and Federal Government alike are kept for mercenaries, who like Job's war horse "attended the battle from afar off," while the true men and brave soldiers stand aloof to view the men they suffered to promote. With such rewards as the Government offers to abject cowards and corrupt poltroons by promoting them over good and true men, we may reasonably expect the next generation to be a race of mercenary knaves that will refuse to fight for their own families and firesides.

We were pained to notice last week, a gallant Confederate captain, that stood the heat of the battle and the fatigue of the march through many a hard campaign, removed from a poor clerkship to make room for a fat, young African just from college. The captain we refer to was a brave officer and when old Virginia was passing through agony and bloody sweat he came promptly to the front in her defense. He has a large family to support, and he is a member of the new and successful political party. Yet he was removed by his friends to make room for a fat, young freedman who has no family to support. Well may the factor of such events repeat the words of the boiled prophet of Khororsan: "See if hell, with all its powers to damn can add one curse to the foul thing I am." Even the foul prejudices of the most narrow minded, bigoted and malignant partisan will fail to justify such paltry treason against nature as the base act betrays. Shame on the dirty despots that do such unclean work! "I'd rather be a dog and bay the moon than such a Roman!"

Owen Family Papers

****

Third Newspaper clipping (No Date)

Captain H.T. Owen, a gallant ex-Confederate, who was removed some weeks ago to make room for a Readjuster Negro, has been appointed to a temporary place in the second auditor's office.

Owen Family Papers

****

Fourth Newspaper clipping (No Date)

Somebody will get hurt before this Legislature adjourns. It has just leaked out that Mr. Owens, the Capitol clerk discharged some weeks since and a Negro substitute, in the auditor's office put in his place, has found out that a certain member of the House was instrumental in having him (Owens) discharged. Late Tuesday night, or rather early yesterday morning, Owens went to the member's room and told him to get up and dress himself, as he was going to thrash him. The member dressed himself and they went into a rough-and-tumble fight, keeping it up until both got out of wind, when a member coming to the rescue they declared a truce. The most ludicrous part of the fisticuff was the crying out of the attacking party in the midst of the melee not to strike his vaccinated arm, and his opponent was so considerate as to respect the request of the man who was thrashing him. After pummeling the delegate, Owens added insult to injury by making the delegate drink with him. The fight is the subject of much amusement among the legislators.

Owen Family Papers

****

Henry's friends apparently supported him in this altercation and on Oct. 8, 1880 sent him a letter and 20 cents for his fine.
****

Commonwealth of Virginia
Land Office
Richmond Va. Oct 8th 1880

Capt Owen
Dear Sir,

Your friends, on duty at the Capitol, feeling a common cause with you in the matter of your recent difficulties, request the pleasure of settling the fine imposed. Upon our part, this is a spontaneous commendation and appreciation of your course coupled with a regret that chivalry should ever be forced to commit a breach of the peace in defense of manhood. Enclosed find 20 cents the amount of your fine, the privilege of paying which is demanded by your

Friends

****
C. Linkenhoker figures into the drama being played out in the Auditor's Office. He is supportive of Henry.
****

Commonwealth of Virginia
Second Auditor's Office
Richmond Sept 3rd 1882

Dear Capt.,
I came back to Richmond last Wednesday and was very sorry to hear that you was not coming back to Richmond but such is politics. If there is any thing that I can do for you, you will please let me know and I will willingly do it.

Politics will be tolerable lively this fall and I would not bet on any man's election. I have not any news to write. I hope to hear from you soon,

Your friend
C. Linkenhoker

Payne sends his pious
regards to you.

****
The authors know that Henry eventually landed in the position of 2nd Clerk in the Second Auditor's Office. One final letter on this subject was written much later from William Smith to Henry.
****

Hot Springs, Ark.
Jany 11th 1884

Capt H. T. Owen
Dear Capt,
I received your kind letter a few days ago and would have answered it at once, but I have been confined to my room for more than a week. I caught a dreadful cold and it settled in my eye and it has given me a good deal of pain, and even now, I can scarcely see to write.

I feel satisfied that Col Ruffin will make an excellent auditor and besides it will enable him to support his family. I am so glad he appointed you one of his clerks. Are you 2nd or 3rd Clerk?

I hope our Legislature will legislate for the good of the entire people and will not be radical or extreme in anything. They should carry out strictly the Lynchburg Platform. I think they have made a good beginning on the debt question. Genl Wickham will be a useful member of the Senate.

This is a wonderful place for the invalid but I would not advise a "seeker of pleasures" to come here. The people are the roughest you ever saw. I haven't seen a person here that does not swear "like a trooper" and a great many of the women do. No regard whatever is paid to the Sabbath and the town is literally run by a lot of gamblers. The civil authorities amount to nothing. I think a young man could make more money out here than he could in Virginia but his morals would soon be corrupted and the money would do him no good.

Every thing is very high here, board from $36.00 to $80.00, baths 50 cents, doctors $25.00 per month etc, etc.

A large hospital for the army and navy is being built here now and it will be a great thing for the poor soldier and sailor to come here and have his broken down constitution built up.

It is an outrage that everything is so high here. It precludes the "poor man" from getting the benefit of the baths and water.

The Government should never have sold the property and then it could be managed differently.

My eye is paining me so I will have to stop.

You must write me a long letter and tell me all the news. I will always be glad to hear from you.

Your friend truly,
William Smith

Direct to P.O. Box 101

****

As if the preceding correspondence did not introduce enough information about political corruption, more is revealed in the following letters on the eve of an election.

****

Richmond Va.
1881

Dear Sir,

Upon the eve of another campaign, which must prove decisive, we observe that never before, in the history of Virginia politics, did so many grave questions, each involving momentous, vital results, crowd together as now to claim the serious consideration of every citizen of the State and earnestly invoke the active support of every patriot for the party advocating Justice,

Progress, and Reform. Free Suffrage is the fundamental principle of Liberty, upon which depends freedom of conscience, free speech, a free press and religious toleration. A price fixed by law, per capita, for the privilege to vote, virtually sells the ballot and throws the delinquent suffrage upon the market at the mercy of political gamblers.

The School System appeals from past Legislation to the sense of honor and justice of a sovereign people, who control representation, for a redress of its wrongs. It claims only the legitimate rights and dues appropriated by the Constitution for its support and protests against persistent robbery and misappropriation of its funds to other purposes. Geographically made the arena of a long distinctive war, where vast armies swept away in their wrathful march, the wealth, the institutions, the very manner and customs of the inhabitants and, in wide sections, obliterating even the landmarks themselves with the force of a tidal wave. The barren land and impoverished people were burdened by an immense debt, based in great part on property destroyed by that war, without indemnity, and largely increased by fraud and compound interest. These are some of the issues at state in the approaching Gubernatorial contest, which must prove the fiercest conflict on record and result in the most signal victory or disastrous defeat in the annals of Virginia politics.

Wisdom as well as necessity, our present welfare, our future prosperity, the full development of the agricultural and mineral resources of our State depend upon and justice to the immigrants, justice to the widows, to the orphans, to ourselves and to posterity demand their readjustment. We must make this fight to win and in order to win we must have immediate and thorough organization of our forces and obtain from the other parties recruits to the number of 90,000. We must also nominate a candidate the most popular with the people, regardless of all personal preferences.

From the best information obtained here from all sections of the state it appears that our greatest hope of success lies in the nomination of Hon John E. Massey.

It is admitted by both friends and political opponents that Mr. Massey possesses great executive and administrative ability. His high moral character as a citizen and his known capacity and integrity as a legislator; his long experience in State affairs, having served several sessions in each house of the General Assembly; his thorough knowledge of the debt question, being the author of the principle laws to secure an honest administration of the public revenue; his position as a public man in the past and his broad and liberal views on State policy at present, all give assurance of a high toned and honest administration and particularly fit him to be the candidate of the party of Progress and Reform.

Ours is a new party with new issues, depending for success upon the number of voters obtained at the polls and our leader must be one who understands the power of honest reassuring and persuasive argument with the people and not seek by aggressive means to antagonize all men who exercise a right to differ in opinion with us. We ask that in the primary meetings called to select delegates to our nominating convention the people may be fairly represented and with an honest able leader popular principles and untrammeled by national issues we may enter the battle with every prospect and assurance of a grand and glorious victory in November next.

(Unsigned)
****

George H. Southall pens a letter to Harry H. Dyson in which he includes a short poem. He, also, asks for a favor from Mr. Dyson.
****

Lynchburg Virginia
Nov 20th 1881

Hon. H. H. Dyson
Dear Friend,

As the smoke of battle has cleared away and the peoples ticket has been fully vindicated by the large majority received against all tricks and subtifuges known to political tricksters and demagogs and unprincipal politicians that thought themselves the very elect but God in all his wise and infinite mercy decreed that they were not the elect but were pharasites like to be heard for their vain boastings and traducing others and crying aloud "we are not as other men are we are the very elite" and still crying aloud to the people "behold the earth is the Lord's and the fullness thereof to his Saints. We are the Virginia Saints, and Virginia, with all that it contains, is ours to dispose of at our own sweet will." The 8 of November has passed. A great revolution has taken place. Now behold the lamentations of the so-called elite Elect party crying aloud to the people "I recant, save me or I perish." The answer comes reverberating from the mountain valleys to the sea shore "depart ye workers of iniquity I know you not." The great Liberal reform party has triumphed. Virginia is free. Redeemed from the curse of bonbon rule she will go forth prospering, and to prosper, the bonbons of Virginia must move into this century or be crushed. Perhaps they don't know that a new era has dawned. Noble birth is a good thing. The possession of land and money is to be desired but this century will not bow down to the one or humbly salute the other. Men do not now seek the protection of those who <u>assume</u> to be their superiors but strike manful blows for themselves. Brains, not fortune, now rules the day. Bonbonism today stands with fear and trembling they see bearing down upon them a great army over whose columns banners of progress are flying. At its head rides the gifted and gallant leader Gen Mahone. A man of the people, a soldier of renown, a foe worthy of any steel, cool, dauntless, full of vigor. We welcome Gen Mahone as the apostle of a new and better feeling amongst the whole people and promise him that we will do our best to keep his banner aloft in the lofty struggle to which he has devoted himself. When the men who now boldly malign Mahone are dead and forgotten his illustrious name will be honored for courage in war and wisdom in peace, the brave ex-Confederate, the young Virginian returning in good faith to his fathers allegiance backed by his parole and rewarded with the choicest blessing of force. Government will find in Mahone the leadership which illustrates an honorable past and guarantees a glorious future. A leadership under which the land of Lee and Jackson, the land of Longstreet and Mahone shall be as prosperous and happy in peace as she was brave though unfortunate in war.

> Oh thou lion hearted warrior
> Seek not of the after time
> Honor may be deemed dishonor
> Liberty may be called a crime
> Stand as of yore with kindred lances
> Of the valiant and the true
> Hands that never failed their country
> Heart that never baseness knew
> Stand and till the latest trumpet
> Wakes the dead from earth and sea
> Virginia shall not boast a braver chieftain
> Than when she speaks of thee

Harry, I guess you think I am crazy or there is a screw loose somewhere as I have digressed to such an extent. I got off on our glorious victory and almost forgot that I had commenced to write a letter. I am still very unwell but hope soon to be myself again I have a bad cough and expectorate a great deal. Sometimes I begin to think that I have consumption. I suppose you and friends have had a nice time enjoying a great victory and the overthrow of bonbonism. No one can conceive what a relief it is to Va and the whole people. In a few years we then can see what a grand and beneficient blessing it was. We can't realize as yet but we can see enough to see the inner lining of the bright cloud that will shed its radiant light over the whole of this grand old State and make her what she should have been years ago, one of the foremost states in the union, and in 1884, she will wheel into line and become republicanised and go forth side by side with Pennsylvania, Ohio and other prosperous states.

Give my respect to Capt Owen. I guess he feels good over the victory. Would like to see him and hear him talk over the result.

Harry, I want you to do me a favour. It is this. I want to get off the road. It is wearing me out very fast. I want a post office inspector's place. Va is not represented. This position was formerly called Special Agent. D. B. Parker, Chief of Special, is a friend of mine, said he would recommend me several years ago but I never applied. I understand the duties of the post office department and think I could fill this position with credit to Department and honor to myself. Bailey, our late Supt, has poisoned the mind of the officials at Washington against the Lynchburg & Bristol RPO because most of us favoured a coalition ticket at Lynchburg. He has done everything he could against us and officials might object to my receiving any promotion, as they hate to give up a man that understands the distribution of the mails. I want you to draw a petition and get the Chairman of the Republican Committee and Readjusters Committee of Nottoway to endorse it. Capt Reeves will endorse it as chairman of the State Central Committee. Col Brady told me he would do all he could for me and I deserved a better place and ought not to run the road. He said this to me without my asking him in Petersburg a few days after the election. If there is any other place that I can get I am not scrupulous about it so it will pay me and not have such hard laborious work as in the road. You see Gen Mahone about this matter. He I know will do all he can to procure me a good place. I would not object to a position in Washington or elsewhere. My main object is to get off the road because I can't stand it. I have been badly mashed up twice and I am not as young as I use to be. Please attend to this at once and let me hear from you, as we are victorious. I don't suppose there will be any changes in the capital offices. Hope you may remain unmolested. I any one makes a fight against you I will do all I can for you. I know a good many of the members elected.

    With many wishes for your future welfare and happiness, I remain as ever your sincere friend,

Geo H. Southall
****

    A letter within a letter is the subject of the next paper. It is unsigned, but addressed to the Honorable John E. Massey.

****

Green Bay, Pr. Edwd Co. Va.
16th Nov., 1882

Hon. John E. Massey
Dear Sir,

    I see from the papers you intend to contest for your seat in Congress and are collecting evidence of the fraud practiced against you in the election by the magnificent party with its great idea of "a free ballot and a fair count." When asked a few days ago "what will Mr. Massey do about it?" I replied "If Mr. Massey was alone concerned he would submit without a complaint but the whole state is interested and all our rights are involved in an honest election and Mr. Massey has just begun his fight for our rights and I feel confident that he will contest for his seat just to expose the fraud and corruption of this campaign if for no other reason." I will not trespass upon your time by comments, tired as I know you are by the hardest work in the bitterest political campaign in Virginia history made by you almost alone, without help or aid from the democratic orators of the State and against a powerful foe treacherous, unprincipled and whose whole argument sunk into personal abuse of you. I want to tell you how matters were managed here as the information may be of use to you and if so you will have to get Hon. A. M. Reilly or some other counsel to instruct us how to proceed as to be in time with the depositions. My statement is this - On the 28th of October I received by mail a lot of 45 blank printed tax

232

receipts and the printed notice of my appointment by H. R. Hooper as his Assistant Collector of Delinquent Taxes for Leigh District Pr. Edw. Co. Va. My first impulse was to refuse to have anything to do with this matter, but then upon reflection, saw that some other person would act for Hooper and we apprehended and feared that the tax receipts would be given out gratuitously and I might be able to prevent this so I posted the notice at the door of the voting place and two others at two grist mills in the district. I made no canvass for taxes and only two persons applied to me to pay their taxes. The first was a negro man named John M. Foster whose name was not upon the delinquent list but the explained that he had been overlooked by the assessor last spring and now wanted to pay his cap tax so as to be qualified to vote. I took his dollar and gave him a receipt signed "H. T. Owen for H. R. Hooper Collector." The second man was white Geo. W. Reid whose name was not on the delinquent list but he had changed his residence from another township and said he owed a cap tax so I took his dollar and gave receipt signed as above.

On the 4th of Nov I recd a note from Dr Champlin as follows:

"Farmville Va.
Nov 2nd 1882

H. T. Owen Esqr.
Dear Sir,

Whenever you collect a delinquent tax be sure and sign my name to the ticket and if you have issued any with your name take them back and give them another with my name signed instead of your own. I found while in Richmond that there may be some dispute in regard to them unless this is done but with my name there can be none.

Yours truly
H. R. Hooper Collector
Per Champlin"

This of course, put a stop to my collections as I had no idea of idea of signing anybody else's name to anything and thought O had the case blocked against fraudulent tax receipts being used. I saw then that I had no legal authority to collect any tax and as Foster and Reid could tie off and not vote I would give their money back and they would not be any worse off. But Monday night 6th inst

233

Champlin and C. H. Bliss Jr. (sheriff) came over and held a meeting here. Champlin asked me to attend and give receipts at the meeting. I asked him if there would be any money paid by those getting the receipts. He replied that there was twenty five dollars to use in Leigh Dist. I asked him if he had the money and proposed to pay 25 capilation taxes. He replied that he did not have the money but Ben Hooper (candidate) would assume the payment of all delinquent taxes in the County. I then told him that if I gave any receipt it would have to be for the money and I would sign <u>my name for Hooper</u> but not sign Hooper's name alone to anything and that I would not attend the meeting. He relied that "he had over fifty blank tax receipts to which he had signed Hooper's name and all he then had to do would be to fill in the voter's name." I said yes, but the judges will not receive them nor will then take those I signed and he replied "If I can get them in it is all we want" and we then separated, I going home, and he to the meeting where I am told there were about twenty colored men. The next morning before the polls were opened I stated the whole matter to Mr. Jones Registrar here and asked him to see the judges of election and urge them to refuse every ticket presented by any man who exhibited a tax ticket signed by Hooper unless they could prove Hooper's handwriting which is easy to do as he writes a somewhat peculiar hand. I am Postmaster here and my wife was away to see a very sick married daughter. My grown children were all in N.C. and I could not leave the office as there was a crowd in all the time up to noon. I then went down to the voting place and found the Judges had taken in over one hundred tickets voting on Hooper's receipts and also the two I had given. I felt out done and protested against the outrageous fraud tolerated but the Judges thought the election would be contested afterwards and it would make no difference. Mark now there were about 20 men at the meeting on Monday night and all others using Hooper's tickets must have received them on the ground Tuesday. There was a crowd around the door as I came out from voting and stated to an intelligent readjuster my suspicions that tickets were being distributed then to be used at the window. He replied "yes, there is a man with his pockets full of Hooper's receipts ready to give them away now to anybody who wants to vote for Wise." The man alluded to named Cason (a Republican and Constable here some years ago) was wearing a satchel with a strap over his shoulder and came up just as the statement was made about his having his pockets

234

full of tax receipts and said "yes" and the first speaker added " and after they are used for voting he (Cason) and Davy Bagley (a negro canvasser with a carpet sack under his arm) will collect all these receipts and carry them back to Farmville to Hooper tonight."

(no closing and unsigned)

****

F. G. Morrison wrote to Henry about Henry's letter in the Dispatch of November 19, 1882. He congratulates Henry on sticking to his views about election fraud. He mentions that was there no fraud, John Massey would have been elected Governor. Also, he mentions Harry Dyson's son is being instructed by the 3rd Clerk in the Auditor's Office.

****

Britton's Hill Henrico Co. Va.
Wednesday Nov 22/82 7 P.M.
(Address No. 608 East Broad St.
Richmond Va.)

Capt. H. T. Owen
Green Bay, P.E. Co. Va.
Dear Sir,

By the caption you will see where I am and after I have finished what I am doing, or rather have been doing lately my attention was called to your letter in the Dispatch of the 19th or after reading it, I have concluded to let you hear from me not that I have any election frauds to report, but to congratulate you on the stand you took in the matter therein mentioned, would that there were more of your sort, but alas, I fear the number is very small. If I am to judge from what I see in the papers, I mean letters and in the Dispatch, John E. Massey would have been elected by a large majority and were I in his place, I would contest every inch of ground 'til I got my rights, even if half the time he was elected by large majority, yet we are told that we are to have "a free ballot, and fair count." God save the world.

Well I will now give you some idea of what I am about. If you will remember I commenced about the 1st July with Dr. Withers in the "Virginia Marriage Aid Association as Sec. where I continued 'til 30th Sept. When I went in not knowing the character of the business, but on a stated salary and stated terms – that I was to leave very day time enough for the 4 P.M. accommodation train on the R.F.P. Railroad, not be required to canvass any nor would any hand

235

(official) be required of me. On all points they seceded from what was of first agreed, and finally I was given to understand that my move would be preferable to my company as an officer of the concern, my mode of bookkeeping and perhaps were too old fogeyish and told that I understood the books at the 2nd Auditor's Office but no where else. "How is that for High?" So I balanced up everything and turned all over to 30th September and left. Since then I cannot tell anything about it but I am fearful it is not doing well but do not know. Since then I procured a job of writing, which lasted me ten days for which I received a small sum, which lasted about as many hours as there were dollars. Now I have nothing to do in town so am doing what I can here at home.

As I have until Jany next a D. H. ticket or pass in the accommodation train to and from Richmond, I go in occasionally to see how things are going on and generally call at the 2nd Auditor's Office. I always find Shack seated at his desk with his blue paste board over his eyes, Brownell Likenhoker and Leath doing some little at funding, Baptist at those old books posting from the transfer book and yesterday I found an addition to the force in the person of young Dyson, son of 2nd Auditor, who was being instructed by Baptist. Wish you could have heard him, Baptist. I had indulged a faint hope, from what had passed between Mr. D. and myself not long ago, that I would go back there, but I made up my mind as soon as I saw his son there that I stood no chance.

So having a little business to be attended to today (22) I attended to it yesterday and thereby saved myself the trip today. I have been at home all day doing various things but most of the day making a mat for my pit 4 feet wide, 8 feet long, which if you could see you would say to me "for what purpose?" I have to tax my neighbor for the broom straw, as I have none.

Two weeks ago I was gathering, hauling and shucking our little crop of corn, much of which was very late, so I cut it down green and cured it for forage. Our bread corn was on one acre of ground and a finer crop I never saw yielding about ten bbls, more or less, of the largest ears I ever saw some few of them (three) measuring 14 inches long, very few under 9 and having less than 12 rows of grain on the cob, and some as high as 24. The average would be about 17. The corn is yellow as gold and makes elegant sweet bread, but yellow of course. I got the see from the Department of Agriculture at Washington and planted on

236

moderately good land. I had two cows but one I sent away today to be sold as she was very nearly dry and would do better in something else than as a consumer of food. I can now go through safely as I shall have but one horse and one cow to feed. I have two pigs but they make their living rooting in the sweet potato and artichoke patches and taking the refuse from the kitchen. I tether them about anywhere so they cannot range at will and find it a great convenience as they can clean out wiregrass too.

I am writing at a small table on which I keep my writing materials and will give you an inventory viz – portfolio and contents, 1 box metal and 1 box quill pens, I write with the quill, 1 box needles and thread and one box rubber bands, 1 awl blade, ½ doz awls of various kinds, ½ doz pencils and pieces of different kinds, 1 stand for pen holders and pens, 1 ink stand and sponge for wiping pens, a wrench for awl handles, 1 pr scissors, 1 handle full of awls, 2 short tape lines, 1 lot slips for labels, 1 small hammer, some buttons and gun wads, 2 gimlets, 1 pounce bottle and many small pieces of cedar, some old spools, 1 screw driver, 1 trade mark from bacon marked C.O.D. "Clark's Old Dominion," 1 drill bit, 2 or 3 rulers, one or two catalogs of Carswell's pumps, 1 copy Don Quixotte, 1 parcel gum Arabic, spectacle case, paper fasteners, string, flower seed, matches, 1 lamp by which I am writing. Are not these enough? And not all.

I have put out 25,000 onions and have more to put out. My bees have done well; I send you one of my labels.

Let me hear from you and direct to 608 East Broad Street, Richmond where I get all my mail matter. I do my own printing on a homemade press. We are all well. Remember me to "Owen's" twins but not Meckins.

When you write tell me the news. With kind regards to your good lads and a share for you. I am as ever your fnd,

F. G. Morrison

****

Henry admonishes Colonel Frank G. Ruffin that the letter dated November 19, 1882, was not written for the public. (Mr. Ruffin must have sent it to the Dispatch.) Again, Henry expresses his feelings on voting irregularities and wishes Massey had been voted into office.

****

Col. Frank G. Ruffin
Dear Sir,

Yrs of yesterday to hand and I thank you for the two copies of the State which I recvd. In regard to my letter from which an extract was taken by the Dispatch on the 19th I have to say, it was not intended for publication and I am very sorry you allowed it to be used as it has been. It was written with the hope that after a consultation with some of Mr. Massey's friends you would direct how the information could be put in shape to be used by him in the contest for his seat in the U. S. Congress.

I know nothing of the management at the two precincts in Lunenburg except from rumor and at the time wrote my letter (which I read to Mr. Jones, Registrar here) we had no Poll book nor a delinquent list by us but supposed all on the list had voted on Hooper's tickets as signed by Champlin. After my letter appeared in the Dispatch Mr. Jones went to Farmville and brought back one of the Poll books (which properly belongs here) and Judge Watkins sent me a Delinquent list so we compared the two and found only about 27 or 30 names on the D. list upon the Poll book. The rest of the names on the list (about 100) are either dead, moved away or did not vote. We had arranged to secure all the information possible of irregularities here and elsewhere in a quiet manner, for it requires caution to procure such information from the Negroes, who are not really suspicious, besides being tutored "know nothings" for Mr. Massey's use, but the appearance of my letter put a stop to everything of the kind and they have gone to work to cover up their tracks. I have recvd messages by the dozen and postals and people have come to my house to talk for hours together about this letter and the election news and the canvass until I have to leave home early every morning to escape annoyance. I have seen somewhere that while Philip, king of Macedon, was carrying on war against the Albanians the latter intercepted a letter written by Philip to his wife Olympia and they returned it unopened saying the contents were sacred and by their laws private correspondence was thus respected. This was about 550 years before Christ and with all our civilization and enlightenment we have made no progress but really retrograded beyond the barbarian in some things. You know I am not going to quarrel with you about anything and I look upon the whole thing as thoughtless or impulsive on your part, a thing you are seldom attacked with. I do not see that my letter would do Mr. Massey any good unless it was placed in the form of a deposition and sworn to an in that case the other side would perhaps have to be notified. I would like to help Mr. Massey in any honest way I could, but cannot afford to become a martyr as I have a whole family of little ones who depend on me for bread and patriotism wanes very fast when the meal barrel gets empty.

I suppose, according to the election returns, there were about 127,000 men in Va. who did not vote and most of these were democrats who stay at home and grumble. The men who stayed away here were not the delinquents but democrats who had paid their taxes but have become tired of politics. I know some democrats who wanted to see Mr. Massey defeated for the U. S. Senate and for Auditor too because if elected Auditor they said the breach in the Readjuster Party would be healed, whereas if defeated he would be the champion of our cause against Bossism and then when he made his fight they hung back and allowed the enemy to walk over us. Now it will be harder to defeat Wise and Mahone next time than this for they will now proceed to thoroughly organize their forces and the Federal patronage in their State will be so completely under their control they will be immensely stronger than at present.

I do not think it possible that any party will ever have in Virginia again, so much material upon which to make a fight nor such an opportunity to gain a victory of 30 or 40,000 majority.

(No signature – page possibly missing)
****

In this letter to Henry from C. M. Reynolds, he asks Henry to endorse Frank G. Ruffin for the office of Secretary of the Commonwealth.
****

Carolina P.O. Botetourt Co. Va.
Nov. 12th 1883

Capt. H. T. Owen
Green Bay Va.
My Dear Sir
Our mutual friend Col. F. G. Ruffin desires the place of Secretary of the Commonwealth under the nav Region and a word from you in his behalf to some of the members of the Legislature

would benefit him but I hope it will be agreeable to you to speak that word. I need not speak to you of his services, his desert or his ability as you know all and appreciate all. Whilst he prefers the office above alluded to, his impecunious condition would constrain him to accept either one of the Basement Bureaus that might be tendered him and his genius, as you know, is equal to any occasion.

I do not suppose Napoleon after the battle of Waterloo felt much worse than Mahone now does. Repudiated at home and abroad, Marius in the Swamp, without the moral consolation which Marius had. With much respect.

Yours truly
Corbin M. Reynolds
****

Henry writes to Judge Watkins stating he has received a letter from Corbin Reynolds, former State Treasurer, and asking him to support Ruffin for office.

****

Green Bay Pr. Edwd Va.
22nd Nov. 1883

Judge F. N. Watkins
Dear Sir,

I recvd a letter last week from Col. C. M. Reynolds (former State Treas.) requesting me to write to some of the members elect of the Legislature in behalf of Col. F. G. Ruffin for Sec'y of State and while I replied to him that, he ascribed to me more influence than I possess, certainly more than I ever having enjoyed, yet being anxious to serve Col. R. I wrote at once to all the members I know and had a hope of enlisting in his cause and have also written to other gentlemen, not members, but possessing influence valuable to him if used to advance his interests.

As the revolution of fortune wheel has put the star of your party in the ascendancy and your voice is again potent, will you not give the Col. a helping hand.

I can't tell you anything of the Col's ability nor his deserts that you do not already know well and to know him well, as I do, is to love him thoroughly. You know he was reduced from comparative affluence to poverty by the torch of the incendiary and when his barns, stables, machinery, farming implements, etc. were being destroyed and his dueling of ten ablazes at midnight by a mysterious, unseen hand of a fiend, who mocked at the numerous

240

sentinels on watch and baffled the skill of expert detectives, enough to turn him to a raving maniac, eleven fires in a year, he still maintained his integrity and exhibited the fortitude of a Job.

After many after ups and downs (struggling with poverty, the best evidence of his continued honesty) we find him a Readjuster Clerk at $100 per month and as you know with half the brains of that party. Here too, when the hour of trial came, he displayed readily and promptly the instincts of a gentleman and that high toned honor of a Virginia Cavalier.

Though dependent upon his salary for his bread and there was no necessity for a martyr, yet when Mahone issued his order requiring a written pledge binding the candidates for the Leg. to Caucus ediction and to tax the clerks and employees 10 cents on their salaries for campaign funds, Col. R. wrote him a friendly remonstrance, couched in the kindest terms, a manly protest, at once demanding attention and the highest respect. The former it received but instead of the latter, it was treated with scorn and spoken of with indignation and then the war began.

On one side a fearful boss with 90,000 ignorant followers, ready to crush, some ready to assassinate any refractory subject while the proud tyrant, backed by untold wealth and Federal patronage, trampled out the life of everything that dared to oppose him, and on the other side one single humble clerk, without money, and then without political friends, stood up alone with his pen and singly did battle for Right. He lost his place, of course, but his ink never failed and his pen rested not. Look at his work. He drew off at the Capital eighteen clerks and employees (all the brains there) either one of whom could have remained by paying the 10 cents assessment and sustaining Bossism. No one man in the State has contributed so much in the late campaign as Col. F. G. Ruffin. His pamphlet of letters has been scattered by tens of thousands over the State and principally among Readjuster Democrats without whom there would today be a disastrous defeat to lament instead of the great victory we now celebrate. We shall want his services again in 1884 and he should then be able to write from a position of affluence befitting his ability. If we mean to recognize him and remember his past services he deserves this or some other good place. In justice to ourselves we cannot ignore this man and if we wish to rebuke Mahone, Elam & Co. there is nothing else we can do that will so effectively accomplish the end as making Col. Ruffin Sec'y of State.

Now Judge, a word from you to the members will do Col. R. more real service than a hundred letters from me and will you speak that word. I copied his Mahone letter and his letters to Beverly and carried most of his correspondence so I know the man of whom I speak. His moral character is the purest, his record without blemish. The people want him to have anything he wants and would elect him today for any office in their gvt.

Yrs truly
H. T. Owen

Strictly Confidential

After receiving Col. Reynolds letter to obey, which was a pleasure as well as a command, I wrote to Mr. Massey, Senator Newberry Twyman, Lovenstein, Williams and to Hon. G. C. Cabell and Geo. D. Wise asking them to aid Col. R. I have a letter from Mr. Wise saying he will follow my suggestion and do all he can for the Col. but I got a letter from Col. R. himself saying he had written to Williams and could not hear from him. So he wrote despondingly. I replied that perhaps B. F. Williams was not as expert in deciphering his hieroglyphics as I am and it would probably take the Senator a week to find out what he was writing about, or wanted him to do. That if he didn't improve his abominable hand he would miss his chances for the place in view. The fact is Senator Williams was from home last week (at the North I think) but what's the odds. If he finds out that Col. R. writes such a hand it will spoil everything. I wrote the Col. that if I could find his writing master I would kill him very dead so he could not turn out any more such people. I want the school law amended so as to require children to be taught to write with both hands and then if they have no gift of nature in one they may possess some art in the other and write legibly. There must be a special clause or act in regard to Col. Ruffin and Dr. Ben Smith requiring them to stop writing altogether. Dr. Wing (State Treasurer under Dupont) P. M. of Norfolk, and a fast friend of Col. Ruffin, said he was trying to read one of Col. Ruffin's letters and was half way through before he found out that he had it upside down. Then I asked "How in the thunder did you read it?' "Well," said he, "I knew what he was writing about and that is all that is necessary with anybody."

I hope you will write to such members or other gentlemen of influence and use your own for Col. Ruffin's election to this office.

Very resp and very truly
H. T. Owen
****

Henry received the following letter from Frank G. Ruffin
****

Richmond Nov 26, 1883

My friend,

You know there is the title of Brigadier General, Major General, Lieutenant General and General. In lieu of that intimation I say "my friend."

I have a letter from Mr. B. F. Williams received today. It is all that I could ask. He said he had received your letter and would answer it in a few days. He was then busy he said. He wrote from a place called <u>Gulf</u> North Carolina where he expects to remain for some time and as soon as I find the place on the postal map I will write and thank him. Excuse ----- but let me sum up. I have a letter from him which as I interpret it, is on my side from Judge Lynch. "up to Mr. -------" or from Mr. Massey, (who declines to take the auditorship because his duty calls him to Washington and who tells them all he asks is that they recognize me) ditto from Judge Boon, ditto from H. T. Owen, the first victim to Mahoneism, ditto from Judge Staples, ditto from Mr. Holmes Conrad, ditto from Mr. Taylor Berry, same too from Amhurst and Nelson and me of my "trainers" etc., etc.,etc.

Then, as appears in the Dispatch's list of candidates in yesterday's paper, I am the only Readjuster candidate for an office, the only one out of some 20,000 to 25,000 voters whom we brought back to the democratic party that ----- away. Is not this wonderful moderation now under all these circumstances it seems to me that policy ---- would dictate my appointment.

But, as you say, Republics are ungrateful. I have been approached once with a suggestion of compromise and replied that I had no office that I could deliver if I were to contract for it, and no right to control the votes of my friends. Besides that, it was not for me and this to say what and which office we should have, but it was the right of the Legislature to dispose of them in the best interest of

243

the country and the party and not thought if I had any right to just any office it would be in the ground of capacity to render service as from prior approved ----.

The fact is I lack the dexterity of the manager of men and I must play the hand dealt me.

But why am I running on this way when I only took up my pen – no pencil – to thank you and let you see that I can write a tolerably good hand when I was not in too much of a hurry.

I hope you will see the election returns properly reported by the returning Board but it is the opinion of a good many people including some cool and judicious men that if the had not been aware that the people would not submit to fraud and the perpetration of fraud would have been the commencement of a revolution whose first move would have overwhelmed the perpetrators they would have returned a majority of one in the Senate.

If you can't read this letter I shall be in despair.
Your friend
Frank G. Ruffin
****

The next unsigned letter is to the Editor of "The State." It may have been a draft that was never sent.
****

Richmond 4th March 1884

Editor of The State
Dear Sir,

In your issue of yesterday there is an editorial headed "A Remarkable Scene" in which it is said "one of the issues upon which the Mahonites gained the colored vote was their assertion that colored schools have colored teachers and colored trustees. This seemed to be the demand of the colored people then" etc. etc.

"The presumption is fair that had the Mahone party triumphed, their promises to the Negroes as to the schools would not have been carried out."

"The Democratic party has acted in accordance with the wishes of the colored people on this matter."

With high respect for your usual sound judgment upon matter of public interest, must yet venture to say, I think it possible you have made a mistake and reached a wrong conclusion in regard to this subject. It is not separate schools, separate boards of trustees the negroes want? Oh, no!   They demand mixed schools, mixed

244

trustees, mixed juries, mixed hotels, mixed cars, mixed theatres, mixed society, mixed marriages and if you will put the question in that shape you will see how quickly and gladly they will jump to its adoption.

You can remember, no doubt, how the negroes applauded Gov. Cameron when he appointed negro school trustees for Richmond about a year ago, and his example was followed by Coalish leaders in other sections of the State who recommended, and had appointed, other Negro School Trustees, which met the hearty approval of the Negroes in every instance. During the summer of 1883 a negro Stump speaker of local influence in South Side Virginia said while conversing with several men (white and black) "Governor Cameron's appointment of colored school trustees in Richmond is a step in the right direction. The Republican Party is a progressive party and we mean to go ahead until we break down every barrier which now separates the two races. We want mixed schools and mixed boards of trustees to control these schools. As a part of the tax payers we are entitled to representation on these boards and if representation at all, then to that representation in proportion to our population. This will give us control of the schools in many South Side Counties, but we hope to be able to run them successfully. We want the law prohibiting intermarriage between races repealed, and in the next General Assembly we shall initiate a step in that direction. We do not expect to succeed with our first effort but all we want is a single representative bold enough to ask for the repeal of that obnoxious law and we will re-elect that man over any opposition, and continue to agitate this question until we succeed." Addressing the white men he said, "Your opposition to and prejudices against   intermarriage is only a flimsy sentiment that will disappear with the repeal of the law. You fought against our freedom a long bloody war and died by thousands to perpetuate our bondage. You refused every overture of peace and every compromise looking to gradual emancipation until you were overpowered and forced to liberate us. You then "accepted the situation in good faith" but opposed as vehemently our right to vote as you had our freedom, and were only prevented from inaugurating another bloody war in resistance to our right of suffrage, by your recent sad experience. You were equally as much opposed to our education and only gave us admission to the Free Schools as a necessity, and for the advantage of the Whites. You opposed the

245

Civil Rights Bill, violently, yet after its passage we could ride on the cars in first class coaches and your prejudices passed away. We only ask for the repeal of the law prohibiting intermarriage between the races and then you will see the negro is able to take care of himself and in fifty years there will not be a black man in America. Personally I have no interest at stake, as I am an old man. If my wife should die I would not marry again but if so would prefer a colored woman. I only say these things are coming and will come within ten years. Separation of the races is impossible. Amalgamation must come at an early day or there will be bloodshed."

his talk was made when the Coalish were jubilant with the hope and bright prospect of sweeping the State by 30,000 majority. Being set back several degrees, they are quiet and many numbers of that party do not, probably, see nor believe their party is leading up to mixed schools, mixed society and mixed marriages.

****

In the final letter of the chapter, Henry writes to George C. Cabell to ask for support of W. Chase Morton as a Revenue Collector in the 2nd District of Virginia.

****

Commonwealth of Virginia
SECOND AUDITOR'S OFFICE
Richmond Va
20th Jan'y 1885

Hon. Geo C. Cabell
Dear Colonel,

Mr..W. Chase Morton makes application for the appointment of Revenue Collector for this, the Second District of Va., under the recent consolidation and he hopes to have your cooperation with Hon. Geo. D. Wise in procuring the position.

He is the son of Hon. Jackson Morton, at one time, U.S. Senator from Fla., and nephew of Hon. Jere. Morton M. Congress from Va. and on his mother's side, cousin to Hon. W. S. Archer of Va. and Branch T. Archer Sec'y of War for the Republic of Texas.

I mention these facts to show his stock because there is more in the blood of men than there is in the blood of horses. Mr. Morton's family are now all poor, but he is peculiarly well fitted to perform the duties of the office, with which he is thoroughly

246

conversant by reason of an experience as First Clerk in this department under O. H. Russell for six years. I understand he has been a life long Democrat and was selected by Mr. Russell on account of his worth and obtained solely upon his merits as an almost indispensable clerk in the Office. Upon the removal of Russell Col. Brady tendered the Chief Clerks place here to Morton, but in a subsequent interview intimated that he was expected to support the Readjuster party. The offer was declined by Morton saying he had been with Russell for six years and the subject of politics never interfered with their business matters, nor had politics been a subject of discussion of conversation, that Russell knew his politics and respected his principles and his position. I have known Mr. Morton for a year and have been associated with him in our daily work in this office where I have constant opportunity to judge his qualifications and usefulness as a clerk worth of any position of trust and responsibility.

I am very respectfully
and truly Y'r friend and obt.svnt,
H. T. Owen
****

There is much to be learned about the politics of Henry's lifetime. The authors know he was out of a job for while concerning all the upheaval in the 2nd Auditor's Office. It appears the matter was settled to Henry's satisfaction as he writes from the 2nd Auditor's Office after all the politicism is settled. He was very loyal to Harry Dyson. He let his views be known without any hesitancy. He wanted nothing to do with blank tax receipts or receipts with someone else's name on them. Henry's war with politics and political figures exemplifies his integrity as a man.

Henry wrote an article on the subject of politics in Virginia.
****

Article Written by H.T. Owen - Published by a newspaper. Date and name of newspaper unknown. Date is probably in January or February 1882.
****

Political Corruption (For the State)

There is one thing about which no cavil of a doubt as to its rapid progress can be raised, and that is political corruption. It is a no longer a subject of jest - it is a fact in our history, and no intelligent man thinks of denying it. There is corruption in the highest places, in political measures, in the leaders of movements, in parties, in the dispensation of office, in the management of the Press - aye, corruption amongst many, very many, of the class known as politicians by profession - a growing corruption, or still worse, a growing indifference to corruption, among the masses of the people. More or less intermixed in all governments, it has recently attained such magnitude in our State as to arrest and fix the attention of the most superficial thinkers. The pure men of all parties deplore this; the impure avow and defend as well as practice corruption. Never before, if corruption existed, did the party in power avow and glory in it, and defend it upon party grounds.

Now, what is political corruption? It is to pervert in any sense, and in any way, the measures, the appointment, the powers of government -- whether legislative, judicial, or executive -- from common to private ends, from catholic or universal to individual or partisan arms - whether on a larger or small scale, whether secretly or openly, whether with a redeeming hypocrisy or an unblushing avowal of rascality-this is political corruption.

It is a disease of the body politic, a rottenness of things political, and an unnatural violation of the purpose for which government is created. It is worse than private dishonesty, inasmuch as it is a breach of the highest earthly trust. It is worse than private gambling; for it puts at stake, not the gambler's own property, but that which has been committed to him as a sacred deposit in the names of thousands of living men. It adds the meanness of theft to the lawlessness of robbery; it is lying; it is perfidy; it is the foulest, the rankest, the most heaven daring perjury.

Its baseness and its wickedness are in exact proportion to the supposed honor of the stewardship and the high religious nature of the trust. It is a violation of the solemn oath taken and imposed for this very purpose-to guard against the intrusion of the private feeling or the private partisan interest in the management of a commission so sacredly intended for the common good.

From the President of the United States down to the most petty State officer, all are required to lay their hands upon the holy volume wherein God reveals his abhorrence of perjury, or raise them in reverence toward heaven and swear in the name of the God who made them that they will rightfully and faithfully and according to its fair meaning, true spirit, and well-known ends, support a constitution and laws, made in pursuance thereof, and whose every principle is in direct opposition to such public trust to partisan aims.

Now, suppose we could see a Legislature duly sworn in, regularly organized, and smoothly proceeding with its work suddenly called upon to halt, to forget oaths, religion, and conscience, and await the command of a party leader or the dictation of a caucus, in order to reward with office men hired during the campaign? What would we say? When we hear that a majority of the Legislature of a certain State thinks nothing a violation of this oath of office unless it by chance or otherwise is calculated to disturb the equanimity of temper of one single man; when we see faithful men put out, and incompetent, blind partisan politicians put in their places, what are we to think?

Can you reverence such a government? Can you respect it? In the name of conscience then how can you obey what you neither reverence or respect? No reasoning can gauge the depth of such corruption; no statement can adequately set forth the vileness of such perjury on the part of the sworn servant of the people to throw their oaths to the wind and cling in support to a single man. No epithets are to strong to express the loathing with which such actions should be regarded by every man of every party, black or white, who has a true love for his country and a self-respect left in his bosom.

Compared with the ordinary caucus-spouter and getter-up of caucus resolutions, the carpetbagger and scalawag make pretensions to respectability, for they did have some independence of character, while the first-named allow themselves to be driven like "sheep to the shambles."

****

One of Henry's sons, Benjamin Hilton Owen received a copy of some of his father's political writings. He mentions this in a letter of February 25, 1888.

****

Clover Depot, Va.
Feby 25th, 1888

Dear Pa,

Your article in the Whig received several days ago (but no letter.) I would have acknowledged receipt before but have had a great quantity of work to do. I have been writing all night for the last two weeks. I have been doing more R.R. work than I ever done before, besides I am Secty of our lodge and have all the writing to do for that. I have had several debates lately and one fight. Got to debating with a fellow and beat him. He got mad then and wanted to fight. Well, as all had gone but a few men when he wanted to do the fighting and he seemed to get pretty wrathy, I furnished him with a little of that article too and a sufficient quantity to give him entire satisfaction.

I got mother a pass about two weeks ago to go to Richmond. I expect you saw her. I heard from home this P.M. All is well. Mich is well and a little boy has arrived at his house. Herman is doing very well and still holding his position.

Your affectionate son

B. Hilton Owen

****

In addition to his interest with his work and politics, Henry led a very busy life following the war. On September 10, 1869, he was appointed by the Union Military Governor of Virginia to a position of Commissioner in Chancery to the Circuit Court of Prince Edward County, Virginia. On March 24, 1896, he was notified that he had been elected as an honorary member of the Pickett-Stuart Camp of Confederate Veterans in Nottoway County. Henry also held a full membership in a Richmond Camp of the United Confederate Veterans. The Camp Commander at Nottoway asked Henry to give a eulogy for a member of Company C, 18th Virginia Infantry Regiment at a meeting to be held on April 7, 1896. On December 20, 1898, Henry received a letter stating he had been elected an annual member of the Virginia Historical Society.

In addition to his active civic, political and religious life, Henry spent countless hours researching Owen family genealogy in Virginia.

CHAPTER 15 - THE WAR RE-LIVED AND HENRY THE WRITER

"The bursting shell in mid-heaven or upon the earth scattered death wherever its fragments flew, and the shrill shot overhead or bounding madly across the field would both alike dip through a line of prostrate men and tear away with a wail to the rear, leaving a wide track of blood behind."

Henry T. Owen, March 26, 1881.

****

Though it lasted only four years, the memories of the War of 1861-1865 lasted a lifetime for thousands of its participants. Henry T. Owen was one of many who reflected on the skirmishes, the battles and even some of the minor incidents of that devastating war. He often felt compelled to record on paper his experiences and the experiences of others who fought for the causes they felt were right and just.

In the many letters he sent and received following the war, his long, sometimes poetic descriptions give us an insight to the horrors and destruction of close combat. In addition to the letters and notes, he wrote several newspaper articles that were published by various Virginia newspapers. Some were published by the Philadelphia Times in Pennsylvania.

In a letter received from J.A. Holland dated December 21, 1878, Henry's description of the Battle of Williamsburg is verified.

****

Franklin Co.
Near Glade Hill
Dec 21st 1878

Dear Capt.,

Yours of 27th now is received and in reply I have to say that the battle of Williamsburg came off on the 5th of May and I am surprised that the gallant old Capt Irby should have made such a great mistake.

In regard to the abandoned artillery my understanding has always been that Capt Claiborne was the chief action in firing the gun and I know too that the battery was in front of Company "C" when the Regt was halted. Dr. E. D. Withers, Benj. Harrington and

John Enright all know the fact. I remembered at the time or since that Lt Shields had anything to do with the gun. I have received the papers on Gettysburg and have read them very attentively and have also had others to read them. Some of the 51st, some of the 24th and some of other Regts and all agree to the correctness of your statement. I am indeed much obliged to you for them and if I should pass your way I will take great pleasure in calling on you.

With kind regards
and best wishes
J. A. Holland

****

In April 1880, another correspondent, answers an inquiry regarding General Garnett.

****

Madison – 30 April 1880

My dear Sir,

In reply to your note I have to say that I was a member of the Va. Vol. Regt (Col. Hamtramck) and was with it during the period of its service in Mexico embarking with it at Old Point Comfort in February 1847 and discharged at the same point about 1 August 1848. The Regiment, however, never had a chance to meet the enemy in battle having reached Genl Taylor's command after the battle of Buena Vista and having remained with that army until the war closed.

I really do not know if Genl Garnett was in the Mexican War but I think he was an officer in Scott's army.

Very truly and respy yours
C. L. Kemper

Capt. H. T. Owen

****

Charles Pickett who was a staff officer to Gen. Longstreet wrote to Henry in October 1881 and gave his version of one of the battles near Petersburg. Item 4. (answer to question 4) in the letter was missing.

****

Norfolk Va
Oct 4th 1881

Capt H. T. Owen
Richmond
My Dear Captain,

252

Yours of 29th Sept to hand. I am sorry that I shall have to rely entirely on my memory for the facts you desire to know. It has been a long time since the occurrence referred to still I will endeavor to give you my recollections. According to the best of my knowledge Genl Beauregard, in order to protect Petersburg, was obliged to withdraw from the Bermuda Hundreds front. I don't believe that the works were occupied by the enemy for some hours after he left. Now to answer your questions categorically.

1 – The Division was encamped the night before the battle on the Darbytown Road very close to Malvern Hill and started on the march about day or shortly after on the morning (of I think the 17th of June). We crossed the river on pontoon bridge at Chaffin's Farm. It was a very hot day and the troops were dreadfully worn out. Hunton's Brig was in advance. Genl Pickett and his staff together with Genl R. H. Anderson commanding Longstreet's Corps were riding along slowly in advance of the troops when a party of the enemy who were thrown across the dirt road opened quite a lively picket fire on them. This point was about directly in rear of a point about a mile north and in the rear of the "Clay House." A line of skirmishers was thrown forward and the road soon cleared. This was somewhere about 2 or 2:30 P.M. Very soon the other Brigades were turned forward after formed and moved forward towards the works. After getting into fair position Genl Lee in person gave directions that a heavy fire of artillery all along the lines should be opened and that on cessation of the fire a simultaneous advance should be made along the whole line to the front. During this fire Gen L. determined for some reason, I think to get reinforcements, to countermand the order for attack but although the order was sent out yet the men were so excited that on the cessation of the artillery fire they made a dash and in a very short time were in possession of the line of works which had been held by Butler's people. This attack was made about 5 o'clock and it was the occasion of one of the highest compliments Genl Lee ever paid to a command. He sent a dispatch to Genl Anderson to this effect: "We tried to stop Pickett's men but could not."

2 – I cannot give you the numbers of troops in the Div at the time as all my papers were destroyed on the retreat. I only know that all four of our brigades were there and none with too full ranks.

3 – As at what hour the battle began and when the works were taken you will find embraced under 1st answer.

253

5 – To my knowledge there were no reinforcements. I think some other Div (whose I don't remember) was halted in the main road to our rear about the time of the attack with a view to assist us but they never were brought into action.

6 – The actual attack lasted but a very short time as our men rushed forward with the greatest enthusiasm and don't think the loss was heavy on either side, but here again, the absence of records puts me at a great disadvantage. After the line was taken there was desultory firing kept up till in the night. And nearly all night there was a heavy mortar fire directed to our lines but I believe with little or no effect.

Am only sorry that I can give you so meager an account but hope it will serve your purposes. Try Capt W. Stuart Symington, Baltimore. He has a good memory and may aid you.

And now may I ask what is your object, has someone been misrepresenting us?

By the way Capt Robert Bright, Williamsburg could also probably give you some details.

With high regard
I am Very truly yours
C Pickett
****

On March 17, 1881, Henry received notice from the *Philadelphia Times* that his manuscript on the Battle of Gettysburg had been accepted. The article was published on March 26, 1881 and is in Chapter 10 - Gettysburg. The Times had earlier published Henry's manuscript of the Battle of South Mountain.

****

The Times
Philadelphia
March 17, 1881

Mr. H. T. Owen
Richmond Va
Dear Sir,

Yours of the 15th at hand. Your Gettysburg Ms. is accepted and will be published shortly. The other is unavailable and is herewith returned.

Very truly Yrs
The Times
M.
****

Henry combined several incidents in one article that was published by the *Philadelphia Times* in early 1881. It included a sad story of the fate of a deserter. Henry told a friend, "I wish I could have been of more comfort to the wretched man."

****

"On the 27th of June 1863, we received an order from General Lee that we were about to enter the enemy's country, calling upon every soldier to abstain from all damage or destruction of private property, urging the officers especially to see this order obeyed, that private rights were respected and reminding them that we were not waging war against peaceable citizens, and defenseless women and children."

Henry T. Owen - March 21, 1881

Published in the *Philadelphia Times* in about 1881

STORIES OF PICKETT'S MEN

Noteworthy Incidents In the Division Just Before the Battle of Gettysburg

By Captain H.T. Owen

Formerly of Pickett's Division - Army of N. Va.

On Thursday morning, the 25th of June, 1863, Pickett's Division left camp near Castleman's ferry, on the Shenandoah river, moved up the road towards Berryville and then turning to the right took the road to Martinsburg, Va. Soon after leaving Berryville, when the troops had marched rapidly over four or five miles, General Garnett, who had been detained in the rear, came riding up with several aides and couriers on their way to the head of his brigade and overtook Sergeant Thomas Brightwell, limping along the road, a mile behind his command. General Garnett and staff were going at a gallop, but he halted and asked Brightwell why he was lagging behind his company and Brightwell replied that he had a bad boil on his ankle and was unable to keep up. "Let me see that boil," said the General. And Brightwell, turning down his sock, displayed to view a large purplish, red boil on his ankle, situated just where the top of his hard, rough shoe chafed and inflamed it at every step he made. General Garnett then inquired if he had reported that morning at the surgeon's call and showed him the boil. Brightwell

255

replied that he did report to the surgeon and was informed there was no room in the ambulance for him; he was not excused from duty, but told to keep up with his company as best he could. General Garnett then asked: "What regiment do you belong to? What is your surgeon's name?" And learning these, he turned to his courier and said: "Ride out and overtake Dr. --- . Tell him to report to me here and you come back with him to show him where I can be found." He then deliberately dismounted and took a seat on the roadside and waited patiently for an hour, when the doctor was brought back and the General asked him:

"Did this man report at your sick call this morning?"

"Yes sir."

"Did you see that boil on his ankle?"

"Yes sir."

"Why then did you not get him in the ambulance and send him to the hospital?"

"There was no room in the ambulance and I thought he might manage to keep up with his company."

"Then sir," said Garnett, "take him up behind you, and if you don't manage to find room for him in some wagon or ambulance, then let him ride your horse until he is able to walk."

The General then galloped on to the front and left the Doctor to take Brightwell up behind him and bring up the rear of the column, but he soon found room in an ambulance to deposit him. Brightwell was well enough in a week to go into the battle of the 2nd of July; came out unhurt and in reorganizing the remnant of our regiment I appointed him temporary sergeant major. His appointment was afterwards confirmed and he held the position to the close of the war.

An hour or two before sunset, the command reached the wooded hill a little south of the village of Darksville, but before going into camp the regiments were drawn up in a line to hear read a number of very important general orders. One was from General Lee, similar to the order issued to the whole army at Chambersburg on the 27th, informing the men, "that they were about to enter the enemy's country, calling upon every soldier to abstain from all damage or destruction of private property, urging the officers especially to see this order obeyed, that private rights were respected and reminding them that we were not waging war against peaceable citizens, defenseless women and children, but against soldiers well equipped with arms in their hands, etc."

A STORY OF A DESERTER

Another order read here was for the execution of John Riley, which was to take place the next evening. After the line was dismissed and we had eaten our rough camp supper I laid down to rest, but got to thinking about John Riley, and although very tired, it was several hours before I could get to sleep. John Riley was an Irishman, and all that is known of the man is found in the reports of the "general court-martial convened at the camp of Major General R.H. Anderson," and reads as follows:

Headquarters Army Northern Virginia - June 14, 1863
General Order No. 71.

Continuation of the proceedings of a general court-martial convened at the camp of Major General R.H. Anderson's Division, by virtue of General Orders No. 45 Headquarters Department of Northern Virginia, at which were arraigned and tried the following named prisoners:

8. Private John Riley , Company E, Eighteenth Virginia Regiment.

Charge: Desertion.

Specifications: In this that the said John Riley, a private of Company E, Eighteenth Virginia Regiment, having entered said company as a substitute on or about December 3, 1862, did, between dark on Saturday night, December 13, and daylight Sunday morning, December 14, 1862, desert from his company and regiment while in line of battle and in the face of the enemy, near the town of Fredericksburg, Va., and did not return thereto until arrested in the city of Richmond, Va., and brought back under guard on the 10th day of January 1863, he having been previously advertised as a deserter and a reward of $100 offered for his apprehension.

Finding: Of specifications, guilty; of charge, guilty.

Sentence: And the court does, therefore, sentence the said prisoner, John Riley, Company E, Eighteenth Virginia Regiment, three fourth of the court concurring, to be shot to death with musketry in front of his brigade, the time and place of the execution to be fixed by the General commanding.

HOW RILEY ACCEPTED THE VERDICT.

The decision of the court was kept a profound secret, and when the division started South in February, 1863, the prisoners confined in the guard houses were taken along, and all through that campaign in the swamps of Eastern North Carolina and around

Suffolk, Riley, with the other prisoners, tramped hundreds of miles, oftentimes marching all night loosely guarded, along narrow roads with dense swamps and dark forests lining the route on both sides and overlapping branches shutting off every ray of light; yet with a hundred opportunities to escape he never attempted to do so. I felt pity for this miserable, unfortunate man, a foreigner, far from his native land, among strangers and condemned to death, with no one near in whom he could confide nor a single friend to receive his last message. In the morning I talked with the adjutant and learned that nothing could be done to stay or delay the execution; that when he offered to let Riley ride in the ambulance that day, he replied: "I have already walked many hundred miles and think I hold out one day more;" and when the day's rations were issued to the prisoners, Riley declined to take his, saying, "I am not hungry and don't think I shall need anything to eat today."

AN ATTEMPT TO BEFRIEND RILEY

Before we reached Williamsport, I got permission to have a talk with Riley, hoping I might in some way do the doomed man a kindness. The captain of the guard kindly allowed me free access to the prisoners, but said he thought I would have all my pains for nothing, as Riley had refused to talk to every one else. Going forward, I found a squad of about a dozen prisoners with a strong guard before, behind and on each side of them. They were at this time marching along a broad turnpike forty or fifty feet wide, and Riley was about the middle of the road. Knowing my errand or divining it, the guards and other prisoners fell away a little and gave me an ample opportunity to converse with Riley. Walking along with him for some distance in silence that he might notice my presence and that I might not appear abrupt, I spoke in a low voice and said: "Mr. Riley, I feel a great sympathy for you in your present unfortunate situation and feel anxious to do something for you if there is anything I can do?" Without raising his head or even looking at me he moved off a few feet towards the opposite side of the road and marched on in silence for a hundred yards, and then said slowly: "There is nothing you can do for me."

EITHER MOROSE OR STOICAL

A long silence followed and we marched on side by side, with a space of five or six feet between us, as I kept the middle of the road while he had moved away to the right. After ten minutes silence I asked, "How old are you, Mr. Riley?" He moved off a few feet farther and after a longer silence than before, replied: "Forty-

Six." I again waited awhile and asked: "Have you a father or mother living?" The same shrinking away still farther and a longer pause before he replied; "I had both a father and mother when I left Ireland for America." I then asked; "How long have you been in America?" and after a very long silence he answered, "Thirty-four years." I then asked him; "When did you hear from your parents?" Still moving away and marching nearly a half mile before he replied; "Not since I left Ireland at twelve years of age." By this time he was on the edge of the road as far off as he could get from me, and although I asked him several other questions and offered to write to any of his friends or relatives if he wished me to so and waited long for his answer to each question and proposition, yet he never replied to anymore. We had now marched several miles together; my presence and questions seemed to annoy him, and as I saw no prospect or chance to serve him in any way, I excused myself by saying this to him: "I hope I have not appeared intrusive. If my motives have been misunderstood and you mistake my sympathy and my anxiety to serve you for any idle curiosity respecting your past life and history, I shall regret my efforts to help you."

To this there was no reply and I returned to my company. We crossed the Potomac and passed through Williamsport about 3 o'clock on Friday evening, and after going a mile or two selected a large open field on the right of the road for the execution. Riley asked for the services of a priest and a messenger was sent to seek one, but returned unsuccessful. The brigade was drawn up in double ranks, forming three sides of a "hollow square" the fourth side, down hill being left open. In the center of this open side and in full view of every man in the columns, which faced inward, a strong stake was driven into the ground and left about three fee high. A band of music entered the square around the right flank, followed by four soldiers bearing on pikes an empty pine coffin; close behind this walked John Riley, with a chaplain at his side, dressed in a long flowing black robe, and then came the captain of Company E at the head of the twelve armed men, drawn by lot from his company to perform the execution. The band struck up that mournful refrain;

Her bright smile haunts me still,
'Tis years since last we met.
* * * * *

I have sailed 'neath alien skies.
* * * * *

Every danger have I known

That a reckless life can fill,
But her presence hath not flown,
For her bright smile haunts me still.

THE END OF RILEY

This funeral cortege, starting at the right, marched close along in front of the line all around the three sides of the square and then to the stake, where Riley's hands were tied at his back and he was made to kneel, so the bandage slipped over the stake behind him. A cloth was placed across his eyes and he was asked if he had anything to say. His only reply was; "Goodbye, boys." Every thing being ready, the captain waved his sword, a volley followed and John Riley lay a mangled corpse. He was buried near the spot and sleeps in an unmarked grave. I doubt if his name was Riley. Twenty years after this execution, while looking over some musty records, my attention was called to this singular endorsement made upon the Riley papers at General Lee's headquarters;

The sentence of Private John Riley, Company E, 18th Virginia Regiment, will be duly executed ten days after the publication of his sentence to his brigade in the presence of the same, under the direction of his brigade commander. By command of General R.E. Lee. R.H. Chilton, A.A. and I. General.

INCIDENTS OF THE MARCH

On the 27th the division marched a little beyond Green Castle and camped in a large grove of oaks to the left of the road and the men began to burn fence rails and to carry a farmer's wheat shocks into camp for bedding, saying they had obtained permission from their Colonel. Several officers waited upon the Colonel and protested against this destruction of private property as a violation of Lee's orders, but the Colonel became angry and said: "He was surprised that officers who had seen such wholesale ruin of private property in Virginia should now lift their hands in holy horror at the burning of few Yankee fence rails and the using of a little wheat for soldiers' bedding." When some instances of this sort were reported to General Pickett as violations of Lee's orders, his reply was; "We are not obliged to everything General Lee says."

While the pioneer corps under Lieutenant Morrissett were tearing up the railroad near Chambersburg, a crowd of citizens gathered around the men and claimed that the road was private property and a good many hard things were said about the Confederates, and the grumbling continued until a preacher from the town came along, with a large pair of goggles over his nose, and peering up and down the track awhile at the burning sills and twisted rails, stepped up to Morrissett and said; "I had no idea this road needed repairing!"

As the division marched through Chambersburg in rear of Lee's army, a large-sized, middle-aged Dutch woman, with a long white apron on, bare-headed, sleeves rolled up above her elbows, with her arms akimbo, stood upon the sidewalk and said;
"Mint Got! it's the whole Sarouth I see, ish it? A soldier replied; "Mostly, madame," and on we went.

CHOPPING DOWN FLAG-POLES

Coming to a tall flag-pole seventy or eighty feet high, with the stars and stripes floating from the top, some soldiers began chopping on it, when a dozen boys, old men and women came up and asserted; "It was a real Union flag, a Bell and Everett flag, but further on we would find a Lincoln flag." So the pole was left standing, and when we turned the corner and reached the end of the next street there was another pole and flag precisely like the first, but the boys followed us, keeping pace along the sidewalk, and other boys had joined in, all of whom now claimed this as regular secesh flag, put up in honor of Breckenridge and Lane and it was a pity to cut it down. But the pole was cut and fell, breaking into many pieces, and the boys then said: "There was no secesh about it. It was a regular Union flag, and never mind, you will be paid for it when you get across the mountains." A rough soldier asked; "Paid how?" A boy replied: "The furder you go that way, the furder you will have to come back, if you get back."

Owen Family Papers

****

The incident of the battle of Gettysburg and the part taken there by the division had already appeared in the Weekly Times of March 26, 1881.

****

Henry was always interested in Virginia politics and became more involved in that arena after the war. In a letter, which he did not intend to be published, he speaks of irregularities in the polls in Prince Edward County.

****

ANOTHER PUBLISHED NEWSPAPER ARTICLE
(Date, newspaper, and other information unavailable)
FRAUDS IN THE FOURTH
How The Coalitionists Worked The Tax-Receipt Dodge in Prince Edward.

The Methods of the "Fair Count" Party Shown up by a former Readjuster

The following extract speaks for itself. It was written to a friend in this city by Captain H.T. Owen, of Green Bay Post Office, late a Readjuster clerk in the second Auditor's Office, and a man of high character. It was not intended for publication. But it is nonetheless valuable on that account;

"I want to tell you of some of the frauds practiced here at the election, and when the time comes to use the information for Mr. Massey we will bring it all out.

"The Auditor appointed by R.H. Hooper (our county clerk) collector of delinquent taxes for Prince Edward County, and Hooper assumed the authority to appoint nine assistant collectors, whose names were printed on a public notice and posted conspicuously at each voting-place in the county. My name was one of the nine, and I received the notice and a lot of forty five blank tax-receipts by mail without any letter or instructions how to proceed. My first impulse was to refuse to act at all, but the election-day was just a week off, and if I refused to act someone else would act for them and give the tickets out without receiving any money. So I went about my business quietly, and merely said, if any delinquent wanted to pay his tax, I would receive it for Hooper and pass it over to him. Only two men offered to pay and I gave each one a receipt, signing my name for Hooper. On Saturday preceding the election Champlin wrote me not to sign my name to the tax-receipts for Hooper, as there might be some trouble about it if I did so, but to sign R.H. Hooper's name. This of course opened my eyes, and closed collections here with, as I thought, the game blocked on them. But Monday night Champlin and Bliss came over to Green Bay and distributed about one hundred tax-receipts to delinquents and to all others who wanted them, and did not receive a dollar. Now came my advantage again. I refused to give any tickets to Champlin or anybody without the money, and asked Champlin if he had the money to pay for these parties, and he said no; but he would sign Hooper's name, and that Ben. Hooper, the congressional candidate assumed the payment of all the delinquent taxes of Prince Edward. I

262

informed the judges of election of this, and asked them to throw out every ticket signed by Hooper unless they could recognize or approve his handwriting; but they concluded to take them, and thus one hundred men voted here on fraudulent tax receipts; and the worst of it all is, after the parties had voted these receipts were collected in some instances (perhaps in all) and carried back to Farmville to Hooper. Some Negroes tell us they returned their tickets as soon as they were used for voting to a Negro named Bagley, who walked about the grounds with a carpet-bag collecting up the tax receipts as soon as a Negro had voted.

"Some men whose taxes had been paid by employers, who still held the receipts, were supplied with these tax tickets to vote. Their names not being on the delinquent list, it seems made no difference. When we got the papers next day, and saw the question raised in Richmond about the Snelling receipts, we then knew that I had no right to act at all for Hooper nor could the Auditor himself appoint more than one collector for any county, city, or town in the state.

"One precinct in Lunenburg County closed polls at 4 1/2 PM -- before the people were done coming. At another the voters were not required to show tax receipts till a citizen protested and it was therefore done.

Yours truly, H.T. Owen

P.S. --- I am satisfied there were about six hundred fraudulent votes allowed in our county.

"Mr. Massey has been cheated by false counting and fraud out of not less than 10,000 votes.

"As so many voted without paying any tax, don't you think I ought to give the $2.00 back to the two men I collected from? Who has the right to the money, these two men or the State Auditor?"

Owen Family Papers

****

One Spring morning, Henry took a stroll around Richmond (year unknown.) In his notes, he reflected on what Richmond once was and what it had become after the war.

****

Rambling Around Richmond
(By Henry T. Owen)

One beautiful spring morning, after the absence from the city for sixteen long years, I landed from the cars at the R&D Depot, a stranger to the many widespread changes wrought here during that eventful period of time by devastating war, by fire, by flood, by death and by many removals, due in some cases to disastrous speculation to a worse fate and in other instances by fortunate traffic to some better lot, and pushing my way through a noisy crowd of men and boys, black and white, and then pressing on through a lane of yelling hack and carriage drivers dressed in uniforms of blue, I slowly walked up Virginia Street to the corner of Cary.

Here I was met by the roar and ceaseless din of rattling drays and paused awhile to look about for some landmark, some familiar place or friendly face, but alas, all around me was so wonderfully altered that I soon felt bewildered and lost in the midst of a busy multitude whose hurrying feet kept up a constant clatter as they swept by and occasionally jostled the old countryman loitering along the sidewalk and halting at intervals to gaze up at the tall, dingy looking buildings whose dark shadows still reached across to the opposite curb stones.

Moving on slowly I found the houses all changed and the people themselves changed beyond any recognition. The entrance to the Columbian on Cary Street was closed and the front of this once celebrated hotel was altered into lofty commission houses and grocery stores, and going around on Shocoe Slip, I found this old building and all others had passed entirely away, and in their place, had been erected an extensive mart of trade occupied by wealthy tobacconists and grain merchants. Around me there were ample evidences on every side, of thrift and prosperity but in pursuing my way up the street I found neither house or number nor any sign or name, nor a single familiar face of grocer or shop keeper by which to remember Cary, so turning across, I sought the American Hotel which once stood upon the corner of Eleventh and Main but that too was gone and its ruins had been razed and upon the site now stands the grand, imposing, establishment of "Levy Brothers." On the opposite side of the street, a little higher up, on the opposite side of the street still stands the United States Custom House and Post Office, a magnificent building of native granite which had withstood all the wear and tear of time and revolution. This was the first familiar landmark of the old city I had found and I greeted it with great pleasure as an old friend and a well established point by which other places could be located, and starting down Main towards the Old Market, I found the many of the houses on the left entirely new while some others were strangely familiar, with apparently the same

264

windows and show cases filled with nearly the same articles, the same entrances, and the same, well worn steps thereto, but the faces of the salesmen were different and the signs and numbers on the doors were altered. Over on the right, the houses were all larger, higher, and more magnificent in appearance. Here on the next corner below "Levy Brothers," I found a new "American Hotel" and further on I inquired for "West and Johnson" and learned they had moved up town. J. W. Randolph had also moved higher up to the other side of the street, and so on down. I found numerous changes caused by removal and death and began to realize what great and wonderful changes had taken place here, since that weary, worn, ragged, hungry, rear guard of a broken army made its last, hurried, tramp along the streets of Richmond, with the city on fire in a hundred places, with the proud banners of a victorious foe floating in hot pursuit and dark, serried, ranks of the enemy pressing close upon their heels, while almost in their grasp. The sidewalks were strewn with a mixed medley of clothing, bacon, shoes, flour, notions, hats, soaps, silks and bread, the gutters running with wine, molasses and liquors, while crowds of wild, distracted, citizens and drunken mobs were rushing to and fro, yelling, cursing, weeping, fighting, praying, robbing and running away to escape across a burning bridge and join in the wake of that scattered band which like the ancient Parthian hosts, fought desperately, yet wasted as they fled.

****

In April 1884, Henry visited Hollywood Cemetery in Richmond and went to the grave sites of three Confederate Generals. He was apparently upset that these grave sites were as he put it, "neglected." He wrote an article and it was published in the Charlotte Gazette.

****

THE CHARLOTTE GAZETTE
Devoted to Home Interest and Literature
Leonard Cox, Editor
Charlotte Court House, Virginia
Thursday, May 22, 1884

THREE NEGLECTED GRAVES
By Capt. H.T. Owen

After wandering through Hollywood for several hours in a vain search, I was at last directed to the spot, on a gently inclining knoll, and that part of the cemetery which slopes down towards the river near the Old Pump House, where there was buried more than twenty years ago a military chieftain whose wonderful career in war and revolution amid constant dangers by field and flood, in widely separated countries, furnishes a brilliant record of a life filled with romantic incidents, heroic deeds and marvelous adventures.

Standing here alone, with the winds moaning overhead and sighing through the cedars at the foot of the grave, I pondered over the history of this man's life.

A Virginian by birth, a Tennessean by adoption, a lawyer by profession, nearly forty years ago, when only nineteen years of age, with the rank of lieutenant, he entered the service of his country, then at war with Mexico, and with a large number of other volunteer recruits joined Gen. Scott's army in the siege of Vera Cruz.

After the capture of that city, when the American army was on the eve of marching inland towards the capitol of the country, our hero was seized with yellow fever, but exacting a promise from his men that he should not be left behind when the army moved, the next morning he was strapped in a hammock, swung between two mules, and thus carried up to Jalapa, where he arrived in an insensible condition.

As soon as he was fit for duty, after his remarkable recovery from a disease almost universally fatal, he reported to Gen. Scott and was detailed for special service in a separate command.

He was now captain of a large company of one hundred and four men, well mounted, handsomely uniformed, splendidly equipped and in perfect drill; and was selected to lead the advance of triumphal entry into conquered cities.

He participated in all the battles of the campaign and was several times honorably mentioned in Gen. Scott's official reports for important services and gallantry on the field, and today, after the long lapse of two-score years, there still hangs beneath his fading portrait on the wall of his father's house, a splendid sword, a treasured gift and memento of an act of chivalrous courtesy worthy of "ye knights of ye olden times."

During a battle in which the Mexicans were routed and pursued by the cavalry, a veteran general was overtaken while vainly attempting to rally his men in face of the tide of invaders that were bearing them away; but too old and too brave to run, he continued to fight until he was completely surrounded by his foes and compelled the surrender of his sword to the dashing young officer commanding the dragoons. Not a single word of the other's

266

language could either understand, but, with the utmost courtesy, respecting the gray hairs and courage of the aged patriot, his sword was returned with a sign that he should be permitted to retain it and while a prisoner he was treated with all the kindness and courteous attention due his exalted rank. Several weeks afterwards when the prisoners were all collected at headquarters for exchange or parole, the Mexican General requested Gen. Scott, through an interpreter, to send for his captor and when he arrived, said through the same medium that "he wished, in presence of the American commander, to express his thanks and gratitude to the young Captain whose valor he had witnessed in battle and whose hospitality he had afterwards enjoyed while a prisoner. At the mess table his cup had been the first filled, his plate the first helped with the most savory morsels; at night he had occupied the Captain's couch while its owner, wrapped in a blanket, had slept upon the ground. He had been treated like a conqueror instead a captive, and he wanted now to present as a gift, which the Captain had declined to receive as a capture on the field. He wished it to be accepted as a token of his friendship and admiration of the man whose strange foreign tongue he had been unable to understand, but whose language of good manners was more eloquent than words." The sword was again refused, but at the urgent request of General Scott it was finally accepted and is retained in the family mansion as an heirloom.

After the Mexican war closed our hero settled in New Orleans and engaged in the practice of law; then we find him a member of the Louisiana Legislature, and in 1848 he canvassed the State and acquired considerable reputation as a public speaker.

Then we find him in mid ocean with two vessels lashed together, standing on deck making an eloquent, stirring address to the volunteers of the Lopez expedition and a few days afterward severely wounded in leading the attack upon Cardenas. Defeated and narrowly escaping capture by a Spanish war vessel the volunteers sought refuge in the harbor of Key West.

Returning to the United States, we find him collecting recruits and hastening to the relief of his early friend and college classmate, Genl. William Walker, who was in imminent peril after his defeat at Rivas.

During the revolution in Nicaragua our hero met with the most wonderful of his numerous remarkable escapes from death. The boiler of a steamboat exploded and he was blown from the hurricane deck into the river, but so entirely without injury that he easily swam to shore, taking a wonderful man with him. Again, after a few years, we find him back in Mexico fighting on the side of the Liberals, and during a four-years' war he war he attained the rank of general of brigade.

In 1859 he crossed the ocean and tendered his services to Garibaldi, was accepted, given the rank of brigadier general, and aided materially that celebrated leader in gaining numerous victories over the Austrians, attracting general admiration of all the foreign correspondents, who frequently mentioned the American officer who galloped to the charge under showers of shot and shell as gaily as most men ride to a banquet.

When the tocsin of civil war sounded here its echo reached him in that far-off land and he hastened home to meet the invader upon his own native heath.

Though suffering from wounds received in Italy he hurriedly organized a battalion of troops, and reached Manassas in time to take part in the memorable battle of the 21st of July 1861.

Placed on the extreme left of a line of battle eight miles long, it fell to his lot to meet the advance of the Federal troops, and for more than one hour, with only 394 men and two pieces of artillery he fought a desperate battle, and held in check Heintzleman's division of 9,000 men. Gen. Beauregard said; "This man has won for himself and his command the proud boast of belonging to that heroic band who saved the first hour of the battle of Manassas."

When reinforcements at last reached that part of the field the battalion was found cut to pieces, and its gallant commander stretched prone upon the earth, with a bullet hole through both lungs from which bloody air-bubbles were escaping on both side as he breathed.

Hauled away to Manassas Junction and placed on a bed, he was informed about midnight by a very eminent surgeon that "he could not possibly live to see the day." His reply was, "I don't think you know much about it. I don't feel like dieing yet." "But," said the surgeon, "there is no instance on record of recovery from such a wound." "Well, then," he rejoined, "I will put my case on record." And to the surprise of everybody he did recover, which, the surgeon thought, was chiefly due to his resolute will.

After an active campaign in the Valley he came with Jackson to begin the "Seven Day's Battle Around Richmond," and in leading a charge at "Gaines Mill," near Cold Harbor, on the 27th June, 1862 our hero, at the age of 36, the handsomest man in the army, was killed. His last request, "Bury me on the field, boys!" was complied with, but his body was afterwards brought to Hollywood and re-interred in this spot among beautiful shafts and marble slabs, reared on every side, carved and sculptured by exquisite art to represent angels, doves, kneeling lambs, lilies, encircling vines and all the emblems of love, purity and innocence, rising in profusion along the landscape to decorate and commemorate the last resting place of the thousands who occupy around this only neglected grave.

A piece of marble ten inches high, planted at the head, was marked upon its face---"C.R. Wheat" - "LA".

No rank, no date of birth or death, no title, no record of any heroic deed of his eventful life is given, and even his land of nativity rendered doubtful by the claim set up by a distant people who perhaps loved him more because they knew him better.

By "H"

"Bury me on the field, boys!' and away to the glorious fight; You will come this way again, boys, in your triumph march to- night.
But when you pass this spot, boys, I would not have you sigh-
In holy cause of country, boys, you would not gladly die?

"Bury me on the field, boys, ' where a soldier loves to rest,
And sweet shall be my sleep, boys, upon my country's breast;
For she is dearer far, boys, than aught this world can give,
And gladly do I die, boys, that she may proudly live."

Another Neglected Grave - The Second.

About fifty yards further on up the ridge, westward, within full view of the church steeples and spires "whose silent fingers point to heaven," within hearing of the sound of tolling bells, the rattle of machinery, the hum and bustling clamor of busy life in this large city - capital of the State and once of the Confederacy - there lies buried a once noted Virginian in another neglected grave.

Buckling on his armor he, too went forth to battle in defense of his native State, and the student of history, searching through the musty records of the great civil war, will find frequent honorable mention of this man's name in the bulletins and reports of every conflict of arms by the Army of Northern Virginia in all its many bloody campaigns; and old soldiers still lingering on the stage can recall the times when this man's clarion voice in the van of battle led them on to almost constant victory; but, alas! when he fell, then disastrous retreat and constant defeat followed in continued succession to the end. Thoughtless visitors and heartless idlers, straggling through Hollywood, with loud talk and boisterous laughter, no respect for the living, no veneration for the memory of the dead, have trampled a well-trodden path across the beautiful plot of green grass here, without inquiring, perhaps not caring to know, who sleeps below this little neglected mound of earth.

A half dozen sorrowing friends stood at the bedside of Stonewall Jackson, weeping, watching, waiting in breathless suspense while that great man, struggling in the tangled meshes of death, imagined during the brief fever of delirium which preceded dissolution that he was engaged in a desperate battle with the Federals, and needing reinforcements, wanting help, cried out; "Tell A.P. Hill to prepare for action!" and a few minutes later, when his failing his strength in the conflict with death, pictured to his fancy the enemy outflanking his position; "Tell A.P. Hill to move up on my right!" then he "crossed over the river and rested under the shade of the trees!"

Gen. Lee at Lexington in 1870 more than five years after the war, and he, too, in the hour of death thought a battle scene and wanted the counsel of his great lieutenant who had proceeded him to the tomb half a dozen years and was far beyond the hearing of that last call of his great commander, "Send for A.P. Hill!"

Cut in the granite curbstone that borders the carriage road ten feet from the grave, we find, "Lt. Gen'l A.P. Hill."

But no greater monument in history is needed for Hill than the fact that he was the last man thought of and called for by two such men as Lee and Jackson.

Pausing here, I could hardly realize that so many years had elapsed since the ragged rebel, like the ancient Parthian, never routed, "But forever fighting as he fled,"
looked back from the hills across the river upon burning bridges and a city wrapped in flames, and thought of the words of the patriotic Pole when led to execution;

> "Whether on the scaffold high,
> Or in the battle's van;
> The proper place for man to die
> Is where he dies for man."

The Third:

The sun was going down, the shadows of twilight settling along the bottoms, and chill blast howled mournfully across the bleak landscape, when I found, away off in the Northern part of Hollywood, half a mile from the graves of Wheat and Hill, in the most lonely, unfrequented spot in the cemetery, where the grass is withered, and rains wash little gullies down the barren hillside, without a single tree, or bush, or briar the spot where lies buried another Virginian General, of distinguished merit in his day and generation, but who seems overlooked and entirely forgotten now in this neglected grave.

Twenty years ago this man's brilliant deeds in battle had already won for him a reputation for such undaunted courage that he was selected to lead his division as a forlorn hope in one of the most desperate assaults of modern times.

"Charge the enemy and remember Old Virginia!"

This reminded his followers of the devastated fields, smoking ruins, desolated hearthstones and deserted altars of their native State. It nerved their arms and fired their breasts with a determined will to carry the frowning position of the enemy or die in the effort, as they moved gradually through the smoke of battle, in face of a hundred blazing guns, the field for a mile became thickly dotted cavaliers from the Old Dominion, and the last scions of many noble families, whose ancestral fame extends back through history and tradition a thousand years, went down by dozens on the crimsoned field, with their faces turned sternly toward the foe.

"At two we began the fell onset,
And charged up the enemy's hill,
And madly we charged them at sunset,
Their banners were floating there still."

But the valor displayed in that desperate assault attracted attention throughout the world, and though our leader was afterward overlooked and neglected while other generals were provided with positions of honor and profit, and though he died poor and sleeps in an unmarked grave, apparently forgotten grave, yet his name is inscribed on a gilded page of history and he occupies a niche in the temple of fame that will endure as long as patriotism is cherished and liberty finds admirers to applaud heroic deeds in its defense.

And now, when every incident of the march, the skirmish, the bivouac, every scrap of a faded battle flag and bit of yellow, time worn paper containing the monogram or autograph of the great leaders has become an interesting relic of priceless value; when museums, libraries, and societies are seeking diligently after these and everywhere for manuscript orders and records of the war, to be treasured up and preserved, and when our Capitol park is decorated with the finest, statuary in the world to perpetuate the memory of

271

our great jurists, orators, statesmen celebrated in the annals of the State, in the time of peace, can we not do something, and ought we not to try by subscription among the old soldiers to raise a sufficient means to have a small marble slab to mark the graves and a railing erected to enclose and protect from intrusion and insult his sacred dust of such renowned warriors and patriots as Wheat, Hill and Pickett, who exposed their persons to the dangers of the hundred battles and freely sacrificed their lives when the hour demanded in defense of the home, the institution, the principles of our people.

Whatever change time has wrought in our opinions or made in our dreams of Southern Empire, however unwise secession may now appear or however well we love the Union today, these men are not to blame for representing the hour and generation in which they lived.

Richmond, April 16, 1884

Owen Family Papers

****

The authors believe this article may have spurred and interest on the part of the survivors of Pickett's Division to raise funds for a proper monument at Pickett's grave site.   In a meeting held on November 10, 1887, the Executive Committee of Pickett's Division Association met.   They met again on November 14, 1887.   The following are extracts from the minutes of these two meetings:

****

"It was agreed that the Committee take immediate steps towards the erection of the monument to be placed on Gettysburg Hill, Hollywood." (Hollywood Cemetery- Richmond, Virginia)

"Captain Reeve, from the Monument Committee, reported progress and asked that the Committee be enlarged by the addition of a member of each brigade and one from the artillery.   The suggestion was adopted and the following appointments were made: Garnett's Brigade, Captain H.T. Owen; Armistead's Brigade, E. Marable; Artillery, Captain William I. Clopton."

"Captain Taliaferro, Chairman of the Committee on Finance, stated that in a few days the Committee would issue a circular. He thought the Monument Committee might safely go to work, as he apprehended no difficulty whatever in raising the necessary funds. In this circular $2,500.00 will be fixed as the estimated amount that will be needed to defray the expenses of the reunion of the survivors here in July next, and to pay for the monument to be placed over

General Pickett's grave in Hollywood. ---The reunion here in July promises to be a grand one. Mrs. Pickett will be here, and it is probable that the Philadelphia Brigade will be present. Old veterans of the Division who have not seen each other since the war will meet, and to them it will be indeed pleasant."

(The monument was erected and the reunion was held.)

****

Among Henry's papers were found four poems. One was never completed. The other three we include here. Henry may have composed them himself, or they may have been copied from another source.

****

WAS THERE NO FRIEND

Was there no friend on whom depend
For counsel good and true
No aged matron to warn you of your future
And tell you what to do
By whom advised and by whom devised
This step you did pursue
A wrong was done when first begun
By them as well as you
Had you no friend on whom to depend
For counsel good and true
Printing at your patron some wise old matron
With a warning what to do
No gossip to relate poor Sallie's fate
Jealous of your name
The tale related of her sad fate
Her misery and her shame
Did you not see how it would be
With this man of crime
If it lasted, your name be blasted
Only a question of time
No whispers low of wicked Joe
His crime and sinful plans, schemes
How he deceived those who believed
Could dissipate your dreams
With one eye shut winking of smut.

****

AS ON THEY RUSHED

As on they rushed into the strife

Each heard the battle cry
"Strike for freedom, your home, your wife
and follow me to win or die"

With death in front and on the flanks
Still pressed the brave brigade
With ghastly gaps and shattered ranks
After the cap on the leader's blade

Brave Armistead's men were in the strife
And each heeded his battle cry
"Strike for your freedom, your home, your wife
and follow me to win or die"

Amid havoc and death from center to flanks
Rushed forward the doomed brigade
Closing ghastly gaps and shattered ranks
After the cap on their leader's blade
and follow the cap on his blade.
****

AT THE FORD OF THE RIVER WE HELD THE FOE BACK
The blast of the bugle had called us in line
The enemy had flanked us and was marching behind

At the ford in the river while the night was all black
The contest was furious but we held the foe back

As a courier came dashing to the General in line
"The enemy has flanked you and is marching behind"

While here you remain to hold this foe back
Send word to the Capital to prevent the great sack

"Go" said the General "and carry the word
To the city in danger, which you have just heard

The road is torn up the wires are down
You must beat in the race or they'll carry our town

Ride hard and tell them to muster their men
For the enemy will be there tomorrow at ten.

274

A FINAL SALUTE TO HENRY T. OWEN

Henry T. Owen left little in the way of property, cash or other assets to his heirs. What he did leave cannot be measured in monetary value.

To his descendants he left the principles of honesty and honor. He left a legacy of integrity and valor and, best of all, he left the ideals of love of family, respect for all, and an undying devotion to his beloved Southland and his native State of Virginia.

One of the impressive principles that live on in Henry's letters is his kindness towards others. In the Chapter 11, he reveals a lovely diversion from the rules of war when he takes a Federal prisoner to breakfast at an unknown person's home. He knew Captain F. R. Josselyn was hungry and he afforded him a good meal at a local residence. More amazing is that he corresponded and visited with Josselyn's sister after the war. Josselyn's family was very grateful to Henry and were able to tell him how they felt in letters and in person after the war.

Also, left behind were insights into Henry T. Owen's belief system. He was very firm in his beliefs as he wrote about them in his letters to his wife, children and other people. He did not hesitate to state what he believed even if it went against what everyone else thought. He professed a strong belief in religion and wanted his family to share in his belief in God. He wrote of a strong belief in home schooling. He wanted his children educated and he wanted them to be able to read and write.

When Henry T. Owen made his scrapbook, penned to paper his writings, and passed all of this on to the next generation, he could not know that this historic material would be preserved for many to read, ponder and enjoy.

The hours he spent, writing his memories of the war, his views of State and National politics, his belief and devotion to Christianity, were not in vain. We, his descendants and others who have read his work, surely must say, "Here was a man of honor."

Perhaps, our recently found cousin, Kimberly Ayn Owen, said it best when she found Henry's gravesite in Riverview Cemetery in Richmond, Virginia. "Standing there, that morning, looking at Henry's headstone, I gave Henry a salute." Yes Henry, we all salute you for preserving a priceless treasure of information.

2601 East Franklin Street, Richmond, Virginia

(Photo by Kimberly Ayn Owen)

Residence of Henry T. Owen and his wife Harriet Robertson Owen from July, 1901 until his death on October 8, 1921. Harriet Robertson Owen died February 18, 1918. At that time Henry's daughter, Harriet Louisa Owen Whiteside (Hattie), widow of James Whiteside moved there and lived with Henry until his death.

REFERENCES

Henry T. Owen Papers, 1822-1929 (Accession 28154) Personal Papers Collection, The Library of Virginia, Richmond, Virginia.

"The Virginia Confederate Rosters," The Library of Virginia, Richmond, Virginia.

"18th Virginia Infantry," by Dr. James I. Robertson, Copyright 1984, H. E. Howard, Inc., Lynchburg, Virginia.

Owen Family Papers

CHRONOLOGICAL LIST OF SOME OF THE NAMES IN THE LETTERS

Letter to Harriet July 5, 1856
"Your Pa" - John Archer Robertson of Rock Castle, Crewe, Virginia
Letter to Harriet Aug 28, 1861
Mr. Irving – (Charles) Co E, attorney, Lt. In Mexican War, later appointed aide to Gen. Jackson with commission of captain.
Tom Cousins – friend of Henry, civilian ?
Lt. Gibbs –(Robert A.) Co C, elected Capt. Jan 2, 1862, died of "camp colic" 1864.
Mrs. Smith – mother of some of students Henry taught..
Milly – (Elizabeth Mildred Owen) eldest daughter.
Letter to Harriet Oct 9, 1861
Pat – (John Patterson Robertson) brother of Harriet Robertson Owen
Mr. Harper – (James M.) Capt. Co A, resigned May 28, 1862
Dr. & Mrs. D. J. – (Jackson) doctor, Nottoway County
Gen. Cocke – Brigade commander, committed suicide, replaced by Gen. Pickett.
Letter to Harriet Nov 6, 1861
Mr. Smith – resident Nottoway County
"Meckleface" - bull
Mr. Jackson – doctor, Nottoway County
Mr. Clarke – neighbor, Nottoway County
Mr. Dalton – neighbor/farmer, Nottoway County

277

Mr. Southall – neighbor, Nottoway County

Richard Irby – Co G, Lt. At muster, elected Capt. 1862, wounded Second Manassas, died 1902.

James A. Robertson – Co C, enlisted Mar 10, 1862, wounded Williamsburg, died May 10, 1862 - cousin of Harriet Robertson Owen.

Capt. White – "Tigers" unit, offered as attorney for Henry in 1861 court martial.

Gen. Jackson – (Thomas J. "Stonewall") General of Shenandoah Valley Campaign.

Gen Beauregard – (Pierre G. T.) commanded Army of Tennessee after Gen. A. S. Johnson, killed.

Maj. George C. Cabell – Co C, 3rd in command 18th VA Inf.

"Sis" Helen - Harriet's sister - Helen Louisa Robertson born May 10, 1842 - married James Ingram

"Cousin Carey" – (Carolina E. berry) 2nd wife of John Archer Robertson Carolina Kaltison Roberts

  Robertson, mother of Harriet Robertson Owen died October 24, 1856. Harriet's father, John Archer Robertson then married Carolina E. Berry, niece of his first wife.

<u>Letter to Harriet Mar 12, 1862</u>

Gen. Johnson - Commanded troops at First Manassas.

Col. Bain – stationed at Camp Wise, Richmond.

<u>Letter to Harriet Mar 14, 1862</u>

"Mr. Morton" – (Samuel H.) Co C, 5th Sgt. captured at Gettysburg.

Leath - (Tyree Glenn Bacon) 1st Lt Co C.

Charley Mottley –

<u>Letter to Harriet Mar 18, 1862</u>

Archer - (Robertson) Co C, wounded at Gaines Mill, lost leg, died 1890 in GA. Archer was brother of Harriett Robertson Owen

Joe Leath – (Joseph E.) Co C, wounded at Frayser's Mill.

Tom Cockman – Joined Co C in Richmond then deserted.

<u>Letter to Harriet Apr 10, 1862</u>

Longstreet - Gen. James, in command of I Corps, Army of Northern Virginia

Pete Temple – (William P.) Sgt, Co C, wounded and captured at Gettysburg

Sarah - her baby died

Womack – related to Henry by marriage

Letter to Harriet Apr 11, 1862

Uncle Bogy – Boygy - slave and a tailor

Gen. Magruder – (John Bankhead) commanded a Wing in Peninsula Campaign

Mrs. Mottley - Lived on Main St. Richmond – relative of Charley Mottley

Tom Jones – (Robert Thomas) Co C

Capt Jones – belonged to another Regiment

Pat – in another Regiment

Morton – (Samuel H.) 5th Sgt. Co C., captured at Gettysburg.

Letter to Harriet Apr 20, 1862

Ada –

Billy Mottley – in another "troop" in Peninsula Campaign

Meredith Watson – in another "troop" in Peninsula Campaign

P. Fowlkes – in another "troop" in Peninsula Campaign

Dick Dyson - in another "troop" in Peninsula Campaign

Letter to Harriet Apr 24,1862

Capt. Graves – (William P.) Co A "Danville Blues"

Louis Morton – resident Nottoway County

Tom Jones – (Robert Thomas) Co C

Letter to Harriet Apr 27, 1862

Tyree G. Leath – 1st Lt. Co C

M. P. Vaughan – 2nd Lt. Co C

A. A. Watkins – 3nd Lt. Co C, later promoted to 2nd Lt. killed at Gettysburg.

Gibbs – (Robert A.) Lt. Co C., dropped from rolls Apr. 26, 1862

Branch Leath – (James B.) Co C

Tuck Fowlkes – (Edward T.) Co C

Letter to Harriet May 6,1962

Upson Robertson – (Upson A.) – cousin to Harriet - Co C., killed at Williamsburg

Otis Watson – (William O.) Co C., killed at Williamsburg.

Sgt. Wilkinson – (Charles H.) Co C., wounded at Williamsburg.

Frank Dalton – (Francis W.) Co. C., wounded at Williamsburg.

Tom Jones – (Robert Thomas) Co C. wounded at Williamsburg.

Pryor Robertson – (Theoderick P.) Co C. wounded at Williamsburg -brother of Harriet

Mr. Davis – Co C, wounded at Williamsburg, joined Company days before.

Mr. Allen – Co C, wounded at Williamsburg, joined Company days before.

Jimmy Robertson – (James A.) wounded at Williamsburg, died May 10, 1862.

<u>Letter to Harriet May 11, 1862</u>

Tom Jones – sent home to recover from wounds.

Lt. Watkins – sent home to recover from wound.

Uncle Boygy - slave - tailor

<u>Letter to Harriet May 21, 1862</u>

Mr. Temple – bond holder

Mr. Slaughter – Friend of Henry, in another Regiment

Tom Ives – In Company C at one time, wounded

Sam Morton – (Samuel H.) Co C

Pete Temple – (William P.) Co C

Jimmy – (James A. Robertson)

Davis – wounded at Williamsburg.

Allen – wounded at Williamsburg.

Lt. Sorey – (Edward N.) Co B, suspended from rank Mar, 1862 after being AWOL.

Verser – (Richard C.) Sgt. Co C, killed at Williamsburg.

<u>Letter to Harriet June 1, 1862</u>

L. Taze. Robertson - (Littleton Tazewell) Co C., killed at Seven Pines- cousin of Harriet

Joseph L. Jenkins – Co C, killed at Seven Pines.

Sydney Foster – (Algernon S.) Co C, killed at Seven Pines.

James C. Baughan – Co C, mortally wounded and captured at Seven Pines.

Charles V. Vaughan – Co C, wounded at Seven Pines.

Lt. Madison P. Vaughan – Co C, wounded at Seven Pines.

T. Pryor Robertson – Co C, wounded at Seven Pines - brother of Harriet

R. Hudgens – (Ransom) Co C, wounded at Seven Pines.

Hiram O. Fowlkes – Co C, slightly wounded at Seven Pines, deserted 1862.

Joseph H. Phaup – Co C, slightly wounded at Seven Pines, wounded and captured at Gettysburg.

Jacob T. Osborne – Co C, slightly wound at Seven Pines.

N. A. Mottley – (Napoleon) Co C missing

Samuel H. Morton – Co C, missing at Seven Pines later found, captured at Gettysburg.

Dick Verser – Sgt., Co. C, killed at Williamsburg

Lt. Watkins – (A. A.) wounded at Frayser's Farm and Second Manassas, killed at Gettysburg.

Col. Withers – (Robert Enoch) Commander, 18th VA Inf.

Letter to Harriet June 12, 1862

Lt. Lowery – From another Brigade – visited friends in "Danville Blues" company.

"Great Jackson" – (Gen. Thomas A. "Stonewall) Commander Shenandoah Campaign.

McClellan – (Gen. George B.) Federal commander Army of Potomac.

Col. William S. Guy - Friend from another Brigade

Peter La Neve – young son of Samuel A. La Neve of Co C.

Mrs.. Leath – Mother or wife of James B. Leath, Co C

E. H. Stokes -

Letter to Harriet June 16,1862

Lyons - Co C Lt., sent to bring back stragglers.

John A. Allen – wounded and captured at Williamsburg, died May 18, 1862.

Lt Watkins – (Aurelius Augustus) Co C

Letter to Harriet June 21, 1862

Sam Spencer – Co K, caught and identified deserter, Byrnes.

Byrnes – (Robert) Co K, deserted one day after enlisting, sent to prison.

Lyons – Co C Lt.

Mr. Mann – James , Attorney Nottoway County and later a member of the Pickett-Stuart Camp of the United Confederate Veterans

Letter to Harriet June 28,1862

Mr. Gill – Co – went home with arm wound.

Col. Robert E. Withers – Commander, 18th, wounded at Gaines Mill.

Carter - wounded at Gaines Mill.

Robert Holloway – Co C, wounded at Gaines Mill.

Capt. Lyle – (Mathew) Co K, killed at Gaines Mill.

Capt. Irby – (Richard) Co G, wounded at Second Manassas.

Letter to Harriet June 30, 1862

Mr. La Neve – (Samuel A.) Co C, wounded at Frayser's Farm and Gettysburg.

McClellan – (Gen George B.) Federal commander, Army of Potomac.

Clay – (Henry Clay Owen)

Pryor – (Theoderick P. Robertson) Co C - brother of Harriet

Archer – (Robertson) Co C .- brother of Harriet - lost leg in the war

Mr. Morton – (Samuel H.) Co C

Letter to Harriet July 16, 1962

Archer – (Robertson) - brother of Harriet

Henry Dyson (Horace H.) Co C, AWOL July 5, 1862.

Letter to Harriet July 27,1862

Mr. Dalton – (Francis W.) Co C

Giles Miller – (Giles A. Jr.) Co C, 5th Sgt.

Gen. Johnston (Joseph E.) Commander, Army of Northern Virginia before Lee.

Col. Carrington - (Henry A.) second in command of 18th VA Inf.

Leo Hawkes – resident of Nottoway County.

James W. Jackson – "killed Ellsworth in Alexandria."

Letter to Harriet Aug 31, 1862

Capt. Holland – (James A) Co A, wounded at Second Manassas.

Capt. Irby – (Richard) Co G, wounded Second Manassas.

Capt. Booker – (Richard A.) Co F, wounded at Second Manassas.

Col. Carrington – (Henry A.) second in command, 18th VA Inf. wounded at Second Manassas.

Lt. McCulloch – (Robert) Co B, wounded at Second Manassas.

Lt. Glenn – (James P.) Co D, wounded at Second Manassas.

Lt. Jackson – (Nathaniel H.) Co F, wounded at Second Manassas.

Col. Crump – Brigade Commander Killed at Second Manassas.

Gen D. H. Hill – Div. commander under Gen. Longstreet.

Letter to Harriet Nov 7, 1862

Bill – shared shelter with Henry

Jackson – Gen. Thomas A. "Stonewall"

Letter to Harriet Mar 14, 1863

Gen. Pickett – (George E.) Div. commander in Longstreet's Corps.

Gen D. H. Hill – (Daniel) Div. commander in Longstreet's Corps.

Letter to Wife & Millie Owen (daughter, Mildred) Apr 6, 1863

Meadows – (James F.) Co H & Co D,

Letter to Harriet June 13, 1863

Lee – (Gen. Robert E. Lee) Commander Army of Northern Virginia

Mr. Campbell – Handled Henry's matter with Sec. of War.

Clay – (Henry Clay Owen) eldest son

Millie – (Elizabeth Mildred Owen) eldest daughter

Pat - (John Patterson Robertson) - brother of Harriet

<u>Letter to Harriet June 21, 1863</u>

Dr. Jackson – Nottoway County, father of Lin Jackson

Lin Jackson – in Cavalry unit.

John Ewing – Nephew of Henry - Henry's sister Ann M. Owen married Thomas Ewing. The

Ewings had two sons, William H.H., and John J.

Uncle W. Henry – Confederate Cavalry

Sec. of War – James Seddon

<u>Letter to Harriet July 18, 1863</u>

Capt. F. R. Josselyn – Co F, 11th Mass. taken prisoner at Gettysburg.

Lt. Watkins – (Aurelius A.) Co C, killed at Gettysburg.

Mrs. Robertson –Harriet's step mother or grandmother

George Anderson – Co C, deserted July 1863

Joseph Leath – Co C

Hiram Fowlkes – Co C, deserted, died in prison, 1863.

<u>Letter to Harriet July 22, 1863</u>

Major Simpson – 17th VA Infantry

Tyne – (Anderson?)

Joe Anderson – deserted July 1863

George Anderson – Co C, deserted July 1863

Mr. Hudgins – (Ransom) Co C, wounded at Seven Pines.

Mrs. Bettie Varner – Sister of Algy Varnier

Algy Varner – Co E

Mrs. Slaughter –

Franklin -

<u>Letter to Harriet July 24, 1863</u>

Lt. Watkins – (A. A.) Co C, killed at Gettysburg.

Burke – (John Leigh) Co C, one brother Edwin J., wounded and captured at Gettysburg and brother Henry H. died of smallpox in May 1863.

Joe Holt – (William J.) Co C, missing July 1863, possibly taken prisoner.

Miss Mary Eckolls – fiancée of Joe Holt

<u>Letter to son, Clay Sept 7, 1863</u>

Mr. Medley – Owned house where Henry went to school.

Mrs. Gallion – Taught school at Mr. Medley's house.

Cousin Polly -

<u>Letter to Harriet Sept 27, 1863</u>

Joe Leath –

Mr. Irving -

Clay – (Henry Clay Owen) eldest son of Henry T. Owen

Michael – (Michael M. Owen) second son of Henry T. Owen

Letter to Harriet Dec. 21, 1863

(None)

Letter to Harriet Feb. 8, 1864

Pat

Sam Wilson Scott

Mr. Brown

Cindy

Cousin Bettie

Tom Campbell – farmer, Nottoway County

Mr. Ewing

Letter to Clay (son) Apr 18, 1864

Mr. Irving – (Charles) attorney, originally in Co E, later a Capt. on staff of Gen. Jackson.

Gen. Pickett – (George E.) Div. commander in Longstreet's Corps.

Gen. Jackson – (Thomas A. "Stonewall") commander of Shenandoah Valley campaign.

Gen. Wheat - Lt. in Mexican War

Mr. Talley – (Chastine H.) Co C, captured at Howlett's House, Aug 25, 1864.

William Henry Talley – Son of Chastine Talley, visited Regiment at Richmond.

Cousin B. –(Bettie)

Mich – (Michael M. Owen) second son of Henry T. Owen

Gen. Longstreet – (James) commander I Corps, Army of Northern Virginia

Gen. Loring – (William W.) commanded Confederate forces in Western Virginia.

Letter to Harriet May 16, 1864

Beast Butler – Benjamin Franklin Butler, Brig. Gen. MA Militia

Gen. Beauregard – Pierre G. T., Brig. Gen., commander defenses south of Richmond

Gen. Heck –

Bill – brother of Henry T. Owen, William J. Owen

Gen. Lee – Robert E. Lee

Letter to Harriet May 20, 1864

Clay – son, Henry Clay Owen

Gen. Lee – Robert E. Lee

Major Cabell – George C. third in command, 18th VA Inf.

Gen. Winston -

<u>Letter to Harriet Aug. 22, 1864</u>

Mr. Brown

Dr. Thaxton – dentist, Nottoway County

Pryor – T. Pryor Robertson, Company C - brother of Harriet

Ben – Benjamin L. Robertson, Company C - brother of Harriet

Gilliam – Marius Gilliam Robertson, Company C

Charley –

Joe –

Bill – brother of Henry T. Owen, William J. Owen

Wm Henry – William Henry K. Robertson, Company A, left arm
amputated May, 1864 - cousin of Harriet Robertson Owen.

<u>Letter to Harriet Oct. 1, 1864</u>

Pryor – T. Pryor Robertson, Company C

Stephen Scott –

Ken -

Cousin Bettie –

Grant – Ulysses S., Lt. Gen., general-in-chief overland campaign

Col. Carter – 3rd VA Cavalry

Capt. Palmer – 3rd VA Cavalry

Bill – brother, William J. Owen

<u>Letter to Harriet Oct 9, 1864</u>

Calvin –

Ben - (Benjamin Robertson) Co C

Cousin Bettie –

Sister Ann – Ann Owen Ewing - sister of Henry

Mother H. Rob - (Robertson) Harriet's stepmother or grandmother

<u>Letter to Harriet Nov. 3, 1864</u>

Weldon – (Sold barrel of apples)

Mother – Mrs. William Jack (Sally Marshall) Owen

Bill - Henry's brother, William J. Owen

Pryor - Robertson, Company C

Junins Lipsomb – Clement J., Company C

Miss Sallie Hardaway -

Cousin Bettie –

<u>Letter to Harriet Nov. 22, 1864</u>

Hon. Clifford Anderson

Mr. Campbell

Judge Gholson

285

Mr. Smith

Clay - son, Henry Clay Owen

Capt. Richardson – Provost Marshal, Castle Thunder, Richmond

Letter to Harriet (Undated) 1864 (No. 52)

Clay - (Henry Clay Owen) son

Pryor – (Theoderick P. Robertson) Co. C

Ben – (Benjamin L. Robertson) Co. C, captured at Sailor's Creek

Mother – (Mrs. William J. Owen) Henry's mother

Bob –

Cousin Martha –

W. Henry – (William Henry Robertson)

Mr. Ewing –

Sister Ann – Ann Owen Ewing

Mr. Temple – (William P.) Co. C, captured at Gettysburg and Sailor's Creek

ALPHABETICAL LIST OF NAMES IN LETTERS

Abner, Anderson - Private Co. A, 18th Va. Infantry
Ada
Allen, John A. - Co. C, wounded at Williamsburg, had joined
Company just days before.
Ann, "sister" -Ann Owen Ewing - sister of Henry T. Owen
Anderson, Hon. Clifford - judge in Nottoway County
Anderson, George - Co C. deserted in July 1863
Anderson, Albert J. B. - Co I, deserted
Anderson, Tyne - resident Nottoway County
Bain, Col. - stationed at Camp Wise, Richmond.
Baird, Edward R. - Capt. Aide-de-camp to Maj. Gen. George Pickett
Baughan, James C. - Co. C, mortally wounded and captured at
Seven Pines.
Beauregard, Pierre G. T., CSA Gen. commanded Army of
Tennessee after Gen. A. S. Johnson was killed.
Bill - William J. Owen - brother of Henry T. Owen
Bettie "cousin" -
Blanton, Z.A. - Capt. Co. F, 18th Va. Infantry
Booker, Richard A. - Capt., Co. F, wounded at Second Manassas.
Boygy, Bogy - slave - tailor
Bright, Robert A. - Staff Officer to Maj. Gen. George Pickett
Brown, Mr. - resident of Richmond.
Burke, John Leigh - Co. C, brother Henry H. died of smallpox, May
1863, brother Edwin J., wounded and captured at Gettysburg.
Butler, Benjamin F. - Brig.Gen., Mass. Militia.
Byrnes, Robert - Co. K, deserted one day after enlisting, caught sent
to prison.
Cabell, George C., Maj. - 3rd in command 18th VA Inf.
Calvin
Campbell, Mr.- Handled Henry's matter with Sec. or War.
Campbell, Tom - farmer, Nottoway County
Carey, "Cousin" -
Carrington, Henry A. - Col., second in command, 18th VA Inf.,
wounded at Second Manassas.
Carter, Charles K. - Sgt., Co. B, wounded June 27, 1862, Gaines
Mill.
Carter (?) - Col., 3rd Va. Cavalry
Catherine

Cindy

Clark, W.F. - (Rank Unknown) - Co. I, 56th Va. Infantry

Clarke, Mr. – neighbor, Nottoway County

Cocke, Brig. Gen. Philip St. George CSA Brigade commander, committed suicide in 1862, replaced by Gen. George Pickett

Cocke, Edmund R. - Capt. Co. E, 18th Va. Infantry

Cockman, Thomas – Joined Co. C in Richmond then deserted.

Coleman, E.B. - Private Co. F & H, 18th Va. Infantry

Cousins, Tom - civilian friend of Henry

Crump ? – Col., killed at Second Manassas.

Dalton, Francis W. "Frank" – Co. C, wounded at Williamsburg.

Dalton, Mr. – neighbor/farmer, Nottoway County

Davis, ? - Co C., wounded at Williamsburg, had joined Company just days before.

Dyson, "Dick" – in another regiment during Peninsula Campaign.

Dyson, Horace H. – Co. C, AWOL July 5, 1862

Eckolls, Mary (Miss) – fiancée of William J. Holt

Ewing, John - Nephew of Henry T. Owen - son of Ann Owen Ewing and Thomas Ewing

Ewing, Mr. & Mrs. -

Foster, Algernon Sydney – Co. C, killed at Seven Pines.

Fowlkes, Edward T. "Tuck" – Co. C

Fowlkes, Hiram O. – Co. C, wounded at Seven Pines, deserted 1862, died in prison 1863.

Fowlkes, P. – in another regiment during Peninsula Campaign.

Gallion, Mrs. – Henry's school teacher.

Gholson, "Judge" -

Gibbs, Robert A. – Lt.,Co. C, dropped from rolls 1862, died of "camp colic" 1864.

Gill, James C. – Co. G, wounded, went home June 27, 1862 to recover.

Glenn, James P. – Lt., Co. D, wounded at Second Manassas.

Grant, Ulysses S. – Union General-in-Chief Overland Campaign.

Graves, William P. – Capt., Co. A,

Guy, William S. – Col. And friend from another brigade.

Hardaway, Miss Sallie -

Harper, James M. – Capt. Co. A, resigned May 28,1862

Hawkes, Leo – resident Nottoway County

Hayes, John S. - Dispatch bearer and orderly to Gen. Robert E. Lee

Heck (?) –

Helen, "Sis" - Helen Robertson Ingram - sister of Harriet Owen

Henry "uncle W." – in a cavalry unit

Hill, Daniel H. – Gen., Division commander under Gen. James Longstreet.

Holland, James A. – Capt., Co. A, 18th Va. Infantry - wounded at Second Manassas.

Holloway, Robert G. – Co. C, wounded June 27,1862 at Gaine's Mill.

Holt, William J. – Co. C, captured at Gettysburg.

Hudgens, Bettie – wife of Ransom Hudgens

Hudgens, Ransom – Co. C, wounded at Seven Pines.

Irby, Richard – Co. G., 18th Va. Infantry - Lt at muster, elected Capt. 1862, wounded at Second
Second Manassas, died 1902.

Irving, Charles – Co. E, attorney, later appointed to Gen. "Stonewall" Jackson's staff.

Ives, Tom – In Company C at one time

Jackson, Dr. and Mrs. – doctor, Nottoway County

Jackson, James W. – "killed Ellsworth in Alexandria."

Jackson, Lin - in cavalry unit.

Jackson, Nathaniel H. – Lt., Co. F, wounded at Second Manassas.

Jackson, Thomas A. "Stonewall" – CSA General of Shenandoah Valley campaign.

Jenkins, Joseph L – Co. C, killed at Seven Pines.

Jefress, William H. – Co. G. & Co. K, wounded at Williamsburg.

Johnston, Joseph E. – Maj. Gen., CSA, commanded Army of the Shenandoah.

Jones, Dr. – doctor, Nottoway County

Jones, Robert Thomas – Co. C, wounded at Williamsburg, sent home to recover.

Jones, Capt. – belonged to another regiment.

Josselyn, Frank R. – Capt., Co F, 11th Mass., taken prisoner at Gettysburg.

Ken

Kemper, James L. - Brig. Gen. Longstreet's Division

La Neve, Peter – son of Samuel A. LaNeve, Co. C, visited camp

La Neve, Samuel A. – Co. C, wounded at Frayser's Farm and Gettysburg.

Leath, James B. "Branch" – Co. C

Leath, Joseph E. – Co. C, wounded at Frayser's Farm and again at South Mountain.

Leath, Mrs. – resident Nottoway County

Leath, Tyree Glenn B. – Co C, 1st Lt., wounded at Frayser's Farm, died 1875.

Lee, Robert Edward – Gen., Commander Army of Northern Va.

Lipscomb, Clement J. – Co. C

Longstreet, James – Lt. Gen., commander, I Corps..

Loring, William W. – Gen., commanded CSA forces in Western Virginia.

Lowery – Lt. from another brigade, visited "Danville Blues."

Lyle, Mathew – Capt. Co. K, killed at Gaines Mill.

Lyons – Co. C Lt, sent to bring back "stragglers."

Magruder, John B. – Gen., commanded a Wing in Peninsula Campaign.

Mann, James. – Nottoway County Court House

Marshall, Charles - Col. Staff Officer to General Robert E. Lee

Martha, "Cousin" -

McClellan, George B.- Federal General, Army of Potomac.

McCulloch, Robert – Lt., Co. B, wounded at Second Manassas.

Meadows, James F. – Co. H & Co. D (gave biscuit to boy near Washington NC.)

Medley, Mr. – owned house where Henry attended school.

Miller, Giles A. Jr. – 5th Sgt., Co. C

Morrissett, William J. - 1st Lt. Co. F, 18th Va. Infantry

Morton, Louis – resident Nottoway County

Morton, Samuel H. – Co. C 5th Sgt., captured at Gettysburg.

Mottley, "Billy" – in another regiment during Peninsula Campaign.

Mottley, Charley –

Mottley, Mrs. – Lived on Main St., Richmond. Mother of Charley Mottley

Mottley, Napoleon A. – Co. C, missing after Battle of Seven Pines.

Osborne, Jacob T. – Co. C, wounded at Seven Pines.

Owen, Elizabeth Mildred (Milly, Millie) – eldest daughter

Owen, Henry Clay – eldest son

Owen, Michael M. – second son

Owen, William J. – brother of Henry T. Owen

Owen, William J. Mrs. (Sally Marshall) – Henry's mother.

Palmer – Capt., 3rd Virginia Cavalry.

Pat -

Phaup, Joseph H. – Co. C, wounded at Seven Pines, wounded and captured Gettysburg.

Pickett, Charles - Staff Officer, Longstreets' Division - brother of Gen. George E. Pickett

Pickett, George E. - Gen., Division Commander in Gen.Longstreet's Corp.

Polly, "cousin" -

Pryor, Roger A. - Brig. Gen. 5th Brigade, Longstreets' Division

Richardson – Capt., Provost Marshal, Castle Thunder, Richmond

Robertson, Archer – Co. C, wounded at Gaine's Mill, lost leg, died 1890 in Georgia.

Robertson, Benjamin L. – Co. C, captured at Sailor's Creek.

Robertson, James A. – Co. C, enlisted Mar. 10, 1862, wounded at Williamsburg, Died May 10, 1862.

Robertson, Littleton Tazewell – Co. C, killed at Seven Pines.

Robertson, Marius Gilliam – Co. C, captured April 8,1865.

Robertson, "Mother" – Harriet's mother.

Robertson, Theoderick Pryor – wounded at Williamsburg.

Robertson, Upson A. – Co. C, killed at Williamsburg.

Robertson, William Henry K. – Co. A, arm amputated May, 1864.

Sarah – slave

Scott, Sam Wilson -

Scott, Stephen – sold goods to "settlers" near Chester Station

Seddon, James – Secretary of War, CSA.

Simpson, – Major, 17th Va. Inf.

Slaughter, Franklin – friend, in another regiment

Smith, Mrs. – mother of some of Henry's students..

Sorey, Edward N. – Lt., Co B., AWOL and suspended from rank Mar. 1862.

Southall, Mr. – neighbor, Nottoway County

Spencer, Sam – Co. K, caught and identified deserter, Byrnes.

Stokes, E. H. – railroad agent below Richmond

Talley, Chastine H. – Co. C, captured at Howlett's House, Aug. 25, 1864.

Talley, William Henry – son of Chastine Talley..

Temple, William P. "Pete" – Co C, Sgt., wounded and captured at Gettysburg, returned to duty and captured again at Sailor's Creek.

Temple, Mr. – bond holder, Nottoway County.

Thaxton, Dr. – dentist in Nottoway County

Varner, Algy – deserted

Varner, Bettie – sister of Algy.

Vaughan, Charles V. – Co. C, wounded at Seven Pines.

Vaughan, Madison P. – 2nd Lt., Co. C, wounded at Seven Pines.

Verser, Richard C. – Sgt., Co. C, killed at Williamsburg.

Watkins, Aurelius A. – 2nd Lt. Co. C, wounded at Williamsburg, killed at Gettysburg.

Watson, Meredith – in another regiment during Peninsula Campaign.

Watson, William Otis – Co. C, killed at Williamsburg.

Weldon – sold barrel of apples for Henry.

Wheat - Gen., was Lieutenant in Mexican War.

White, Capt. – "Tigers" unit, offered as attorney for Henry in 1861 court martial.

Wilkinson, Charles H. – Sgt. Co. C, wounded at Williamsburg.

Winston

Withers, Robert Enoch – Col., Commander 18th Virginia Infantry.

Womack - related to Henry T. Owen by marriage